Sabra

BOOKS BY TED BERKMAN

Sabra

Cast a Giant Shadow

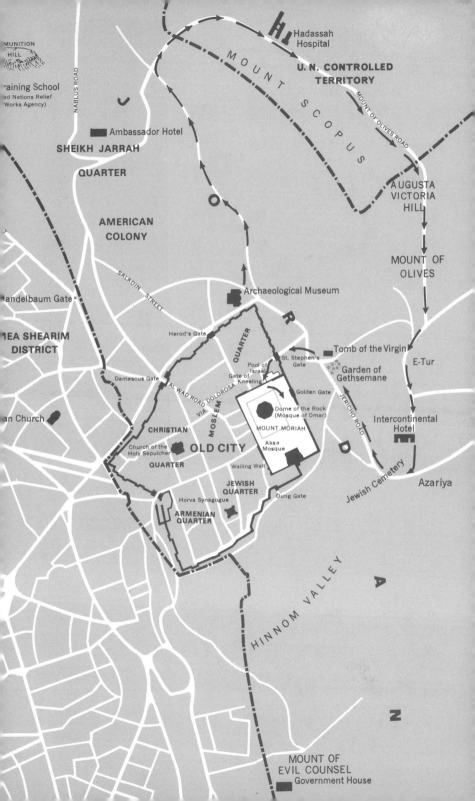

Sabra

TED BERKMAN

Harper & Row, Publishers

New York, Evanston, and London

1817

Maps by J.P. Tremblay

The lines from "Jerusalem of Gold" ("Yerushalayim Shel Zahav") are reprinted with the kind permission of Chappell & Co., Inc. Copyright © 1967 by Naomi Shemer.

SABRA. Copyright © 1969 by Edward O. Berkman. Printed in the United States of America. All rights reserved. No part of this book may be used or reproduced in any manner whatsoever without written permission except in the case of brief quotations embodied in critical articles and reviews. For information address Harper & Row, Publishers, Incorporated, 49 East 33rd Street, New York, N.Y. 10016.

FIRST EDITION

LIBRARY OF CONGRESS CATALOG CARD NUMBER: 69-15298

A-T

CONTENTS

MAPS

A section of photographs follows page 146

In deference to official Israeli Army policy, officers below the very top level are generally identified in these pages only by their first names.

If there must be trouble, let it be in my day,
that my child may have peace.

—Thomas Paine

Almost everything that is great has been done by youth.

—Benjamin Disraeli

Sabra

PERSPECTIVE

SABRA is the Hebrew word for a type of local cactus, prickly-tough
on the outside, succulent at the core, hence applied with grudging
affection to the native-born Israeli who, like the cactus, hides his
inner sweetness beneath a rough exterior.

In this and other respects, the sabra is literally a new breed of
Jew. Hardened by border clashes, burned brown by the desert sun,
educated to a different understanding of his people's history and of
his role and his rights in the world, he stands calmly and firmly on
his own soil, his character stripped to essentials by the constant
presence of danger. Often abrasive outside of his natural environment, he is generally more purposeful, decisive and resourceful than
his overseas cousin; quietly self-contained, he is at the same time
acutely responsive to the needs of others.

The sabra has little time or taste for ritual niceties. His land is
harsh and uncompromising. His language, abrupt and explosive,
lacks the liquid charm of the Romance tongues. Lost, and sometimes
bewailed, is the soft *Gemütlichkeit*, the flexible charm of the Jewish
sophisticate in Vienna or New York. Lost also is the fear. The sabra
has the virtues, as well as the defects, of the frontier.

If he sometimes appears arrogant, it is usually in an attempt to
persuade himself, rather than others, that he can keep up the mir-

acles forced upon him. Living under siege, he finds little in his environment to encourage—or even permit—hesitant gentility. Withal, the aptly-named sabra is not a violent man. Only his surface is prickly. Precisely because he lives close to fundamental truth, he is an extremely gentle parent deeply engaged in family relationships, a loyal friend, a man sensitive to song, story, and sorrow. Some critics have professed to see in the sabra a "Prussian swagger." This is plain nonsense. The fact is that the sabra has an essential humility that makes him uncomfortable in the role of conqueror. As one boy summed up his views on militarism, "I would love to be a pacifist—if the world would let me."

The sabra *spirit* is harder to define. Yet it is an inescapable presence in Israel, hovering over kibbutz apple orchards in the north and army training camps in the Negev; floating through the crowded halls of Haifa's Technion Institute and the crooked alleyways of Jerusalem; turning up unexpectedly in the dimly-lit alcoves of a Tel Aviv discotheque. It saturates the country, penetrates and overwhelms personal attitudes acquired elsewhere.

"Patriotism" and "nationalism" do not begin to describe it, because these words lack the special overtone that in this case is the essence. The modern Israeli feels that his forefathers, hounded since the beginnings of tribal memory, became for the sake of survival the great adjusters of the world, adept at swimming along with the tide. The sabra spirit says that kind of solution is not good enough, not consonant with human dignity or with the freedom-principle of the reconstituted Maccabee tradition.

The sabra stands not merely on his need, but his *right* to live and grow as part of a free people, without favor or apology. Encouraged since childhood to be a free and equal individual, rather than part of a minority under sufferance, he is prepared to demand and even enforce that right. He and his fellows are bound together not only by knowledge of a shared past, but—perhaps more importantly —by the conviction of a future entirely in their own hands.

The Jew in the West, no matter how successful materially, tends to suffer from a sense of spiritual unease. He is always looking back over his shoulder to make sure there is no new Hitler coming over the hill. The sabra knows no such torment. He is an Israeli, as secure in his national identity as a Frenchman born in Paris. Having at last achieved a narrow foothold of equality, he is resolved never to be pried loose from it, short of physical extinction. He will never return—or be thrust back—into the past.

In the historic week that began on June 5, 1967, ancient ghosts rode the turrets of the Israeli tanks. The reservist fighters were frighteningly aware that if their country went under, it would be forever. In 1948, a world still reeling from the stench of the crematoria had, in a rare burst of generosity, awarded a tiny slice of parched Middle East wasteland to the Jews. It was understood that this was a single brief, impatient gesture, not to be repeated.

The framework of this book is the Six-Day War of 1967. But essentially it is a book about people—various in age, upbringing, education and tradition—forced by outward circumstance and inner need to become temporary warriors; about the experience of living, and more particularly of growing, inside an Israeli skin.

The stories in these pages are not isolated cases. Men equally brave were in the unscarred tank alongside, or died in selfless acts that will never be recorded because no one survived them. As with the army, so with its leadership; there were no irreplaceable generals.

Israel is a fact of life, perhaps the central fact of the modern Middle East. Its people, regardless of origin, speak today with the voice of the sabra. They will do so increasingly tomorrow. The values they live by have implications far transcending the borders of Israel —wherever they may be fixed.

The First Day

DAWN: THE PILOT

SHORTLY before dawn on Monday, June 5, Egyptian shells hurtled out of the Gaza Strip into the Negev kibbutz of Nahal Oz, setting wheat fields on fire and killing several cows in their sheds. It was not the first such attack; border settlements near the Strip, like those huddled beneath the Syrian mountain fortresses, had been under constant harassment for nineteen years.

But this Monday was different. Less than an hour after the shelling an Israeli pilot named Major Avihu, sleeping somewhat restlessly in his modest stone cottage at an air base south of Tel Aviv, was awakened by a pounding on the door.

Avihu, a sturdily-built sabra of twenty-eight, had been expecting the summons: "The closing of the Tiran Strait meant we'd have war. As an Arab, Nasser couldn't possibly back down; and he had left himself no loophole. We for our part couldn't accept being choked; and no one else was prepared to be killed for us."

Avihu tumbled rapidly out of bed, remembering to turn off the alarm, which had been set as usual for 7:00 A.M. He pulled on his trousers and headed for his razor, in deference to a tradition among Israeli flyers that pilots, the gentlemen of modern warfare, "die shaven."

In appearance, Avihu was almost comically type-cast as the noble-

4

visaged, hard-breathing air commando of the late, late TV shows. He was long-limbed, trim, and suitably glittering of eye. He was also, however, reassuringly human: irritable if interrupted at his evening newspaper; a chronic speeder on the highways (possibly because anything less than five hundred miles an hour seems like crawling to a supersonic pilot); and frankly limited in his aesthetic interests. "The symphonies and chamber music are for Ariela. I stick to dance music, light tunes—and the news."

His shaving cream had been laid out, with fresh blades. That was the kind of wife twenty-three-year-old Ariela was. They lived with their two-year-old daughter in a colony of comfortably-spaced homes for married pilots. Each unit had a living room, dinette, kitchen and two bedrooms (more if families got larger).

Ariela, her long blonde hair knotted at the back, had a pot of coffee brewing; but Avihu, a career officer and second in command of his squadron, was impatient to join his men. He was not at all sure this would be a call to action—there had been several such alerts since the start of the crisis—but he was painfully aware of his country's peril. A long, straggling border of some 650 miles had to be defended against bitterly vengeful, twice-defeated enemies. Nasser had nearly a hundred thousand men and nine thousand tanks poised to strike in the desert; the narrow neck of the country, only nine miles across from Tulkarm to Natanya, was particularly vulnerable to an armored thrust from the east.

In manpower, tanks, artillery and naval forces the Israelis were crushingly outweighed, but the most ominous threat was from the air. For every plane available to the Israelis, their enemies could muster three. Tel Aviv was seven minutes away from the Egyptian air base at El Arish in the Sinai, and Nasser alone boasted scores of latest-model MIG fighters, twenty-seven Soviet-built Ilyushin bombers and a fleet of thirty long-range Tupolev bombers. Avihu knew that civil defense authorities in Tel Aviv had made plans to handle up to forty thousand air raid casualties.

His bluish beard scraped clean, Major Avihu kissed Ariela goodbye, bent briefly over the crib where his tousle-haired daughter, Imbar, was murmuring in drowsy curiosity, and drove under a brightening cloudless sky to his squadron building. There he changed to his pressurized flying suit and joined the other pilots.

The first order came: pilots to proceed to their aircraft and await instructions. Major Avihu led the other three pilots who would make up his four-plane formation onto the field, where each took his seat in a French-built Mystère fighter-bomber. Up to this point, he still wasn't sure he would go into action.

Another command: "You may taxi to the runway."

Avihu, leading the entire squadron toward the runway, felt the tension rising in his throat. He had a vague sense of unreality. But the operation could still be called off at this stage. It had been in the past.

Then—the green light for take-off.

Now the battle order of Air Force Commander Mordechai Hod rang in Avihu's ears: "Soldiers of the Air Force, the blustering and swashbuckling Egyptian Army is moving against us to annihilate our people. . . . Fly on, attack the enemy, pursue him to ruination, draw his fangs, scatter him in the wilderness, so that the people of Israel may live in peace in our land, and the future generations be secured."

Normally, a pilot running into trouble on take-off could cut his engine, put out the drag chute and stay on the runway. But not this time. Orders were to keep going, finish the runway, and if necessary explode—but in no case to block the next man. A tightly-timed operation, aimed at hitting eleven Egyptian airfields at precisely the same moment, couldn't afford a break in take-off rhythm. Avihu knew that in some air forces such instructions would be regarded as suicidal. He didn't consider them so; there was always the possibility of being able to pull out safely. In any case, even if a pilot thought he was likely to be killed, that was a chance he had to take.

Avihu made his run—first man to leave his base and possibly the first Israeli in the air. Swiftly after came the other members of his formation, in a pattern resembling an unbalanced spearhead. No. 2 flew behind Avihu on his right, with Nos. 3 and 4 spread out to the flight leader's left, farther back.

Their target was Fayid near Great Bitter Lake on the Suez Canal, a MIG and bomber base roughly halfway between the nearby Sinai airfields and those at the extreme west of the target area, along the Nile.

Once in the air, Major Avihu's sense of unreality vanished. This was it. The time of waiting and worrying was past; he was going forward to meet the challenge. A tremendous exhilaration swept over him.

Zooming out over the Mediterranean, he retracted his wheels and settled into the business at hand. For the past dozen years—from the time that he made his first solo flight at age sixteen—his entire life had been pointed toward this moment; mind and heart had been focused on flying in defense of his country. Since acquiring his wings in 1959, he had been at the training controls of one plane or another virtually every day for at least a couple of hours; Israeli pilots spend more time in the air than any of their contemporaries.

The immediate technical demands on Avihu and his comrades were enormous, perhaps without precedent in military aviation. They would be flying through a forest of scanning radar: sixteen Egyptian posts on the Sinai Peninsula alone, plus electronic feelers probing the area from Russian naval vessels, a British station atop Mt. Troodos in Cyprus, and airborne American patrols. No one, friend or otherwise, must know of this attack. Detection would be fatal. They would therefore be obliged to fly at maximum speed compatible with their war loads, and extremely low, all but skimming the waves to duck beneath the searching radar.

Normally, three hundred feet is the minimum altitude considered safe for control of the French-built Mystère, a swept-wing craft capable of 640 miles per hour. Occasionally, senior pilots like Major Avihu had experimented with unofficial stunting at lower altitudes. But those were isolated moments, over land. This had to be a sustained performance, flying in formation on a crucial mission—and over water.

On land, as Avihu well knew, the scenery below—trees, highways, buildings—gives the pilot a gauge for "feeling" his altitude. "Flying over the sea, there is only an endless expanse of glassy surface. Water merges with sky so there's no horizon. Without contrasts to guide you, you don't know whether you're at one hundred feet or ten."

Whitecaps churned up restlessly beneath his wings. Even to a veteran scuba diver like Avihu, the Mediterranean did not look inviting. He hoped he would not be obliged to eject—and was fully aware this might become necessary. Radio silence had been imposed on all formations in order not to jeopardize the mission. As with the take-off, any pilot running into difficulties would manage on his own: fly back to base at low level, or eject by parachute into the sea, no matter how dim his prospects of ever being found. The important thing was not to betray military presence.

The outcome of the war, he had been told, and Israel's whole future, hinged on a successful opening air strike. "We were too small to fight a long war. We had to hit hard from the first, and keep hitting for a quick decision." His primary assignment was defensive: to block Nasser's promised "annihilation" of Israel by wiping out the Egyptian superiority in air power. A strong blow would also aid the outweighed Israeli ground forces.

If, on the other hand, the air attack failed . . . "I knew that if the Arabs won, not even a child would be spared."

To Major Avihu's left, the undulating outline of the Egyptian coast was dimly taking shape. He would soon be across the Mediterranean, that sea into which Arab orators were constantly promising to throw the doomed people of Israel.

Now he was over the sandy, deserted shore. Avihu climbed a little and looked back. His heart sank. Instead of the three planes that should have been following him, there were only two.

A moment later, consulting his map, he got another jolt: flying over the trackless sea, he had ended up some nine miles off his course. What was worse, his angle of entry was such that, unless he changed direction fast, he would wind up far from the mission target at Fayid.

The major kept his cool. One hand on the flying stick, he made some rapid calculations and adjusted his course. Looking back, he saw the other two pilots follow suit. And now, on more leisurely inspection, he realized that the missing plane was No. 3, not, as he had first feared, No. 4.

No. 4 was the youngest man in the formation, the one most likely to crash or be forced to ditch under the strained conditions. No. 3 was more experienced. Avihu decided he had run into some problem and was a pretty good bet to make his way back alone. The major climbed sharply and concentrated on finding Fayid.

He had been flying due south over the desert for about two minutes when he found himself hemmed in by a sudden thick bank of clouds. He was obliged to drop again to one thousand feet. This was bad news. An effective bombing run required a climb to the neighborhood of five thousand feet, followed by a steep dive. If the cloud blanket was maintained all the way to the target, the mission would be blotted out in advance—a total failure.

The major thought to himself, "God is with them. I don't have No. 3, I go off my course, and now clouds. This is the end."

Then, like the Red Sea 180 miles away, the clouds parted. As Avihu led his formation across the Suez Canal toward Fayid, open patches appeared, creating a "4/8 sky"; i.e., one that was about half covered. The other 50 percent provided more than enough room for climbing.

Avihu shot up rapidly to six thousand feet, then shifted to a steep dive.

At 7:45 A.M., he was over the target, dead on course. "It felt like a training run. As I entered the area, followed by the other two Mystères, there was some movement on the ground—probably a reaction to the sound of our engines. We saw a number of MIG-21's taxiing to the runway to take off, but not a single enemy plane got into the air. We smashed them all at the edge of the runway.

"Our first pass was completely unopposed. We hit planes on the ground, we bombed the runway; and we did a very, very good job of it."

The Israelis returned for several more passes, all at low level. Now the Egyptian anti-aircraft batteries came to life, peppering the sky over the airfield with black bursts. But all the Mystères got through unscathed.

After the fourth pass, Major Avihu picked up altitude again and broke off smartly eastward, his formation following. Behind them lay useless, crater-strewn runways and eighteen shattered Egyptian planes. Ghostly-swift MIG-21's sprawled gracelessly on their sides, smoke spiraling up from their shredded wings. Giant, bulbous-nosed Tupolev bombers were pinned to the ground like squashed insects. Each of the twin-jet, swept-wing Tupolevs had a bomb-carrying capacity of 19,800 pounds, along with seven powerful cannons. This "basic bomber" of the Russian air fleet could fly three thousand miles, at close to supersonic speeds. But these particular Tupolevs would drop no explosives on the white verandas of Tel Aviv; and this runway would not, for the moment at least, send MIG's roaring over Israel's border kibbutzim.

With the raid completed, Major Avihu could break radio silence

ISRAEL AFTER THE SIX-DAY WAR

Territory taken by Israel during the Six-Day War

O   MILES   100

M E D I T E R R A N E A

30°

32°

30°

28°

Alexandria

Cairo

Nile

U N I T E D   A R A B

(E G Y P

J. P. TREMBLAY

30°

and report his results back to base. He was delighted to learn that his No. 3 man had returned there safely, forced back by a malfunctioning of fuel tanks. The radio operator was equally delighted with the major's account of direct hits.

The time was exactly two minutes before eight.

Huddled over the incoming messages at Air Force Headquarters in Tel Aviv were Israel's top brass, including the man who created the nation's air arm, Brigadier General Ezer Weizmann. As Army Chief of Operations, Weizmann had backed to the hilt the daring plan advanced by his protégé and successor in command of the Air Force, Brigadier General Hod. Together they had overcome high-level opposition reaching up to Major General Yitzchak Rabin, Chief of Staff, and Defense Minister Moshe Dayan.

The two airmen had insisted that a static defense system was a waste of money; effective protection of Israel lay in the skies "over Cairo, not over Tel Aviv." An all-out smash leaving only a handful of Israeli planes in reserve was a good gamble, they asserted, because the attack would be over before the enemy discovered what it was all about. Confident in their grasp of Arab mental processes, Weizmann and Hod estimated it would take the Egyptians an hour to figure out the scope of the strike, and that the Syrians and Jordanians would need two hours to react. In this detail they were wrong. It was fully four hours before the Arabs could organize a response, and by that time the back of their air power had been broken.

Weizmann, a sabra, is a nephew of the scientist Chaim Weizmann who was Israel's first president, and a brother-in-law of Moshe Dayan. He has long served as a personal model for pilots like Major Avihu. If Hod, broad-mustached, plain-featured, chatty as a Brooklyn dentist, is something of a departure from the glamorous image of the flying ace, his mentor more than makes up for it. Tall and rangy, with hawkish good looks, Weizmann is a gusty, freewheeling man whose abundant energy sometimes spills over into unpredictable channels, especially after a comradely evening at the bar. He has a caustic and unsparing wit, exercised with what often seems to be deliberate recklessness. His reputation as a charmer is so formidable that, justifiably or not, men with attractive wives keep an eye on him. He is as self-centered as he is swift and decisive. Needing luggage once for a sudden trip, he borrowed a suitcase from a secretary at headquarters, simply dumping its original contents—shoes, dresses, underclothes and make-up—onto an office table and marching off.

After an apprenticeship in the R.A.F. during World War II, he built the Israeli Air Force. His were the early decisions on equipment and training, the flair that set the style, the criteria that guided the selection of pilot candidates.

Weizmann is at forty-three only two years older than Hod, but his questioning air and cynical humor make him seem infinitely more worldly. His vitality is overwhelming; people who talk to him feel as if they had been exposed to a needle shower. He likes to coil his long legs around the nearest furniture and, utterly self-composed, pour out ideas in slangy, British-accented profusion.

"The first thing we look for in a pilot trainee is confidence. You see, the game of fighting in the air has built-in ingredients that fighting on the ground doesn't have—for one thing, you have to fly a bloody airplane. With all due respect to an army battalion commander, who has a nastier job in many respects, he does not have to manipulate personally, physically, bodywise, a machine while he's fighting.

"Confidence leads to determination. Obviously, you cannot have confidence and determination and not be courageous—so you look for a man with guts.

"Guts, I suppose, is how able you are to control your fear—because anybody who tells you he never got scared in his life is a bloody liar, especially a pilot. I was flying a couple of days ago with my son and suddenly *bing, bong, blump,* I thought the bloody engine was falling to pieces. I was scared. Actually, it turned out to be a silly thing, something I left dangling.

"But the trick is to keep control when anything like this happens —a knock, an oil drop—to keep calm and determined to get through."

Weizmann thinks the ideal pilot should have superior mental equipment (but not too superior—"above a certain I.Q., a man becomes a little bit abnormal") and a basic love for flying. He sees common nationality and identity of interest as an important fusing force. "Every Israeli knows that the one basic difference between Israel and other countries is that God forbid if we ever lost the war, we would not be just another country that has lost a war. We would be annihilated."

Weizmann feels that the special challenges of Israeli life have bred a new kind of person. "You see, what happened here—Zionism —is a revolution. Nasser is *not* a revolution; he changed certain things, but he didn't change the basis.

"Here, we uprooted people from A and we replanted them in B. Thank God, the uprooting was successful; the soil in B was the soil necessary to make the plant grow properly. Now we can analyze its ingredients: it's Jerusalem . . . it's Jewry, it's the climate, the geography, the pressure from the Arabs. But the sum total, the way of living, has created a human being that is different."

Although snorting at formal religion—"Don't Godify me!"—Weizmann feels strongly about Israel's claim to Jerusalem. "A country cannot be based on a factory here and a kibbutz there, and—with all due respect—a city like Tel Aviv. I cannot raise my two sons on the history of Tel Aviv."

In building Israeli air power, Weizmann scorned all preconceptions—"We have not been influenced by any military religions"—in favor of his own country's peculiar needs. "Small countries tend to have complexes toward big countries: 'Can anything be bad and cockeyed in America? Obviously not; what's good for America is good for the world.'

"This is hooey. It's what happened to the Egyptians: 'What's good for Siberia is good for the Sinai'; and it's all wrong."

Weizmann went by pragmatic tests. "Your first consideration is, 'Where is my market; who is my enemy?' Then you decide on weapons and their organization." In purchasing supersonic Mirages from France in 1958, Weizmann insisted that two cannons be added to their armament, so that they would be capable of destroying planes on the ground. He refused to be seduced by sophisticated arguments about the missile age.

His greatest reputation is as a magician of morale, with an off-the-cuff eloquence that keeps his flyers tightly linked to the over-all defense establishment, yet preserves their sense of being an elite group with a special responsibility. In other situations his untempered candor has apparently antagonized influential political leaders, with a dampening effect on his army career.

Weizmann has been spiritual father of a new phenomenon, a

twentieth-century warrior in the Maccabee mold: the Jewish pilot. "When our trainee reaches the point where he can fly at forty thousand feet, we send him up one night between nine and ten o'clock, tell him not to look down as he rises. He climbs to ten . . . twenty . . . thirty . . . forty thousand. Then we say, 'Look down.'

"And what does he see? The whole of Israel a pearly blaze, humming with life, and around it the Arab states in glum darkness, with only here and there the barest glimmer of a light. When he sees that, he becomes a Jewish pilot."

Just such a pilot is Major Avihu, on whom the impact of Weizmann is plainly visible. Avihu's explanation of Air Force esprit echoes Weizmann's imagery: "At fifty thousand feet, in a supersonic Mirage, I can fly only north and south; otherwise, I'd be out of the country in a matter of seconds. You can see on one side Cyprus, Turkey—on the other, Iraq and Sharm el Sheikh. You have no trouble spotting the Suez Canal. But your own country is very difficult to see; it's under the belly of your plane. You have to turn around and look back to see it. You become very aware of its smallness."

The pilot, says Avihu, develops a special feeling of protectiveness toward his country. "You fly over it, you see it every day—you get the feeling it belongs to you. The man on the ground sees one little corner. We see it as a totality—and we also see its tininess and isolation."

Avihu is the son of a Polish couple who met in a training camp for Palestine "pioneers." His mother came to the Holy Land in one of the "illegal" ships that defied the British ban on Jewish immigration; cast adrift in the Mediterranean several hundred yards offshore, she nearly drowned before comrades dragged her to safety. Avihu was born in a moshav, a modified form of collective farm settlement, in the north. When he was two, his father moved the family to Kefar Vitkin outside Haifa.

The boy's first contact with flying came in Gadna, the national youth movement operated jointly by the Education and Defense Ministries. He started by building plane models. From the moment he took up a Piper Cub alone, there was no looking back. "I knew that for me it would be the Air Force till the end. It's a hard feeling to explain. There you sit, looking down on people who seem to be ants beneath you. You feel like a king—or a poet."

Soon after, Avihu spent a month in the United States, one of five promising youngsters invited as part of an exchange program by the Civil Air Patrol.

For the next several years, his biggest trials and triumphs came from flying. At eighteen, in spite of his mother's misgivings, he entered the Flying Course, extremely rigorous in Israel because the Air Force counts on overcoming its inferiority in numbers and equipment by the quality of its pilots. He sweated and suffered: "Flying was my life; failure would have been unendurable." Exultantly, he passed.

At twenty-five, Avihu was considered "an old bachelor." Most Israeli pilots marry early, if only to have a refuge from the tensions of living under a perpetual state of alert. The girl chosen by Avihu offered more affirmative inducements to matrimony.

He first saw her standing just outside his base, waiting for a lift: a fresh, slender blonde in officer's uniform, with a wide mouth set in a long, gravely-smiling Modigliani face. Avihu pulled up his car beside her. Attractive and knowing it, he has a gruff, teasing manner with women. "What are you waiting here for? Nobody will ever pick you up if you stand on the dividing line."

He swung open the door and the blonde got in. "How is it I don't know you?" Avihu demanded. "I know all the girl officers in the Air Force."

It turned out the girl was a newcomer to the base, and her name was Ariela. Avihu suggested she throw a small party—the Israeli equivalent of a debutante ball.

When she did, he turned up briefly, left with another girl—and a few months later, married Ariela. It was that kind of courtship and it has been that kind of marriage—laconic, challenging and transparently happy. Avihu reports dryly that "on our honeymoon to Europe, my wife was elected the queen of the ship. You can imagine the competition." This thrust, however, is accompanied by an exchange of warm glances.

Ariela likewise is a sabra, daughter of a Vienna-educated engineer and a lady gymnast from Latvia who came for the first Maccabee Games (the all-Jewish Olympics) in 1935 and stayed on. At fifteen, Ariela was sent to a Catholic finishing school in England. She found the atmosphere oppressive. "Being told when to take a bath was a bit too much. And having grown up as a sabra in a free country, I wasn't used to being pointed out as a Jew." She packed her things and flew home.

Ariela is an inventive cook, and a skilled painter in the Hokusai style. She also designs cloth cut-outs of clowns and animals for little Imbar, a honey-haired elf full of unexpected oddities and graces. In 1966 she took a journalism course, and is now a part-time reporter for the daily, *Lamerhav*.

Ariela likes flying and has been up several times with her husband. However, she is comfortable only with Avihu at the controls: "I don't really trust anyone else." She is attuned to the hazards of Avihu's profession, and worries less when he is aloft than when he's on a long auto trip: "It's not that he's a bad driver. But in the air, he alone controls the situation. If he's in trouble, he can eject. On the ground, there are other cars."

Ariela is contented with a way of life that others might find irksome. Their cottage is simple, their recreation limited to swimming, photography, and visits with other couples on the base. They pay the penalty of specialization: Avihu has no great interest in opera, Freud, vintage wines or Carnaby Street fashions. A compassionate man, he is sometimes uneasy about the human consequences of his efficiency. And he is constantly on call.

A pilot of Avihu's talents could be living on quite a different scale, taking his pick of commercial airline jobs that would pay three times his Air Force salary and enable him to live in any glamour capital of the world. When he completed five years of service in 1962, he was free to make such a choice. It never entered his head.

Nor has he had occasion to regret his stance; never less than on the morning of June 5, 1967. Flying back from his raid on Fayid, Major Avihu saw a long column of Israeli armor plowing westward from the Negev into the Sinai. The pilots had done their part, and would do more in days to come. But only ground forces could push back the enemy gathered along Israel's borders.

AFTERNOON: THE SINAI

THE army of Israel—*Zahal* in Hebrew—has to be seen in the field to be believed. Pants and jackets are likely to have no more than a nodding acquaintance. Boots alternate with sneakers, work shoes, and—in the case of a girl mess corporal—ballet slippers. Headdress is splendid in its irreverence for military precedent: helmets and berets vie with chauffeur's gear, religious skullcaps, floppy peaked hats from the kibbutzim, and wide-brimmed Australian bush hats. Beards flourish on equal terms with mustaches, Beatle haircuts, and long orthodox curls.

But this army is serious, without being solemn. Precisely because the grimness of their task is thoroughly understood, Israeli soldiers can afford to relax. Theirs is the friendly raillery of men bound together by more than military discipline.

The fact is that Zahal is still at heart an underground army of volunteers, an underground that, with nationhood, has surfaced. Privates call majors by their first names. Leadership is exercised through logical persuasion and personal example: "Follow me!", rather than "Forward!", is the command to action. Not content with mesmeric chants of "my country, right or wrong," Zahal has a strength based on the commitment of its personnel to its purposes.

Behind that strength, according to one of the army's senior commanders, are two words: "common fate."

Israel Tal is Chief of Armored Forces. Although ranked with Rommel and Patton as a tank strategist, he is not everybody's idea of a model brigadier general. The disparity is not physical. Tal is short, but so is the Uzzi, the swift-firing submachine gun developed in Israel and carried by its noncoms. In battle dress, with his sharply etched features and hard lines creasing his stubbly cheeks, Tal cuts a suitably fierce figure.

His mind and manner are something else. Tal has a university degree in philosophy. With a scholarly precision that nettles less academic colleagues, he lays down opinions on international relations("I am against flags, boundaries, whatever separates peoples; but you can't start with the Jews, they're too vulnerable"); on Zionism ("Our claim rests less on historical primacy than on fundamental justice; the Jew has a right to live which requires no sanction from anyone else"); on Arab refugees ("Tragic, but a consequence of their entire social order"); and, of course, on the Israeli Army ("Our morale is so high because everyone knows that what happens to one, happens to all"). Officers and men alike, says Tal, know that failure in battle means collective extinction; that, regulars or reservists, they share field conditions and opportunities for advancement, and that their families receive the same casualty benefits.

By contrast, in the Egyptian Army an abyss separates the manicured and monogrammed lieutenant from the soldier in the ranks. The lieutenant, who is likely to be the son of a former pasha, plays tennis in Cairo's sumptuous Gezira Sporting Club, whose grounds along the Nile have never admitted a plebeian in other than a menial capacity. The officer enjoys better food, more comfortable living quarters—all the privileges that in a quasi-feudal society accompany birth, rank and education. He feels no special responsibility toward his men—and engenders no special loyalty.

One benefit of Zahal's democracy is operational. Tal points out that in other armies a patrol caught in ambush is usually under instructions to withdraw, because the purpose of its mission has been revealed. An Israeli patrol is expected to assault and carry out its original assignment regardless of the enemy presence. Each man, aware of what is at stake for all and confident that his comrades will not let him down, fights as if the outcome of the war depended on him alone.

Leadership, too, acquires a different coloration. Command assignments have nothing to do with old school ties. "Because there is a common base of education, income and morality," says Tal, "the spectrum of qualities in which there can be a difference is much narrower." Lacking an external source for his authority, and under constant scrutiny from below as well as from above, the officer can emerge from the mass only on the strength of such inherent personal qualities as wisdom or decisiveness. "None but the fittest rises to the top."

Status in civilian life is not a primary consideration; nor is age. A young farmer may command a graying bank director. Under these stern conditions, reservist officers in particular may come from unexpected quarters.

On Thursday evening, May 25, David "Dudu" Sela took the stage at Tel Aviv University's Academy of Music, last of five soloists in an end-of-term cello competition. He was a wiry, intense twenty-three-year-old of grasshopper restlessness and angularity. Thick black hair tumbled down the right side of his forehead.

Dudu settled his instrument firmly on the floor, took his A from the accompanist, and launched into Beethoven's Fifth Sonata for Cello and Piano. His fingers flew along the instrument with deft precision. Reaching the fugal finale, Dudu broke into a beatific smile, head swaying in time to the dancing phrases.

When he finished, wild applause rocked the auditorium. The dean of the Music Academy, Professor Oeden Partos, turned from his inconspicuous tenth-row seat to make a little gesture of respect to a plump, smiling woman across the aisle.

For Dudu's mother, the successful concert came as climax to a stormy adventure in parenthood. For fourteen years her only child had oscillated between music and less gentle pursuits, a troublesome, stubbornly individualistic boy whose willfulness continually threatened to overwhelm his natural gifts.

In one of his earliest escapades, Dudu smashed a long row of pop bottles at the local grocery because he "liked the different sounds" they made. At grade school, he was chronically absent, late or disorderly; his mother, trying to pacify outraged teachers, spent as much time there as he did. When, at the age of nine, Dudu discovered music, the rejoicing was therefore general. It was a logical pursuit for a boy whose mother's colorful pottery brightened the family villa at Herzliya outside Tel Aviv; whose aunt, Hannah Orloff, was a world-famous sculptress; and whose ninety-year-old grandfather was one of Israel's first teachers.

Dudu began with the trumpet but soon shifted to the cello, submitting to private lessons and then, to everybody's astonishment, uncomplainingly commuting to Tel Aviv's High School of Music.

At this point, peculiarly sabra factors intervened. Dudu's father, an official in the Defense Ministry, had held a key army command in the 1948 War of Independence; his mother had been active in the

Haganah underground. Dudu had been introduced to the air rifle at six; a visiting uncle from New York, who protested at such "gangster" training, was told: "Israel will need defenders."

For teen-agers, this militant spirit was channeled into a variety of voluntary youth movements loosely associated with different political parties, and devoted to the outdoor life: camping, hiking, summertime work on government construction projects. Dudu joined one such group, Ha-Noar Ha-Oved, and was promptly fascinated by the world of nature. He began a collection of snakes and scorpions, took to making sudden disappearances on fishing trips, and found it necessary to refresh himself by frequent dips in the nearby Mediterranean. His attendance record at high school suffered accordingly.

Nonetheless, when Israel staged a Casals Festival in 1961, honoring the great Spanish cellist, Dudu was one of three student soloists chosen to perform. His virtuoso showing earned him a place in the national Youth Orchestra when, a year later, it made a concert tour of western Europe. Once again music dominated Dudu's life. He heard the great symphonies of London and Amsterdam, attended the rehearsals of celebrated chamber groups, luxuriated in widening aesthetic horizons.

But he could not completely escape his Jewish consciousness. On a driving tour of Switzerland, his group needed permission to cross a six-mile strip of German territory. The German border guard— booted, self-important, wearing the imperial eagle on his cap— frowned suspiciously at their passports. Dudu turned the car around to follow a winding forty-mile route that would keep them inside Switzerland. "I was not going to cross at that frontier. I felt sure that border guard would kill a hundred Jews on command without blinking an eye."

In a Dutch village, the Israeli musicians were approached by a Jewish boy who told them two huge Germans had beaten him and stolen his bicycle. Dudu and his friends tracked the Germans down. In the encounter that followed, Dudu picked up a few bruises, but he gave more than he took. "If my friends hadn't dragged me away I would probably have killed them both."

Returning from Europe, Dudu faced his thirty months of compulsory military service. Over his mother's objections, he opted for the elite but hazard-ridden paratroops, who during the repeated

Arab incursions of the 1960's carried the brunt of the army's reprisal operations.

Dudu was an excellent paratrooper. He took honors in cross-country running and swimming, qualified for the Officers' Course, and finished No. 2 in his class. He flourished in the congenial atmosphere, the paratroopers being the most informal branch of Zahal. "If anybody tried to salute me, I would reply with such a caricature—I copied it from a comedy film—that the saluter would be forever discouraged. I hate military discipline!"

Nonetheless, Dudu demonstrated in a half-dozen border clashes that he could subordinate his individualism when he had to. He simply could not meet his responsibilities as an officer with his old hit-or-miss approach.

Music as such was no part of his life, except for one memorable, accidental occasion. His unit was speeding north to intercept an anticipated Syrian invasion. Lying in the truck, one of the riflemen began softly humming the opening of a Bach chorale. "They were mostly kibbutz boys, with a good musical education. Someone else came in with the second part, and in a few moments the whole truck was overflowing with Bach, in four-part harmony. On the way to a battlefront. It was quite wonderful."

It was also exceedingly rare. For nearly three years Dudu did not even play a scale on the cello. When at long last he came back to the instrument, he did so very cautiously, uncertain as to whether he would be able to find his way again. The serenity of the vine-covered villa at Herzliya helped. More important was an inner change, a newly focused energy. Almost unnoticed, a crystallizing of vision had come in the army. Dudu began reading furiously. His bedroom, already crowded with African sculptures, instruments, paintings, and an upright piano, was soon piled high with books: Sholem Aleichem's folk tales and William L. Shirer's *The Rise and Fall of the Third Reich,* volumes of poetry, psychology, Talmudic philosophy.

His new seriousness quickly emerged in his playing. Once his technique was restored, he plunged intensively into Bach and Vivaldi, working for hours to capture a single elusive nuance.

He formed his own chamber group, supplementing his cello with two recorders, an alto singer and a cembalo. So radical was the transformation in Dudu that when Chief of Staff Yitzchak Rabin saw him in an orchestral appearance in 1966, Rabin refused to believe his eyes. He came backstage to demand, "Is it really you?"

His main diversion was women. Although he was careless of dress and appointments, as self-assured in his judgments as a Roman emperor, and hardly the handsomest of his circle, Dudu took cocky pride in an active social life. As spring of 1967 rolled around, he was looking forward to the delights of the long, warm Israeli summer. He was vexed to learn that Nasser had other plans.

The May 25 concert at the Tel Aviv Academy was actually a farewell appearance. A few days before, the moment he heard that tank reservists were being called up, Dudu had reported to his paratroop unit for instructions. Months earlier, he had turned down a job offer from the illustrious Concertgebouw Orchestra of Amsterdam, because "this is my place. Here, you have an identity you can take with you anywhere. Here you have something of your own."

Now, that "something" was threatened. "It was a question of fighting, or letting them kill you. I am a very proud Jew. I was not going to permit us ever again to undergo the Hitler kind of holocaust.

"What were we asking? Only to live. When you fight for life itself, it is something."

Dudu packed a kit—shorts, knife, toilet supplies—and headed for the broiling Negev.

At 10:15 on the morning of June 5, First Lieutenant Dudu Sela rode at the head of an armored column smashing westward along the coastal highway of the Sinai. He commanded a half-track, the centaur among armored vehicles, which combines a tank-like forward section borne on steel treads, with truck wheels in the rear. Behind him rolled a scout forte of paratroop regulars in half-tracks, backed by Patton tanks.

His face caked with dust, Dudu had just guided his driver through five miles of treacherous dunes to emerge west of the main Egyptian fortifications at Rafah. Because of the furious din—there was incessant harassing fire from pillboxes, antitank guns and bunkered-in tanks—he had been forced to communicate directions by pressing down on his driver's right or left shoulder.

They had crossed the border from the upper Negev two hours earlier as part of a divisional group commanded directly by General Tal. Tal's northern command had the crucial task of undermining

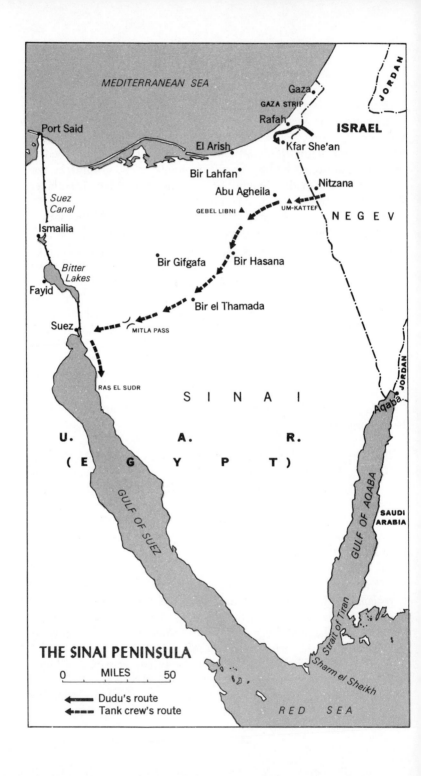

MEDITERRANEAN SEA

JORDAN

Gaza
GAZA STRIP
Rafah
ISRAEL
El Arish
Kfar She'an
Port Said
Bir Lahfan
Nitzana
Suez
Canal
Abu Agheila
GEBEL LIBNI
UM-KATTEF
NEGEV
Ismailia
Bir Gifgafa
Bir Hasana
Bitter
Lakes
Fayid
Bir el Thamada
Suez
MITLA PASS
RAS EL SUDR
S I N A I
U.   A.   R.
(E   G   Y   P   T)
Aqaba
JORDAN
GULF OF SUEZ
GULF OF AQABA
SAUDI
ARABIA
Strait of Tiran
Sharm el Sheikh
RED   SEA

THE SINAI PENINSULA

0   MILES   50

Dudu's route
Tank crew's route

Egyptian morale by breaking through at the western end of the Gaza Strip, around the crossroads of Rafah, where Nasser had concentrated the heaviest defenses ever constructed in desert territory. Against the complex fortifications designed by the Russians, the huge Stalin tanks, the outranging field guns, and the punishing terrain, Tal would have to pit improvisation and sheer verve. As Tal put it, "This will be our first trial of strength against the Egyptian Army in ten years. Other countries in other wars can afford to lose the first battle and then apply the lessons of defeat. We are different. The cost of losing would be too high, so every objective has to be taken. We can think only of decision—not of losses."

Nonetheless, Tal tried to avoid a head-on collision with the twelve-mile belt of mine fields, tanks and artillery clustered around Rafah, by daring maneuvers over the soft sand dunes. Entering from the Negev, the paratroopers were to continue west across the north-south highway from Nitzana, then turn right in the desert and cleave an alley to the coast through the drifting sands. Once near the sea, they would push westward again some thirty miles toward El Arish, the main Egyptian supply base in the Sinai. El Arish, a fishing and date-growing town of thirty thousand, was the site of ancient Rhinocolura ("city of cut noses"), where three thousand years ago the Egyptians kept a colony of mutilated prisoners.

Dudu was part of the spearhead group leading the battalion, with the dual responsibility of clearing the way and drawing fire that would reveal enemy positions. The very nature of the operation, an unprotected thrust deep into a fortified area, created long odds against getting through it unscathed. Dudu was fully aware that sooner or later, something was going to happen to his half-track.

"It wasn't a matter of intuition, but of simple logic. In a brief engagement, there is a chance to survive a mission like this. But in a sustained battle—a real war—we would have to be hit at some point. I knew it, and all the others knew it. The spearhead has to be chewed up for the whole force to reach its objective."

The reconnaissance unit was therefore made up entirely of volunteers. In the Israeli Army, this tends to become a technicality; few men exercise their option to back out.

His first hazard, soon after entering the Sinai, was the northward passage through the dunes: several miles of slippery terrain considered difficult for tanks and impassable for half-tracks. The rear wheels of his vehicles were constantly sinking into the loose sand. Frequently the dunes reared up at chillingly sharp angles. The paratroopers shot for the top and hoped for the best. Most of them got through.

Turning to the north, they began to encounter resistance: isolated infantry detachments, pillboxes, bunkered-in tanks. The tanks were painted sable to blend in with the sand; under the blazing midday sun, it was impossible to detect the Egyptian positions except from the puffs of smoke that followed fire. When a position was revealed, they jumped down from the half-track, fought and returned. They stopped for nothing—not even water.

The Rafah sector had been reinforced so recently that Israeli Intelligence had not been able to keep abreast of the changes. The main buttressing, it turned out, had been with antitank cannon. Now these opened up, line upon line, against the Israeli reconnaissance platoons; long-range guns thundered from the rear.

As the first range-finding shells whistled over the scouting force, Dudu ducked. "Of course I was afraid at the beginning; everyone is afraid." He looked over and saw his cousin Giora standing erect in a half-track, shouting "Follow me!" as he waved his men onward. "I remembered I was a commander. After that, I kept my head up."

The Egyptian fire intensified. Behind the Israelis, the hole punched by Tal's tanks had been plugged up; the half-tracks were for the moment alone on the battlefield, hemmed in by both heavy artillery and close-range fire. The advance was halted; but not for long. Leaping to the ground with rifles, bazookas and machine guns, Dudu and his men charged each obstacle in turn: barbed wire, trenches, bunkers. They had taken the enemy by surprise; it was essential not to lose momentum.

For Dudu, a vivid and terrible moment was the firing of his first shot in combat. "I said to myself, 'You are going to kill another human being.' I remember cursing Nasser, saying, 'Why did you have to do this to us, force us to kill?' "

Later, he was terrified at the ease with which the killing became commonplace. He found himself shooting as if at target practice, becoming annoyed when he missed. "It was awful, this losing all sense of human awareness."

It was midafternoon, and the unit had been in action for some eight hours, when they came to the outskirts of a village called Kfar She'an. Hidden along the low stone houses some two hundred yards away, Dudu spotted a Russian T-34 tank. An Israeli captain riding in Dudu's half-track—his own vehicle had been disabled—ordered a soldier armed with a bazooka to fire.

The soldier became so excited that he fumbled with the release plug; the more he tried, the more entangled he got. Dudu, ever the individualist, burst out laughing: "I couldn't help it." He grabbed the bazooka—"you must be very fast in these cases; if you don't kill him, he kills you"—and pulled the plug. Then he threw himself across one of the soldiers at the side of the half-track, took the bazooka in the crook of his arm, and shot at the tank.

"It was lovely, I must say. The tank went up—*phht!* After that, I swung around and hit an Egyptian truck. It jumped, and went 'boom,' and then you saw all the soldiers running out. It's an awful thing to say, but it was wonderful to see, because a bazooka is such a light weapon, it's really nothing. . . ."

A few seconds later, there was a furious whirring in the air and Dudu's half-track exploded. Almost simultaneously, the Egyptian tank that had hit him with a shell from the left was itself destroyed by an Israeli tank cannon.

But five men in the half-track were dead. Another was blasted to survival through the door of the burning vehicle. Least injured was the soldier across whose body Dudu had been lying, because Dudu absorbed the greater part of the shock.

Dudu's first thought was that he was dead. "I had the sensation of flying someplace. There was a buzzing in my head, *zzew, zzew, zzew*, over and over. Everything was red, really red."

He became aware that his hands were on fire, the skin shrinking. His hands!

It occurred to him that he was having thoughts. Something still worked. He had to get out of this inferno.

His vision was blurred, his whole body in torment. His hands were useless, and his left foot would not move. But he had some leverage with the other foot; using it, he forced his way free. Toppling to the ground, he was dimly aware of bones cracking across his chest.

Dudu staggered up. He tried to drag himself toward a gap between two small houses, but collapsed before he could reach it. He had a faint awareness of bodies on the ground, and of a rescue party approaching. As a blanket enveloped his body, he held up his shriveled hands. "I'm all right now," he mumbled. "Go to the others." Then consciousness receded.

By 6:30 P.M., as the first hints of a sundown breeze stirred from the sea, vanguard platoons of Centurion tanks had slammed forward twenty-five miles. General Tal was running fourteen hours ahead of schedule. Whatever might happen on other fronts, the desert campaign was well under way.

EVENING: THE PROFESSOR

ISRAEL is no travel-poster Mediterranean paradise inhabited exclusively by psalm-singing angels. It has rates of auto death and divorce surpassed only by those of the United States, along with its quota of bureaucrats and fanatics, housebreakers and embezzlers—the usual ugly barnacles of a democratic society.

In the spring of 1967, caught in the doldrums of a lagging economy, increased emigration, squabbling among old-line politicians, and a mass retreat to discotheques by disenchanted urban youngsters, Israel was beginning to look like many a fractioned, restless nation to the north and west.

Until Nasser began thumping his chest.

Self-interest promptly vanished. Elegant Haifa matrons who wouldn't set foot in their own kitchens offered to carry hospital bedpans. In a back-alley Jaffa café, a notorious jewel thief turned up resplendent in army uniform, boasting about how he had invoked *protektsia* (wire-pulling) to get back into his unit: "If there is no Israel, where will I steal my diamonds?" A Tel Aviv dentist, well-known for his insistence on advance payment, recoiled indignantly when a paratrooper patient offered a check: "Would I take money from an army officer at a time like this?"

Jerusalem in particular had a strong front-line tradition. In the

1948 fighting its people had survived months of bitter siege and merciless shelling; Jordanian sentries were still posted across from their Israeli counterparts, sometimes within a few yards of Jewish homes, along the ragged armistice line dividing the city.

Apart from its central district of shops and government buildings, the Israeli capital was a city of immigrants and scholars. The immigrants were dispersed through a dozen "colonies," mainly on the edges of the city; the academic community was concentrated in the southwestern hills, around Hadassah Hospital and the university campus.

The Hebrew University of Jerusalem sits in white-columned grandeur on a wind-swept mountaintop, its clean neo-classic buildings sparkling in the sun. Simple, strong architectural lines match the unspoiled outdoor setting; stone, pine-covered hills, and sky blend to create an Athenian openness. It has a touch of Mexico University in its modern bas-reliefs, and of the American Midwest in its spacious lawns.

Its faculty lives nearby, in California-style ranch houses clinging to the hillsides, in villas on rambling side streets, in modest middle-class apartments. To one such dwelling in the Katamon area, a third-floor walk-up bright with paintings and sun-drenched balcony, the belligerent rumblings from Cairo brought a painful dilemma.

This was the home of Robert Szereszevski, lecturer in economics; sometime poet, full-time husband and father; ardent admirer of Moslem architecture, British theater, Swedish movies and African sculpture; a man with more interests than he had time to pursue, and more friends than interests.

Some men seem born to die on the barricades. Robert was not among them. Tallish and slim, with green-brown eyes behind tortoise-shell glasses, Robert looked less professor than student. He wore rugged open-toed Israeli sandals; brown hair spilled down his forehead, belying his thirty years.

Robert led a busy life. Although he carried a formidable work load—teaching classes in introductory economics and the problems of underdeveloped areas, counseling, and writing books on Israeli history and economics—at the center of his existence was his family. Everything in his crowded schedule could be shifted around, but not the hours between 6:00 and 8:00 P.M. Late afternoon always found him swinging briskly homeward with his eager, distinctive gait: head and chest thrust slightly forward, shoulders swaying in the rolling movement of a crawl swimmer with each long, buoyant stride.

Waiting there were his wife and two small blonde children, a girl of three and a boy of one. Together and separately, the children had their allotted playtime, when Robert would chat, sing, play and draw pictures with them. Sometimes there would be a brief walk to a nearby playground. Weekends also were set aside for family excursions to the beach or the country.

These occasions, and many others, were shared with his wife Yaffa. Dark, slight and girlish, with a small nose set in a delicate face crowned by a mass of wavy hair, Yaffa met Robert at a party nine years ago in Tel Aviv, where she was studying Hebrew literature at the university. He was about to get his bachelor's degree in Jerusalem. They were married soon afterward. Over the years a relationship of extreme closeness and interdependence developed; "brother and sister as well as husband and wife," perhaps because both had been only children.

From the beginning of Robert's career as a "student assistant," then in London where he took his Ph.D., and in Ghana, where he had a Ford Foundation grant, Yaffa had helped with research, diagrams and typing. Back in Jerusalem, where Robert was engaged in half a dozen projects, she set up a protective atmosphere for him and his collaborators: beer, cakes and coffee, and no interference from the children. He was free to concentrate on what had all the earmarks of a brilliant career. At thirty, he had contributed important original studies to the two standard texts on the economy of Ghana, was momentarily expecting promotion to senior lecturer (somewhat higher than the American category of associate professor), and was in line for a major exchange appointment in the United States.

Robert's classes at the university were standing room only—and for good reason. Leftist in his orientation, he regarded economics not as a procession of dry statistics, but as the key to human betterment, inseparable from such considerations as freedom of the individual and ethnic equality. His lectures were punctuated with wry humor: "Countries that make good tanks rarely make good tractors." And he made sure he was understood; he would rewrite an entire lecture if he found a way to make his point more simply. At student-faculty teas, traditionally stuffy affairs where timid students hung back from stiff, self-conscious little groups of professors, Robert was a welcome catalyst. Sooner or later he rolled back the rug, dug up a hora record—and the ice was broken.

He was a convivial host at home, too. He liked a social drink, danced "a kind of distorted twist" (Yaffa's phrase) as well as the waltz and tango, and sang boisterously if inaccurately, favoring sentimental Slavic melodies from his days in one of the Socialist youth movements. At such moments, his friends in the radical intelligentsia were sometimes bewildered. Robert plainly enjoyed the pleasures of the capitalist world.

But there was no "betrayal" involved. He was simply a man of widely varied interests. A rover through bookshops, he read voraciously in Hebrew, English, Polish, and Italian, Camus, Sartre and Brecht in translation, Michael Fry in the London *Observer*, satire wherever he could find it. He relished Pete Seeger's ballads. He was delighted with *Macbird*, and especially the "hero's" outburst, "Why, it's a nigra and a filthy beatnik!"

He also wrote verse, this paradox of an economist, and had more than a touch of the poet in other respects. He could never be bothered to repeat a lecture; repetition bored him. But he would gladly travel to a distant kibbutz to address an audience toward whose views he felt sympathetic. Offered a consultant post by a business firm, he refused to discuss it; his training was not at the disposal of mere money-making. And he scorned pomposity; of colleagues who dangled their academic pedigrees, he gibed, "A man must be pretty desperate if he needs to label himself 'doctor.' "

He was, in short, a confirmed humanist, scornful of material values, adamant in defending the rights of the individual everywhere. And this was the root of his mid-May conflict. He could make no exceptions: not for Jews when he felt they were being coerced into super-Zionism, not even for Arabs.

On the face of it, Robert's problem was academic. Unlike most of his friends, he was not a member of the Israeli Army reserves. He had been refused for military training in 1955 because of the residual effects of a childhood illness. He was therefore under no obligation to serve, and in fact had no visible means of getting into the army. But he was keenly aware that his university colleagues were exchanging their textbooks for military manuals.

Robert was thoroughly Israeli. Although he was born in Poland, and had survived the Warsaw ghetto, he had spent his adolescence in the deeply nationalistic Achdut Ha'avodah (Socialist Workers) youth movement. In 1964 he had turned down an appointment to the London School of Economics because "one must belong somewhere, and Israel is my home." His attachment to Jerusalem was almost fanatical. He would walk alone for hours in the old orthodox quarter of Mea Shearim, totally bemused by its quaint architecture, narrow lanes, and picturesque citizenry "straight out of a Rembrandt canvas." He delighted in contrasting the capital's character-soaked atmosphere with the pedestrian bustle of Tel Aviv (Jerusalem is to Tel Aviv what San Francisco is to Los Angeles: older, wiser, cooler, hillier, more formal and more individualistic). Robert loved the mystery of the city, and the grandeur of the views from its heights —so much so that although he felt that "not seeing the United States is the same as not being in the twentieth century," he never dreamed of spending more than a sabbatical there.

As family man and Jerusalemite, his heart was in Israel. Yet his whole intellectual orientation made him sympathetic to the neglected Arab masses. A scholar trained in the long view, he saw them as victims of history, part of the ex-colonial millions who had been robbed of the personal dignity that was every man's natural inheritance. They were, after all, Semites, the same basic material as the Jews, one-time fellow wanderers of the barren desert. Robert felt that the Arabs, along with other previously exploited societies, had a long-standing claim for damages against the more advanced industrial powers. The pious "white man's burden" of the nineteenth century had now become the white man's obligation: to provide the former underdogs with guidance, education and financial aid.

Conditions for local Arabs had improved enormously since 1948. Infant mortality rates, for instance, had become the lowest in the Arab world. But there were still grievances about land, travel and housing.

Land ownership had long been a complicated issue in Palestine, locked in a tangle of Turkish grants, British mandate laws, and the unregistered claims of wandering Bedouins. The lands abandoned by fleeing Arabs in 1948 compounded the chaos.

More recently, Arab-owned lands in the border areas had been expropriated on security grounds. Robert questioned the authenticity of the security need in some cases, and the reasonableness of the payment in others. Citing the many references to olive trees in Arab folklore, he argued that a tract of land has deep emotional meaning for the fellah as the source of his bread as well as of his status in family and community.

City housing was the other main Arab complaint. It was not bad in Jerusalem or in Haifa, where the races had long dwelt together. But in Tel Aviv, the Arab construction worker was too often denied an apartment the moment he acknowledged his identity. For many ex-Europeans, the Arab was a stranger, a potential threat to be eyed warily.

It was on this theme that Absolom Katz, a crony from student days, had made a bold film. Katz, a radio writer, lived in Robert's apartment building. The two frequently relaxed at western movies together, hissing the fearless marshal. They were also collaborating on a picture-and-text Israeli history book for which Robert was writing pungent little captions: "Yemenite working hard without benefit of ideology"—"Palestinian Conventional Robbery, garden variety." But their closest link was on the Israeli Arab question.

Katz's film, *I Am Achmed*, documented the inner torment of an Arab worker adrift in a Jewish city. It opened in Herzliya, the residential seaside-villa suburb where Dudu Sela lived outside Tel Aviv. The audience greeted it in dead silence. The Israeli government declined to purchase the film for mass distribution. At its next showing, in a private hall in Jerusalem, it was violently attacked by a journalist in the audience.

Robert, rising to his friend's defense, was greeted by strident boos and catcalls; but after he had talked for a few minutes, a thoughtful silence spread through the hall. "The very fact that some of you were ready to start fighting," he observed, "proves that there is a cancer here on this subject, a guilt of sorts. It isn't enough to provide the Arab with modern facilities; you must understand what is in his heart."

Robert was on his feet for ninety minutes. Then a regular-army major stood up. "I have killed many Arabs in combat, but I have never hated. You young boys who are screaming, you have hatred, and that's bad. Because of our forty-year history of fighting with the

Arabs, sometimes we forget to be human. We are humanitarians with respect to the American Negro, or the Vietnamese; what about the Arabs?"

Afterward, people milled around in the street outside the hall for two hours, debating.

Robert did not confine himself to speeches. Like many other Israelis, he opened his home to Arab students—a gesture of enormous significance in Arab eyes. Moslem culture attaches great importance to being welcomed in the home, an importance that is reflected in the ancient saying: "Accept me, even if you do not give me dinner." Arab tradition holds that a man must give sanctuary even to the murderer of his own son.

For Robert, the gesture was practical. Ultimately, he felt, Jews and Arabs would have to learn to live together in an integrated Middle Eastern society. He foresaw the day when a power equilibrium and a compromise would be reached; at that moment, the Arabs in Israel could be an invaluable cementing force.

Meanwhile, he urged restraint on the international plane. He especially counseled patience with Egypt's Nasser, in whom he thought he detected signs of a social conscience. He was skeptical of military solutions, whether they emanated from the Kremlin, the White House, or Tel Aviv. And he mistrusted charisma itself, the intoxicating presence of a Dayan, as dangerous to the democratic process.

Robert was the classic unpurchasable rebel, in a tradition dating back to the biblical prophets; a man who held himself chastely aloof from emotional attachments in the belief that somewhere the voice of calm objectivity must remain intact; an ivory-tower intellectual who nonetheless kept up a running fire of outspoken comment from the tower.

It was a position that brought him into constant collision with the Zionist Establishment. For some time David Ben-Gurion had been insisting that Jews in the Diaspora should either come to the homeland, or in effect give up their spiritual franchise. Under the difficult economic conditions of 1966, when Israelis themselves were beginning to emigrate, the argument of the former premier was gaining ground.

Robert entered a sharp dissent. At a university student-faculty forum, he asserted that every Jew should be free to decide his own destiny; to settle in Israel, or to remain in an overseas country of his choice, where, if he preferred, he could decide to assimilate to the majority. "The task of Israel is to accept all comers—not to push or coerce."

He was promptly challenged in print by Chaim Guri, one of the country's leading poets. A radio confrontation was arranged on a related subject, the "brain drain" that was siphoning off native intellectual talent to the West.

The stocky, dynamic Guri, a sabra and a veteran of the 1948 war, stressed the nation's life-and-death need for Jewish skills and capital from overseas. Robert countered that every man had an overriding "right to act without moral or public pressure"; a Jew in America could legitimately feel that his prime responsibility was to advance American racial equality. And if an Israeli wanted to go elsewhere, that was his prerogative. This in particular outraged many listeners, who felt that Robert was providing a moral rationale to quitters and waverers. But Chaim Guri, curiously enough, was impressed by the sincerity and eloquence of his adversary. They became good friends.

For his own reasons, Robert deliberately resisted the powerful emotionalism of the militant sabra viewpoint. Most immigrants to Israel soaked up the local atmosphere eagerly, often becoming more partisan than the natives. Robert held back from such total commitment. Yosi Gorni, a friend from university days, noted a chronic unwillingness in Robert to "submit and submerge himself, to become one of the crowd." Gorni assumed that this was based mainly on Robert's desire to maintain the detached status of a critic. But perhaps, Gorni speculated, there was something else, some "psychological resistance to committing himself and entrusting his fate to others."

This was a shrewd guess from a man who—like everyone else in Robert's intimate circle—knew practically nothing of Robert's early life.

Robert was born in Warsaw on December 30, 1936, two and a half years before the outbreak of the Second World War. His father, Richard Finkelstein, was a gifted young lawyer; his mother Miriam, a comely girl of twenty-three, was the daughter of a leading engineer-industrialist.

When the Nazi-Soviet pincer closed on Poland, Robert's father answered the government appeal for evacuation. The Poles were quickly overwhelmed, and Richard Finkelstein returned to his family in Warsaw, now under German occupation. The child and his parents moved into the large apartment of his maternal grandparents.

In the fall of 1940, under Nazi prodding, they joined their fellow-Jews in the ghetto. The move cost them most of their worldly goods. Richard, Miriam and Robert now shared a single room, but the family still had a servant.

The Nazi vise tightened. Robert's grandfather, Stanislav Szereszevski, was taken for a time as a hostage. As a member of the *Judenrat* or Jewish Community Council, he early became a marked man. One could not seek relief for the ghetto without antagonizing the occupiers.

Deprived of public services, the ghetto stagnated. In the fetid air, Robert contracted pleurisy. In 1941 his mother, fearing for his life, took him to a nearby rural district, which although it was technically part of the ghetto offered a few trees and a little space where the boy could play in the fresh air. That winter, the Jews were ordered to hand over all their furs; Robert's coat was taken away, with the explanation that "the Germans need furs for their army." Puzzled, the five-year-old asked, "But do they have such small soldiers?"

In July, 1942, the Germans began deporting Polish Jews to concentration camps. A month later, Miriam fled with her son to the "Aryan" side of Warsaw. She went directly to the home of her secondary-school teacher, the wife of an anthropology professor.

The professor—like his wife, a gentile—promptly gave up his room to the Jewish mother and her son. He also insisted on taking Robert out for a walk, in spite of the danger: "The child must have air."

Miriam got in touch with her husband; ironically, there was easy telephone communication between the two sides of the city. Richard begged her to come back. He felt that the advancing Russians would soon liberate the ghetto. Miriam was not convinced. But she was unable to persuade either Richard or her own father to leave the ghetto.

The women of the family accepted Miriam's reasoning. She was joined by her two sisters and her mother. They all became gentiles. Miriam's new name was Sviecicki.

In January of 1943, the Germans decreed their "second liquidation" of Jews. Richard Finkelstein, one of a picked group of intellectuals, was deported to the death camp at Treblinka. Three months later, in the third and final liquidation, Robert's grandfather was shot.

In the grim game of hide-and-seek that followed, Robert's mother was obliged to disappear for two months, leaving him with friends and very explicit instructions: "If anybody asks about your father, say he was an officer killed in the war. And don't forget—your name is Sviecicki."

"Why, mama?"

"Why? Because you're a Jew; and if they ever find out . . ."

Robert nodded. At seven, he had heard enough.

He became the pet of a priest, a former professor of theology at the university, who arranged for him to have the run of the local church grounds and dressed him up so he could be an acolyte at Mass. For a brief time he enjoyed the masquerade.

But when his mother returned, the situation was shakier than ever. Mother and son were constantly on the move—changing flats, keeping to the side streets, avoiding the eyes of strangers. Few could be trusted.

Once, Robert and his mother were picked up on the street by German security men and taken to a police station for questioning. The experience left the boy shaking with fright. Thereafter whenever Miriam had to go out, he stood in the doorway weeping until she returned, oblivious of the attention he was attracting: if he and his mother were to live with danger, at least they should do so together.

Before the uprising of the Polish Resistance in Warsaw in August, 1944, Miriam fled with Robert to a Catholic old people's home where her own mother was staying. The nuns registered the two as guests—a precaution that saved the life of the older woman. Although listed as an inmate, she was allowed to join Miriam and Robert hours before the Nazis swept through the institution, killing all the inmates in their beds and then burning it down.

All Warsaw was in flames. Miriam ran through the burning streets with Robert clinging to her hand—"just another Pole and her son." She had obtained a new set of papers, including a marriage license. Now she was "Mrs. Mayevska," widow of a slain Polish officer, and her own mother posed as the mother of the dead gentile officer.

With the retreating Germans, they were carted off to Berlin, and assigned as "railway slaves" to a work camp. More than once, as Allied planes swooped over the camp, Robert had to be dragged, protesting, to the dubious midnight safety of a half-smashed bunker.

At long last, the Russians reached Berlin. Miriam, her mother and Robert were free to return to Warsaw, where they stayed for nearly a year with her two sisters.

He was nine when his mother took him to Italy, first step toward emigration to the Holy Land. Miriam got a job working with refugees for the Joint Distribution Committee, and enrolled Robert in an Italian school. "I wanted him to feel like everybody else for a change, to mix with other children and not have the sense of being different, special."

He did have a few Hebrew lessons, however. Actually, he was terrified at the prospect of still another uprooting. A photo of him at the time shows a brooding, withdrawn youngster with veiled tragic eyes. He had absorbed, according to his mother, "one central idea: to be a Jew is to suffer."

The Israeli victory in 1948, jubilantly chronicled by the anti-British Italian press, perked Robert up a good deal. He felt the first stirrings of pride.

A year later, when Robert was twelve and one-half, he and his mother reached the new homeland. Out of the muddle of names they had used over the years, Miriam registered him with two: his father's and her own.

To expedite his learning of Hebrew, she sent her boy to the "child village" of Ben Shemen in the north, a kind of Israeli Boys-and-Girls Town where young newcomers are acclimatized to the country's ways. After a year, Robert had a recurrence of his chest illness, so she took him to live with her in Ramat Gan near Tel Aviv.

In high school, he joined the voluntary outdoor movement to which Dudu Sela later belonged, Ha-Noar Ha-Oved ("Working Youth"), which was loosely associated with the dominant Mapai party. Robert entered upon several of his happiest years. After the decade of isolation in Europe, he had a bottomless hunger for companionship. The songs, the hikes, the campfires and especially the new friendships poured into the void, filling it almost completely.

The shock was doubly painful, therefore, when at eighteen he was turned down by the army on physical grounds. In the ultra-patriotic tradition of the youth movement, he had applied for service in Nahal, the tough farmer-soldier corps assigned to key border kibbutzim. The army ruling meant that he would be barred even from rear-echelon service.

Once more Robert had been stigmatized, labeled an outsider. He had given himself wholeheartedly to a group and its ideals, only to be placed again beyond the pale; this time, as it were, of the militarily competent. He was bitterly hurt. It would be a long time before he would risk commitment of his deepest feelings again.

His mother, anxious to soften the blow, urged him to seek admission to Hebrew University, even though the term was at the midway mark. An honor student, he was accepted. For the moment the pain was somewhat assuaged.

Robert was marking papers on the May afternoon when Nasser demanded the U.N. pull-out. He could not at first believe that Nasser, for all of his posturing, would force a showdown. Robert had pictured the Egyptian dictator as a realist in the mold of Ghana's ex-premier Nkrumah. Where Nkrumah had exacted graft as the price for modernizing his country, Nasser imposed cronyism and self-glorification. As ruler of a nation suffering a severe postcolonial hangover, with a massive sense of wounded pride, Nasser would appreciate kid-glove handling; "one could do business with him."

When Aliza Argov, secretary of the Economics Department, expressed fears for the lives of her two children, Robert playfully bet her a chocolate bar that the tension would blow over.

He was jolted by the blockade of Aqaba on May 23. Now he was no longer sure that Nasser could resist the influences and temptations swirling around him. But Robert still argued for efforts to avoid war.

By this time, his friends and colleagues were being called up wholesale, mostly to the city's own Jerusalem Reservist Brigade. Those who weren't were storming recruitment centers to find out why.

The chairman of the Economics Department at Hebrew University, Chaim Barkai, had postponed a trip to America in order to don sergeant's uniform. Another eminent associate, under whom Robert had studied, was going into Barkai's platoon as a private. The younger men were disappearing from living room and campus. Robert felt increasingly isolated, relegated to the sidelines.

On the evening of May 24, a half-dozen friends and neighbors gathered at Robert's apartment. Downstairs, the road in front of the building complex was jammed with buses and other vehicles collecting reservists. Most of those present, including Absolom Katz, were on the eve of departure for the front. Absolom could see that Robert was suffering.

While Yaffa served beer and lemon squash, several of the men spread large maps on the floor and tried to anticipate the likely course of the fighting. Robert pulled out a volume on the 1956 Sinai war and eagerly joined in the speculation. For the firt time, Absolom noted, he spoke in terms of "we."

At 1:00 A.M. the call-up car arrived for a member of the group. Soon after, another excused himself to complete his last-minute packing. The meeting broke up. Tomorrow all—except Robert —would be soldiers.

Two nights later, Nasser addressed the Moslem world from Cairo. With Moshe Maoz, a University lecturer in the history of the Middle East and an expert on Arab affairs, Robert sat before his radio at home. Sentence by sentence, Maoz translated the Egyptian dictator's words pledging "total destruction of Israel" in the coming campaign.

Early the next morning, Robert was at mobilization headquarters, volunteering the use of his car and his driving services. His phone number was jotted down, but army transport was pretty well in hand.

For four days he did petty military errands, chafing, "too honest a man," in the words of his friend Yosi Gorni, "to let someone else do his fighting for him. He had to take a firm position, on every issue. If he was pro-Arab, he let everybody know it. If he was going to oppose them, it had to be with a gun in his hand."

Robert told Yaffa of his decision. She pointed out—delicately and reluctantly, knowing his sensitivity on the subject—that he was medically ineligible for army service. He was without training, had never fired a rifle. But she had no real hope that legal restrictions—or anything else—would stop him.

Robert took his problem to Chaim Barkai, his department chief. Barkai called Nehemiah Oz, a battalion commander in the Jerusalem Reservist Brigade. Barkai and Oz had served together under Chaim Guri, Robert's one-time radio adversary, in the pre-inde-pendence Palmach.

Colonel Oz was acquainted with Robert. A year earlier, on retire-ment from the regular army at forty-one, Oz with Israeli aplomb had enrolled as a freshman at Hebrew University. Unhappy with his economics lecturer, he had audited Robert's class instead. He re-tained a clear impression of Robert as "eloquent, likable—and breakable."

Oz already had several of Robert's colleagues in his battalion. "They were all men of reputation—professors and Ph.D.'s—who be-longed to noncombatant staff units. They hadn't been called up. They wanted to be in the front line, and since they were trained reservists I didn't see any reason to stop them from joining my battalion."

Robert was a different matter. It was clear that he had been kept out of the army in his youth because of some medical condition about which he was stubbornly evasive. It was equally clear that he had an almost physical need to be with his friends. On impulse, Oz agreed to request transfer of Robert-plus-auto to his battalion, which was presumably to be deployed like the rest of the brigade in purely defensive positions.

Once in the unit, Robert asked if he could have some training. He wanted to be able to handle a gun. Oz assigned him to a company headed by Chaim Guri, with instructions to drill the recruit in the rudiments of weaponry and infantry tactics. Unofficially, Oz saw to it that Robert got a uniform.

Robert had crossed to the sabra side.

The training camp was in a wood near the university. The new private was not the most gifted soldier Oz had ever seen, but he was one of the most enthusiastic. Granted permission to take bayonet drill, he lunged and grunted with the others under a blazing sun for half an hour until Barkai told him to quit.

Afterward, panting under a tree, Robert was a happy man. He was where he wanted to be.

The burden lifted from his shoulders settled onto Yaffa's. Visiting him at camp, she was frankly frightened. If the Jordanians attacked, their first targets would probably be the positions held by the bri-gade. She didn't think Robert belonged in combat, and urged him to switch to a staff post. Robert declined to move. He did make one concession: no more bayonet drills at high noon.

David Levhari, a close friend from the Economics Department who did not share Robert's dovish attitude toward the Arabs, was surprised to find Robert carrying a rifle. "I am neither a pacifist nor a conscientious objector," Robert told him bluntly. "I have never said there were no circumstances in which I would fight. This is a question of defending my home and family, my own community."

And what, Levhari asked with mild irony, about his past concern for the Arab masses?

"I'm still sorry for them. But I must protect myself against their leaders."

On Saturday, June 3, Robert came home for dinner. His mother, occupied with social work in Ramat Gan, still had no idea that her son was training with a combat unit. But to Yaffa he confirmed that his status as an infantryman in the Jerusalem Brigade was now official: "If anything happens to me, I am considered a soldier."

Sunday, June 4, tension ran high at the camp. Wives and children, sensing a climax, swarmed over the grounds. At six o'clock, Robert had a visit from Yaffa and his daughter. After they left, Robert entertained Chaim Barkai's family. Barkai had already been dispatched to survey a forward position the company would occupy; his smallest boy was weeping in fear that "the Jordanians will kill Daddy."

The childish tears reflected a real enough danger. The Jordanians had sufficient power concentrated along the frontier—three full brigades, eighty tanks, Hunter fighter-bombers, Iraqi reserves and Egyptian commandos—to effect an armored push to Tel Aviv or Haifa in an hour. Oz was aware that the General Staff did not expect a major Jordanian thrust, but he was taking no chances.

Monday morning, alerted to the outbreak of action in the Sinai, Oz promptly ordered his men into their front-line positions. He did not want to risk having them caught en route by Legion shells.

His mind flashed to Robert Szereszevski. Recalling the 1948 catastrophe at Latrun, where riflemen fresh from the refugee boats were found dead on the battlefield with their safety catches still unreleased, Oz had "a bad feeling" about Robert; "I was afraid for him." Oz told Chaim Guri to send the economics professor back to battalion headquarters for a staff assignment in communications.

When Guri relayed the order, Robert gave him "a sweet, child-like" smile. "But why? I'm perfectly all right here."

"It's too tricky. You were never really supposed to be with a combat unit."

"Please . . ." Robert confronted him directly. "I ask you. No, I'm begging you. Let me stay with my comrades."

"But this isn't training any more. This is war. People will be killed."

"I know. That's exactly why I want to stay."

The poet shook his head. "Well, it isn't right, but . . ."

He agreed that Robert could stay with the combat forces until the matter could be taken up again with Oz. But Robert would be shifted to another platoon. Guri did not want three members of the economics faculty to be facing enemy fire within a few yards of each other.

Robert's new unit was assigned to man an irregular arc of shallow trenches facing the Jordanians. In back of the trenches, less than ten yards away, were several one-story Israeli houses, set among pine and almond trees. Laundry still hung, and the subdued voices of children could be heard by the men in the trench posts. Straight ahead, across some 150 yards of scrubby fields, were the positions of the Arab Legion.

The Israeli trenches, dug out of a hillside at the time of the 1956 Sinai campaign, had lain neglected since. They were about four and a half feet deep, cement-lined, with concrete roofing in only a few places. When Guri had complained about their vulnerability to air and artillery attack, he had been told it was wasteful to spend a lot of money on defenses: "If real fighting starts, we go over to the attack in an hour or two anyway." Even bushes and thorns that obstructed the firing lanes at the position were, by order of the High Command, not to be destroyed; the Israelis were ready to forego military effectiveness rather than give a single jumpy Arab Legion sentry an excuse for opening fire.

In late afternoon of Monday, June 5, Robert was manning one of the advanced observation posts stretching out like an extended finger from the Israeli command dugout toward the Jordanian lines. His partner was a young Moroccan named Avram, a factory hand in a Jerusalem textile mill. The two took turns on lookout duty at the far end of the position, where there was a concrete-sheltered opening about sixteen inches square.

Crouching, Robert made his way to the aperture and peered out. Along with the steady pounding by Jordanian artillery which had begun in midmorning, there had been sporadic rifle fire and heavy machine-gun bursts across the stone-strewn valley. His job was to locate if possible the enemy gun posts, and to scout the area for signs of a Jordanian ground attack.

Robert was facing northeast, with a waning sun behind him and a light breeze stirring from the west. Far to his right, where the walls of the Old City began, a mosque minaret cut the sky, framed between the towering spire of the Franciscan Monastery and, incongruously in the foreground, a television aerial. On his left was a semicircle of new Israeli apartment buildings ending in the Pagi housing project.

Before him, a clump of olive trees fifty yards ahead partially screened the Israeli position. Beyond the trees was a rugged, narrow ravine; then a barbed-wire fence, some irrigated fields and finally a long row of low stone strong points and houses shielding the Arab Legion. Flashes of rifle fire came from apertures in the stone walls. Arab machine-gun posts, perched in taller buildings at the side, were more difficult to pinpoint.

Cautiously, Robert craned his head.

In an arched third-story doorway across the valley, a Jordanian machine gunner squinted into the sunset, caught the movement of a helmet through the branches of the olive trees.

Avram was nervous. The professor was staying at the lookout post longer than the recommended few seconds; too long, he thought. He shouted for Robert to get down.

He was too late. The half-inch machine-gun bullet struck Robert in the forehead. He fell soundlessly.

The Moroccan ran up to him. "I saw that the bullet had pierced his skull. All I could do was say a *Shma Yisrael* [the classic Hebrew prayer 'Hear, O Israel, the Lord Our God, the Lord is One']."

Robert died in the sixth month of his thirty-first year, just nine days away from his father's age when he was killed at Treblinka.

The Second Day

PREDAWN: AMMUNITION HILL

ALTHOUGH spectacular air strikes and massive tank engagements dominated the headlines of the Six-Day War, the battle that will probably emerge as historically most significant was fought by a relatively few men, hand-to-hand, through a tight web of trenches along a knoll on the northern outskirts of Jerusalem. It was launched early Tuesday morning, from springboard positions some two hundred yards above the post where Robert Szereszevski had fallen eight hours before.

Jerusalem has classically been penetrable only from the north. Perched on a mountain ridge half a mile high, it is surrounded by deep valleys forming natural moats in the east, south and west. For three thousand years its invaders, Babylonians and Persians and Crusaders, Pompey and Saladin and Allenby, have charged the ancient citadel from the stony plateau north of the Old City walls. When Herod built three great towers to protect his palace shortly before the Christian Era, he placed them "on the vulnerable northern side."

In 1967, Old Jerusalem was taken from the east for the first time. But the decisive struggle for the city took place the day before, as ever on its northern approaches, where the key defenses of Jordan's crack Arab Legion were overrun. The vital sector was called

Ammunition Hill. It was captured by paratrooper reservists, pitched suddenly into the crucial arena by a combination of two circumstances: the unexpectedly rapid advance of Israel Tal's armor, obviating the need for a paratroop drop behind the Egyptian lines at El Arish; and the surprising belligerence of Jordan's King Hussein.

Initially, Dayan and Rabin had every reason to expect prudence from Hussein. The little monarch, ruler of an artificial kingdom created by the British Foreign Office in 1948, lived under constant pressure from the Palestinian extremists who had assassinated his father in 1951. If he fought Israel and won, he would probably be swept aside by pro-Nasser leftists; if he lost, his throne would be shakier than ever. In the Sinai war that pitted England, France and Israel against Egypt in 1956, Hussein had confined himself to a few token gestures that hardly constituted a second front.

But this time, perhaps under instructions from the Egyptian general thoughtfully sent to Amman by Nasser, Jordanian heavy guns had been thundering all along the front since 10:18 A.M., with 155 mm. "Long Tom" shells reaching into Tel Aviv. Jerusalem Mayor Teddy Kollek, poking his head out of his office on the armistice line dividing the New and Old Cities, was incredulous: "We had sent messages to Hussein making it clear that if he didn't attack in force, we wouldn't."

At 10:30 A.M. Arab Legion forces moved into the Old City, occupying its lofty towers and minarets, especially the terraces and ramparts overlooking New Jerusalem to the west. Scores of Patton tanks assembled on the eastern hilltops; Hussein had seven brigades concentrated against Israel's three in the area.

Shortly after noon, Jordanian troops seized the U.N.-occupied Government House on the strategic Mount of Evil Counsel south of the city. Obviously this was prelude to a general assault on the New City, as well as an immediate threat to the Israeli enclave on Mount Scopus to the northeast. It was also, however, an unexpected and welcome invitation to counterattack and perhaps capture the Old City, in Jordanian hands since 1948.

The first move was to check the Jordanian threat, and seal off the main battleground from north and south. At 2:30 P.M. the go-ahead was given, and troops of the Jerusalem Reservist Brigade swept the Arabs out of Government House. Then an armored brigade in the north advanced through heavily-mined mountain passes above Jeru-

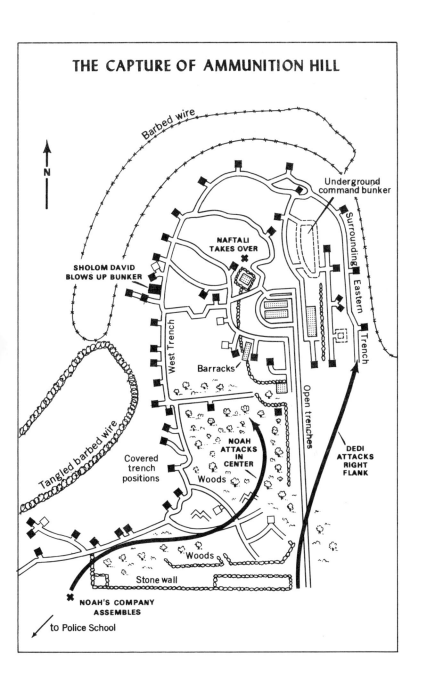

THE CAPTURE OF AMMUNITION HILL

N

Barbed wire

Underground
command bunker

Surrounding Eastern Trench

NAFTALI
TAKES OVER

SHOLOM DAVID
BLOWS UP BUNKER

West Trench

Barracks

Tangled barbed wire

Covered
trench
positions

Open trenches

NOAH
ATTACKS
IN
CENTER

Woods

DEDI
ATTACKS
RIGHT
FLANK

Woods

Stone wall

NOAH'S COMPANY
ASSEMBLES

to Police School

salem to cut the highway leading to Ramallah. With the Israeli 120-man garrison on Mount Scopus holding out successfully, the stage was set for mounting an Old City effort.

In a young citrus grove south of Tel Aviv, a reservist brigade of paratroopers shuffled impatiently in their high crepe-soled boots, waiting to make a scheduled drop at El Arish. Commanders knelt over their maps; ammunition and gas masks were distributed.

Shortly after noon, word came that the Sinai jump was being scratched; Tal didn't need them.

The grumbling of the disappointed paratroopers had scarcely died down when a roar of excitement swept through their ranks: they were to fight on the ground as shock troops assigned to retake the Old City.

Already the brigade commander, Colonel Mordecai "Mota" Gur, was speeding toward Jerusalem with his battalion and company officers to set up a headquarters post. Gur, a personable redheaded six-footer, had been snatched back hurriedly for field duty from administration of the Staff and Command School. He had been raised on the improvisational techniques of the Haganah underground's striking force, the Palmach, and enjoyed a considerable reputation as a combat leader.

En route Gur huddled over maps with his operations officer. Their first mission was to clear the area north of the Old City walls, a heavily-built-up district topped at its far end by a fortified complex. This complex, the crux of the Arab Legion defense system outside the Old City, was grouped around two formidable relics of British mandate days. Across a shallow field from the Israeli lines was a massive three-story stone structure known as the Police School, once used as a training academy and barracks for Jordanian police, more recently occupied by the United Nations Works and Relief Agency. Behind the school to the northeast was Ammunition Hill, so named because it served as a shell depot for British artillery units. An elliptical mount about 150 yards in diameter, the hill was covered with bunkers and gun posts.

Cracking this sector was a rough assignment, but the alternative of striking farther south in the thickly populated area of the Mandelbaum Gate checkpoint would have been even worse. This, like the western wall of the Old City below, was a solid block of Legion defenses.

Gur's main problem was time. His brigade had been geared to a totally different operation, requiring other tactics and weapons. Most of his reservist officers were unfamiliar with the Jerusalem area, since they had not been considered likely candidates for a battle of such importance. Gur set about rounding up aerial photos and other intelligence, commandeering supplies, and organizing evacuation centers for what would undoubtedly be numerous casualties.

Meanwhile, the civilian-soldiers of the brigade were making the long eastward trek through the Judean Hills into Jerusalem. For most of them, it would be the first battle. Because the main highway was choked with armored traffic swinging into action north of the capital, the paratroopers' blue tourist buses traveled over bumpy, weed-grown back roads.

Crawling up the narrow stretches of asphalt along the Jerusalem Corridor, squeezed into the aisles among bazookas, mortars and ammunition crates, the men softly began to lift their voices. Zahal sings. Its music has the immediacy of jazz: lusty marches whose minor-key setting is redeemed by an overriding joy and virility, haunting ballads with a bittersweet echo of the past. On this trip they had just such a tune, with evocative lyrics seemingly preordained for the occasion: Naomi Shemer's "Yerushalayim Shel Zahav" ("Jerusalem of Gold"). Written to commemorate Israeli Independence Day three weeks before, the song had quickly become a national hymn of hope and longing. Matched to a simple, expressive melody, it recounts the Israeli sadness over the lost golden-bronze capital:

> Alone and captive in its reverie;
> In its heart, a wall.

The ballad ends on a note of wistful prayer: "Let me be the violin to all thy songs."

The last of the battalion buses reached the capital by 8:00 P.M. They found a chilly, deserted city. Packs of wandering dogs were scurrying in terror before the thudding Jordanian shells.

The force disembarked in the modern suburb of Beit Hakarem in the west, where the soldiers were quickly overwhelmed with gifts from delighted housewives: coffee, cake, fruits. Trucks roared up with arms requisitioned from the Jerusalem Brigade; the click of guns being loaded echoed through quiet apartment hallways.

An elderly woman emerged from a bedroom carrying a piece of white cloth crudely adorned with a blue shield of David. It had been made in her family's home in the Old City, she said, shortly before they were forced out by the Jordanians in 1948. Would somebody please take it, and fly it over the Wailing Wall? An officer took the flag and assumed personal responsibility for seeing that it reached its destination.

Colonel Gur had taken the precaution of surveying the terrain a few days before; he had been encouraged to do so by Moshe Dayan, who had a faint premonition that King Hussein might be tempted to martyrdom. Now, before sundown Monday, Gur sent his subordinates forward from the command post for personal reconnaissance, accompanied by aerial photos and a group of locally experienced officer-guides from the Jerusalem Brigade.

They climbed to the roof of the Pagi houses, a new project built along the armistice lines in accord with the stubborn Israeli premise that sooner or later Jerusalem would have to become one city again, and its Jewish and Arab inhabitants might as well get to know each other. But now, with its freshly painted apartments evacuated and machine guns in its top windows, Pagi was the scene of a brewing artillery duel.

When the commanders returned, Gur put them through a final briefing. The brigade's assignment covered a substantial slice of territory: a rectangle running eastward from the armistice lines to the Mt. Scopus enclave to the northeast, and due south from there to the Palestine Archaeological Museum abutting on the far corner of the Old City wall. Between the paratroopers and their targets lay the cluster of hotels, consulates and religious institutions of the American Colony, so called because it was developed in the 1920's largely by United States interests; and, farther north in the Sheikh Jarrah district, the Police School and Ammunition Hill.

Against the center of the Jordanian line, skirting the northern edge of the American Colony, Gur would throw his Second Battalion. Once a breach was made, the Third Battalion would follow, then fan south to clear the crowded streets just above the Old City wall.

For the crucial mission in the north, Gur chose his First Battalion, made up like the others largely of untried fighters, but led by a handful of battle-toughened commanders.

Obviously the huge granite-walled Police School was going to be trouble. But even more worrisome, because it was less open to reconnaissance, was the ancient knobby mound behind it. Thrusting up from a sea of surrounding valleys, Ammunition Hill, some historians say, was actually the original Mount Scopus from which Alexander the Great surveyed Jerusalem. It still stood athwart any passage eastward toward the modern Scopus. The circle of guns on its crest, like a gigantic tank turret, dominated the entire area.

Defended by the Legion's professionals, the northern compound would be a hard nut to crack. But Gur had some powerful nutcrackers—including a company commander named Captain Noah.

Eleven months of the year, Noah stands like a young oak in the flat fields of the Jordan Basin. Deeply burned by countless hours under the Galilee sun, he has a thick powerful neck, horny farmer's hands, and sapphire-blue eyes of a Technicolor brilliance. An inch or so under six feet, he seems bigger, filling the space around him. Some of this impression may come from his massive shoulders; but the aura of strength that flows from him is more than a matter of physical dimensions. In tattered sneakers, faded blue dungarees and half-open work shirt, he manages to convey a serene, almost majestic presence.

The twelfth month of Noah's year is also important. That is when he serves as a paratrooper in the General Headquarters Reserve Brigade. In practice, the annual training period tends to be somewhat more than the official four weeks. Israeli reservist officers, especially in the paratroops, do not measure their service time with a stop watch; and senior military leaders have always tended to draft Noah when special maneuvers or difficult reprisal actions were planned. As an officer, Noah could be a colonel in anybody else's army—and possibly in this one, too, if he wished to make a career of soldiering.

Noah knows exactly who he is and where he is going. Self-contained, he makes no effort to be ingratiating. It is as if, having reduced life to what he considers essential, he is impatient with everything else—and especially words. He makes definite, unhesitating answers—or none at all. Time and again he dismisses comment with a quick, self-deprecating shrug that says "It's not worth talking about."

At the core of Noah's world are land and family. For nearly all Israelis, love of the land is something literal and specific. It means a personal affection for every struggling pine, every barren sun-stabbed mountaintop; for the ceaseless thrust of white-capped waves at Tel Aviv, and the shimmering fairy-tale towers of Old Jerusalem. In army training, the recruit is deliberately marched over every inch of his rugged little country so that he can learn its fierce beauty: "To love something, you must first know it."

The kibbutz sabra personifies this feeling. He has daily contact not only with the stubborn soil but also with the determination of the pioneers who preceded him. Here on the land is the heart of the sabra spirit.

Noah lives in Kibbutz Gonen, a picturesque two-square-mile patch of farmland alongside the Jordan, cradled between Israel's Naftali Hills on the west and Syria's Golani Plateau. Less than a generation ago the area was fetid swamp. Today the settlement boasts spacious fields of potatoes, cotton and alfalfa; fisheries, cow barns and sheep meadows; and fruit orchards yielding one hundred tons annually in apples and peaches.

At Gonen, every settler's home has a weapon. The road leading northward to the kibbutz from the Sea of Galilee bears other evidence of its closeness to the Syrian frontier: a burned-out eucalyptus grove, the tangled wreckage of mine-blasted cars and trucks, an Israeli dugout in the woods facing east. And, of course, miles of barbed wire.

The kibbutz was founded in 1951 by members of Mapai, the long-dominant Labor party established by David Ben-Gurion. Within a few years most of the original settlers, discouraged by Syrian harassment from the cliffs eighteen hundred feet above as well as by the primitive living conditions, had returned to Jerusalem and Tel Aviv. In 1958 a relief force arrived from the Assistance to Young Kibbutzim movement. Noah, then twenty-two, was among them. He had grown up in a settlement farther south where his parents, both natives of Poland, met and were married.

He had been a dairy farmer. At Gonen, he shifted to potatoes, launching experiments in mechanized techniques of cleaning and packing. On a typical summer's day, he is in the fields from 4:00 A.M. to 5:00 P.M., with a long midmorning pause for breakfast and siesta.

In late afternoon the other half of his life begins, in a cool, green-shuttered little white villa near the top of Gonen's residential slope. Noah seeks "to live peacefully in a Jewish country." For him this includes hours of listening to recorded music, mostly Bach and the baroque Italians; and "good literature" as available in Hebrew (Kazantzakis is on his bookshelf along with Sholem Aleichem). He hopes to supplement his high-school and specialized agricultural studies with a university degree in history and philosophy.

Above all, Noah relishes his family. In Gonen, unlike some other kibbutzim, the children live not in separate quarters but at home with their parents. When Noah comes in from work, his wife and four children are there to greet him. He has daughters of nine and four, and two boys aged eight and six. His idea of a satisfying evening is to read, play and generally relax with them at home. Gonen is a prosperous kibbutz. Noah has a small stone porch and a tidy lawn spread with bluebells and wildflowers. In the dim twilight, with its paved walks and bike-strewn front yards, the Gonen family quarter could almost be a modest section of Westchester.

Noah's wife, Rachel, is as soft and plump as her husband is hard and trim. Round-cheeked and snub-nosed, not a conventional beauty, she speaks quietly and with conviction.

She first met Noah when they were both starting grammar school at Degania A, the pioneer kibbutz where Moshe Dayan and Air Force Commander Mordechai Hod were born. In his unhurried way, Noah waited twelve years to express his interest, asking for a date just before being inducted into the army at eighteen. They spent the evening sitting on the grass at the kibbutz, talking. They parted in peace, without making any big decisions.

While Noah was away, Rachel dated other boys. Three years later, at the end of his training, she received an unequivocal love letter, quickly followed up by a personal visit. He told her she was his dream girl, and had been for a long time.

Rachel was mildly astonished. "Frankly, I had no such feelings myself then—but I decided Noah was a good gamble. For one thing, there was his sheer physical strength—very important in pioneer life. He can do things that other men won't even try. To this day, when he goes on reserve maneuvers every year, the young boys in the army can't keep up with him."

The couple departed for Gonen, to work in the fields together and share a cabin. In close daily contact, Rachel discovered that her suitor was responsible to a fault, and "very, very patient." Being together "was nice—so we got married." She has never been sorry.

After her first baby, when she became pregnant again and was uncomfortable, Noah simply took over. As the family grew, Noah's protective arm stretched further. "He'll get up during the night to cover them, bring a glass of water, say a soothing word."

Most evenings, during the three- or four-hour stretch between supper and bedtime, Noah tells the children stories, drawing copiously on Grimm and similar sources as translated into Hebrew. In the kibbutz, as Rachel points out, there is plenty of time to give children. "And he does it—with each one of them."

Noah is not a demonstrative man. Even at home, where his concern for his family is obvious, it rarely takes the form of lavish external gesture. "He only reveals himself," says Rachel, "through a look in his eyes." Their most intimate exchanges are nonverbal: a gentle plucking at her husband's sleeve by Rachel when he returns from work, while she scans his face to make sure that all is well; his quick affectionate glance that follows her into the kitchen.

Outside the family, Noah's cool detachment is an irritant to some —especially, as his wife says, "when he turns out so often to be right." His laughter is rare and rather strained. When he was proposed for kibbutz secretary a few years ago, there was some grumbling about his uncommunicative ways. But to nobody's surprise, he won.

Noah went to war with a typical minimum of fuss. He was in the paratroops because an ear problem had kept him out of the air force. To him, fighting is a disagreeable necessity; he professes no special feelings about Israel's angry neighbors, other than dismissal of pan-Arabism as "a cultural myth." In previous actions, he was actively conscious of shooting human beings, and "definitely uncomfortable" about it.

His letters before going into battle were models of military brevity: "I'm alive. Love to you and the children."

His parting from Rachel had been equally untheatrical. Toying with his shirt front, eyes downcast, Rachel said, "Papa, you have to come back. We need you here."

"I'll come back," Noah told her calmly. "Without so much as a scratch."

The paratrooper attack was originally scheduled for midnight. But there were repeated delays in accumulating supplies and intelligence, and several snags in organizing a casualty evacuation system. At 1:00 A.M. Rabin phoned from Tel Aviv to suggest that the attack be postponed until the next morning, when air support would be available along with stronger armored backing than the single tank unit now being detached from the Jerusalem Brigade.

Gur took a poll of his three battalion commanders, noting the unfamiliarity of the terrain and the acknowledged toughness of the opposition. The Bedouin-manned Arab Legion, originally trained by the British, had throttled the highway to Jerusalem at Latrun in 1948, bloodily repulsing repeated Israeli onslaughts. Unlike the Egyptians, the Legionnaires were not terrified of fighting in the dark.

To a man, the brigade's subcommanders still preferred to strike by night. When they were backed by the Central Front Command, Rabin withdrew his objection.

A few minutes later the troops piled into their blue buses again and rolled north on Ein Karem Road, swinging east in the orthodox Geula district and continuing nearly to the bottom of Samuel the Prophet Street. Here they dismounted and formed up on foot, according to battalion and company assignments.

Gur leapfrogged his command post eastward to the top of the Central Talmud Torah at 19 Joel Street in Geula. Here he had a sweeping view of the Ammunition Hill battleground to the northeast and the Old City to the southeast. Huddled in the cellar of the building, in flight from Legion shelling, were a score of women, children and elderly men.

The brigade staff was greeted by a hail of artillery fire, one shell ripping out a huge chunk of masonry a few feet from the colonel's head. A communications sergeant was severely wounded by a high-angle mortar blast as he stepped out into the street; and a truck attempting to bring him to safety was destroyed.

Gradually the battle was fully joined. At 2:00 A.M. the Israelis detonated a heavy charge of explosives within Jordanian territory. Minutes later, two tanks rolled down the slope of Samuel the Prophet Street, blasting away at enemy emplacements spotted during the day. At 2:20, the Israeli artillery opened up. Behind the tanks, now advancing toward the frontier in the Police School sector, the First Battalion went into action.

The sky was a silvery chandelier. Still moonless at 2:30 A.M., it was covered with distant stars, too far aloft to penetrate the blackness of the battlefield. The battalion deployed along the Pagi Settlement walls. To their left, an artillery-battered blockhouse marked the northernmost Israeli position in Jerusalem. Slanting away from it along the crooked armistice line, scarcely fifteen yards to the southwest, was a similar gun-slitted Jordanian outpost. Beyond that, due east of the Israelis across a 150-yard depression, loomed the forbidding bulk of the Police School, stripped of its U.N. staff and transformed into a fortress with gun posts at every window. Here the main body of the estimated two-hundred-man Arab Legion force in the area was believed to be concentrated. The Israelis would be attacking with a little more than half that number —scarcely a comfortable margin in view of the enemy's guns, fortifications and high ground.

The three-story police building, a rectangle about eighty yards wide, was topped by a stone tower nearly doubling its height. Windows darkened, it presented a silent silhouette. An occasional flare lighted the U.N. lettering across its façade.

Directly in front of the building, on a slight rise, the Israelis could discern the outlines of several bunkers apparently linked in a trench system. But a good deal more than that stood between their jumping-off point and the Police School. The intervening hollow was crammed with an elaborate system of barricades and traps, begun shortly after the 1948 war and steadily refined ever since. A series of barbed-wire fences was interlaced with mine fields, and capped at the far end by a succession of stone walls. The whole valley was exposed to withering fire both from the Police School and from Ammunition Hill, whose artillery-studded western slope could be glimpsed dimly to the northeast. The Israelis had hoped to strike across a narrow sector sheltered from the guns on the hill, but the Legion had shifted some emplacements to cover this strip.

The four companies of the attacking battalion were split into two approximately equal forces. One group was to clear and occupy the Police School itself, then continue eastward to the abandoned Ambassador Hotel at the foot of Mount Scopus. The other two companies, headed by Noah and a lanky young captain named Dedi, were to deal with the rest of the northern position, crashing through the defenses around the school and then moving into the trenches honeycombing Ammunition Hill. The whole battalion would rendezvous at the hotel.

Companies and platoons lined up under a rain of machine-gun fire. A spectacled sergeant standing in a half-track directed traffic "as calmly," Chaim Guri said, "as if he were a policeman in the heart of Jerusalem."

The infantry assault could not begin until a path had been cleared by engineers. A squad of demolition men raced forward into no-man's-land carrying bangalore torpedoes, designed by Indian Army officers in the late nineteenth century to breach barbed wire by low-angle explosive charges ripping along the length of a long steel tube. Errant flames from the first torpedo touched off the dynamite pack on an engineer's back, blowing the man to pieces.

For half an hour, Noah and his men crouched by a low wall while the demolition crew slashed with wire-cutters and probed the ground for mines. Finally a flashlight signaled that an opening path had been cut. Noah streaked forward with a long line of paratroopers strung out behind him.

On the captain's heels was a lean, sharp-featured corporal named Naftali Cohen, born in Israel to parents from Yemen in southwest Arabia. Naftali had never been in combat before but he was quietly determined, for his own reasons, to be in the thick of the action. The best way he could guarantee that, he reasoned, was by sticking close to Noah.

They tore through the first gap in the barbed wire. Directly beyond, a white phosphorescent ribbon, fifteen inches wide, snaked along the ground to define a trail safely cleared of mines. On either side of the line lay the first Israeli casualties: engineers wounded by mortars and mines.

Some twenty yards farther along, undetected by Israeli reconnaissance, a second forest of barbed wire began. The demolition squad operating here was handicapped by a damaged bangalore torpedo; they could force only a narrow breach. Noah hurled himself into the opening, enabling several men to climb across him before a dynamite charge ripped open a wider path.

Close to the Police School, a third layer of wire stretched across the field, this one within punishing range of machine guns and bazookas brought up to the roof of the school. Here the torpedo explosion was unaccountably delayed, finally erupting several seconds behind schedule.

Now there were only stone walls, six feet high, blocking the last approaches to the building. Dynamite was laid, and Noah leaped over the fragmented boulders like a steeplechase hurdler, Naftali and the others scrambling behind.

Just before the school-fortress, the first set of Legion trenches began, curving to left and right around the sides of the building to a near-junction at a parking lot in the rear. Above the lot was a grove of small pines and olives; north of that, beyond two outbuildings, lay the really elaborate network of Legion defensive positions, an arterial maze of tunnels, dugouts and bunkers crisscrossing Ammunition Hill.

Even before the Police School, the Jordanian trenches were more formidable than those dug by the Israelis. Plunging down nearly seven feet and lined with concrete, they bulged out into concrete-roofed bunkers at about every twenty-five feet. Passage elsewhere was very narrow—some thirty-six inches across—so that an attacking force would have to blast its way forward in single file.

Noah paused a moment to regroup his company. Plans called for his men to clear the leftward-circling trench. A platoon under one of his lieutenants, a burly gymnastics instructor named Nir, was to go first. Noah saw the lieutenant a short distance to the west, gathering an assault force, and gave Nir the go-ahead to charge.

Minutes later, Noah shouted a curt warning—"Watch out, comrades, this is no training exercise!"—and jumped down into the eastern end of the trench. He emptied his Uzzi along the length of the dug-out corridor, then flattened himself against the wall to reload while Naftali, replacing him, let loose a second volley. Then the paratroopers ran forward into the dim tunnel as more Israelis piled in behind them.

A Jordanian who had ducked into one of the tunnel pockets now emerged, rifle blazing. Two more riflemen were behind him. The Uzzis spat back at them at close range. Within seconds the narrow trench was clogged with dead and wounded.

The green reservists found themselves stumbling over corpses, splattered with blood, battling hand-to-hand against an enemy literally hidden in the walls. Noah materialized out of the darkness, slapping backs, urging the men to "go faster, faster," himself seeming to run forward and back at the same time. In training, he had struck some of the troopers as distant, remote, uninterested in the friendly gesture; here, they found his sturdy self-possession reassuring.

Legion resistance was unexpectedly heavy. Instead of concentrating their stand in the school building itself, Jordanian commanders had chosen to fight in the serpentine tunnels, where they had the advantages of surprise and concealment. Israeli ammunition, passed along by hand-to-hand relay from the rear, was rapidly running out.

Lieutenant Nir struggled back through the trenches to report the problem to Noah. He could not quite reach the captain; the two officers were separated by a medical corpsman loaded with first-aid equipment. As they tried to communicate above the tumult, the medic obligingly crouched and let the lieutenant step over his back. Returning to his platoon by the same route after conferring with Noah, Lieutenant Nir paused to shout an unwittingly comic "Excuse me!"

Noah pushed forward relentlessly. As a combat commander, he had to be in the forefront of the assault. At the same time, he felt obliged to keep the entire picture in view so he could report accurately to the battalion command. In his own mind, the major problem was to avoid getting deeply engaged in combat. The automatic response of a soldier coming under fire is to defend himself any way he can. A commander had to deny himself that luxury, if he was to watch over all the men in his unit, and maintain contact with his superiors. "That means you must resist your instinctive impulses and keep yourself detached."

It was not always possible. Circling toward the rear of the police building, where the trenches became more shallow, Noah came upon the young medic, his left hand all but severed at the wrist by a machine-gun bullet. Another soldier was tightening a tourniquet around the bleeding artery. Noah asked what direction the fire had come from. The soldier raised his head above the trench to point—

and was killed instantly by a bullet through the throat. Noah fired once, toward the trees where he had seen a flash. A Legionnaire toppled forward.

Naftali Cohen, meanwhile, was fighting a war of his own. The rangy, black-haired Yemenite lost contact with Noah in the first trench before the Police School when one of the Israelis stumbled over a Jordanian ammunition box, causing a pile-up behind him. By the time Naftali reached a fork in the tunnel, he was alone. He heard a scraping sound, and turned to see a shadowy figure emerging from a bunker.

Naftali asked for the password. The other man made no answer, but reached back his right arm in an underhand bowling motion and sent something spinning toward the Israeli. It had to be a grenade. Naftali caught it, knee-high, and felt in the dark for the pin. It had not been pulled. He brought the grenade up to his eyes to see better, removed the pin and flung it back. The bunker blew up, and the Jordanian ran.

Naftali took the right fork and soon caught up with the main body of his platoon. As the parking lot behind the Police School came into view, he was gratified to see Noah. "That man had waves of confidence radiating out of him; standing next to him, you had to absorb some of his strength."

Noah sent the corporal and a machine gunner into the shallow trench leading to the parking lot to look for a link-up with the Israeli company coming from the opposite direction.

Emerging from the trench, the Yemenite saw a Jordanian ammunition truck silhouetted against the olive trees. He set it ablaze with a single rifle shot, then felled the fleeing driver. Another soldier appeared in the archway to the far right, this one recognizable by his chin-strap as Israeli. Naftali shouted "Contact!" to Noah; the Police School had been encompassed.

But at terrible cost. Up to this point in the battle, Noah had been advising his superiors that the paratroopers were advancing on their objectives, and the situation was under control. Now, making a quick head count, he realized that Nir's force and his own had been merged into a body of single-platoon strength. Checking with Captain Dedi on his right, he found that one platoon had been reduced to a handful of men. And Ammunition Hill still lay ahead.

Noah radioed for reinforcements. Meanwhile, he gathered his remaining officers and noncoms and plunged northward through a gap between two outbuildings.

Now they were on the lower slopes of Ammunition Hill, in a labyrinth of zigzagging trenches and thickly-shielded concrete bunkers, flowing upward to artillery emplacements and an underground headquarters at the top. The enemy was totally out of sight, revealed only in flashes of fire from the squarish pillboxes above them.

The Israelis split into three groups, Noah diving into the main trench in the center, one of his lieutenants taking the left fork, and Captain Dedi moving to the right. This time, with individual units dissolved and the multiplicity of Legion positions making it impossible to see who was firing or from where, Noah had no choice; he was obliged to fight his way forward himself. Twice he stormed bunkers blocking his path upward toward the headquarters post.

Then he turned back to rally his men. It was a sound judgment. For some of the untried reservists, the pressure and the terror, the gaping wounds of friends, the furious uproar of the guns and especially the relentless presence of a hidden enemy flashing murderous fire out of the darkness, had become too much. A few men lagged at the rear, unwilling to brave the hurricane ahead. Here and there a soldier sat motionless on the ground, paralyzed with shock.

One and all, Noah urged them forward—shouting, pushing, slapping—always in command. And they moved up through the bloodied trenches, raggedly and uncertainly, but steadily ahead.

Sometimes he coaxed fantastic performances out of men whose backgrounds were anything but martial. Near the top of the hill, on the right flank, a large bunker undetected by aerial reconnaissance had pinned down a dozen Israelis in a trench twenty feet below. In the faint beginnings of moonlight, the paratroopers were being raked by bazooka and machine-gun fire; their Uzzis and rifles were completely ineffective against the concrete-vaulted, double-walled Jordanian position.

Noah, loping eastward from the central trench to survey the situation, decided the bunker could be silenced only by close-range demolition. He called for volunteers and turned to Sholom David, a wiry twenty-five-year-old electrician whose father had been an impoverished delivery wagon driver in Iraq.

Sholom primed a grenade, clambered up and sprinted toward the bunker. Flinging himself across the roof, he dropped his live grenade through a gun-slit. But the Legion guns kept firing. The Iraqi shouted for dynamite. Three sacks of TNT sailed up from the paratroopers in the trench. Sholom placed the charges at the foot of the bunker, and blasted the entire casement from its moorings. Miraculously he escaped unhurt.

On the other side of the hill, Naftali was also upholding the Oriental banner. Moments after he entered the left trench, the lieutenant leading his group was hit in the shoulder. The Yemenite corporal suddenly found himself in charge of a dozen men who had lost their officers. He told them to use a grenade on every bunker, and follow up with rifle fire when the occupants came out.

Kneeling to reload his rifle, Naftali became aware that there was a body under his feet. He was too preoccupied to have a reaction. Feelings, time, distance did not exist; everything was swallowed up in the intensity of the moment.

Abruptly, the lower trench system ended. Naftali emerged, blinking. The moon had come up—a thin yellow melon slice, hooked around a single bright unwinking star. Above Naftali, higher up the slope, Arab machine guns were banging away from a new line of defensive positions.

Naftali organized his little group for attack, training two machine guns against the Legion trenches. He felt, as he was to tell friends later, that he was no longer a mere corporal, but a "battle commander giving orders."

The main enemy trench was fifty yards above, with a jog downward on the right that came to within twenty yards of the Israelis. A scattering of trees gave both sides some concealment. Dawn was approaching. In the half-light, Naftali saw helmets moving cautiously along the jog. He told one of the machine gunners to provide covering fire, and slipped out into the open, creeping from tree to tree. Soon he could see four Legionnaires. He opened fire. His machine gunner, picking up the directional cue from Naftali, swept the trench, killing all four.

Now Naftali, joined by three other Israelis, charged straight up the slope, bellowing fiercely. One of the quartet was hit, but a shower of grenades destroyed the Legion gun posts.

Still another trench led to the top of the hill. As Naftali headed toward it, the officer beside him was shot through the heart. He had known the man well, from training days. "Seeing him hit, I felt a tremendous hatred. I wanted to destroy."

There were three Legionnaires in the trench. Naftali shot one through the forehead, another in the face, the third in the body. As he crouched to reload, something hit him—"like a tap on the back." He sprayed the trench again, then sagged to the ground, feeling a "weakness in the right hand." A medic ran up and stripped away the heavy pack—clothing, mess kit, first and second aid, grenade pockets—that had slowed up the Arab bullet headed straight for his lungs.

Hauled up from the trench, Naftali declined an escort back to the medical field station. He stumbled westward toward the Israeli lines. Halfway down the hill he encountered Noah, returning to lead a final smash against the crumbling Legion command post.

Dawn broke at 4:37 A.M., crisp and eucalyptus-scented. A rosy tint spread along the blue-shadowed crest of Mount Scopus. From a stiffly swaying cedar in the heart of embattled Jerusalem, a covey of small birds swooped down, their high-pitched chirping strangely sweet against the barking of the guns.

South of Ammunition Hill, fighting raged on, with Gur's Second and Third Battalions advancing through sniper-filled streets in a pincer move toward the Archaeological Museum above the northeast corner of the Old City. From the thick, sixteenth-century northern wall came the rattle of machine-gun bullets, the whine of recoilless rifles, and the whoosh of antitank fire poured down by Legionnaires stationed along the parapet and in hidden gun niches. The Old City had not been stormed successfully for nine hundred years; and beyond it lay the deadly fortresses in the Syrian mountains.

But on the stubbly, bullet-shattered hill there was only mopping up. A force of some 200 Jordanians, the pick of Hussein's army, had been destroyed; many of their 67 dead were buried where they had fallen, under a crudely lettered marker bearing·tribute from the victors to a courageous foe.

Israel had paid heavily for the two-hour breakthrough; 36 men were dead, and hundreds wounded. Noah, starting with three platoons, could muster less than one at the end. But the crucial bastion, unlike Latrun in 1948, had been wrested from Legion hands.

Among the few to receive a "mention in dispatches"—the closest thing to a decoration for bravery in the Israeli Army—was Naftali Cohen.

Naftali's story typifies the problems, hopes and achievements of a community that has changed the face, if not the heart, of the Jewish homeland. Jews from the Islamic countries now make up more than half the population—and the army—of Israel. Called "Orientals," as distinct from the Ashkenazic and Sephardic Jews of Europe, the Eastern newcomers constitute a "second Israel" markedly different in physical type, education, and cultural pattern. Their integration into the national life has been one of the prime challenges of Israeli society.

These Jews, dispersed from their original home in Palestine, had lived for centuries in the Arab lands of North Africa and the Middle East. Apart from a few wealthy families in such capitals as Cairo and Baghdad, they had been squeezed into urban ghettos where they lived as minor shopkeepers and craftsmen; or scattered like the Arab fellahin over primitively cultivated farmlands. They had shared the patriarchal family life of the Arabs, from which no dissent was tolerated; the nonexistent public schooling; the habit of dining en masse without tableware from a common bowl on the floor. Completely divorced from any sense of identification with a larger political body, they had developed a vast, apathetic self-centeredness. They were traditional and Messianist, without a spark of revolutionary fervor; at most, they sought escape from their second-class status.

Their absorption into Israeli life has not been a matter of a simple joyous embrace on either side. Many European Jews, especially of the older generation, have been frankly reluctant to accept as equals a mass of immigrants of dissimilar habits, tastes, and frequently, color. Others from the West, with the best of intentions, have been unable to shake loose the prejudices ingrained in their past surroundings.

The government, lacking any precedent for coping with the huge influx that began in 1948, has frequently stumbled. Some critics charge that it has failed to integrate Eastern and Western populations sufficiently and has often uprooted old ways before offering new ones to replace them. Although most younger people mingle freely as fellow sabras, discrimination against Orientals lingers in employment and housing, and is often fierce in parental opposition to Ashkenazim-Oriental marriages.

Yet the Israeli experience in dealing with a dark-skinned subgroup has been fundamentally different from that of the United States. A paratrooper sergeant, who in civilian life trains immigrant boys and girls from the Moslem countries at the Youth Village of Nurim near Haifa, argues that America has the financial and educational means to resolve the problem, but not the national will. "It doesn't really want to. We, on the other hand, acquired a huge minority when we lacked both the means and the training to absorb them; but we are making a genuine effort, and we have absolute faith in the ultimate potential of our people." It is clear that, for all the remaining tensions, thousands of Orientals have already been enabled to leap in a single generation from a virtually medieval condition to increasingly full participation in an advanced Western democracy.

In the case of Naftali Cohen, the personal revolution has been practically total. Dark and coarse-featured, Naftali is unmistakably Eastern in appearance. His face is lean and sharp; one is tempted to say hatchet-shaped, but that sounds unattractive, and Naftali is just short of handsome. He has deep dimples, a wide aggressive mouth, and a kind of Bedouin-chief dash. Although Naftali is not a big man, his chest is broad from years of cross-country running.

He was born in Israel twenty-two years ago, the eldest child of a farmer who had just arrived from Yemen. His credentials as a Jew were unshakable: the Yemenites are descended from one of the twelve original tribes of Israel, deported after the first destruction of the temple by Nebuchadnezzar in the sixth century B.C. They went to Babylon on the Euphrates, and then southward to Yemen, at the bottom of the Arabian peninsula between the Red Sea and the Indian Ocean. For generation upon generation, they clung to their God and their ethical tradition. To make maximum use of the precious prayer books transported with them into exile, they taught their children to read the Hebrew Torah upside down as well as right side up, so that two boys could chant the liturgical melody simultaneously.

From early adolescence, Naftali was plunged into bitter and increasing conflict with his surroundings. "It wasn't only my parents, who had all sorts of old-fashioned ideas about religion and how children ought to behave; it was the whole neighborhood, the

Yemenite-immigrant community in which we lived. Everything was prohibitions, restrictions—'You can't do this, you're not old enough for that.' When I rebelled once and went to a party on a Friday night, my father walloped me. There was simply no understanding between us."

Untrained in Western ways and having five people to support, Naftali's father was glad to get a job as caretaker for the high school his children attended in Even Yehuda, an orange-growing village of thirty-five hundred near the coast north of Tel Aviv. The lowly status of his parent did nothing for Naftali's self-esteem. Taunted by a classmate from Rumania who shrieked "Yemenite, Yemenite," Naftali bloodied the other boy's nose. He was gravely censured, and told that he would be permitted to stay in school only as a special favor, because his father was an employee.

Naftali angrily dropped out, relinquishing his educational opportunities in his middle teens. Although free public schooling is confined to the elementary grades in Israel, grants and subsidies for secondary school are frequently extended to promising Oriental pupils. Naftali spent the next year or two loafing, doing occasional odd jobs, and in the evening chasing girls.

At eighteen, summoned for army training, he was an insecure, unhappy boy rapidly going nowhere. By some instinct for self-preservation, he chose the paratroops. "I deliberately wanted to take on the toughest kind of training; not only to harden myself, but because I knew that if I could overcome such a challenge, it would make me feel that I was really somebody."

He was sent first to a kibbutz below Tel Aviv, where the army operated an instruction center for Nahal, the farming-defense corps attached to border settlements. Here, in camp, Naftali had his first pleasant surprise. "Nobody there ever suggested for a minute that I was different from anyone else. From the moment I arrived, I had the same responsibilities, the same privileges and freedoms as the others. In fact, sometimes I would be given a more desirable assignment than one of my Ashkenazim comrades: I might be supervising the packing while he was picking crops in the hot sun, or filling in for one of the girls in the kitchen. It was the first time in my life I had ever been treated that way. It was wonderful."

It was also no accident. The Israeli Army education program has been designed with an acute sensitivity to the needs of the Oriental recruit. Colonel Mordechai Bar-On, the Education Director, is a large, rawboned former guerrilla fighter grown scholarly and somewhat ponderous in staff service. He sees the boys of Eastern background as having been hemmed in at home by outdated, irrelevant conventions that virtually prohibited any deviations in the direction of personal progress.

The Army, with its classless philosophy and absolute equality of opportunity, "offers the entrance ticket to a new life," Bar-On says. Lack of formal education is not such a crippling stigma, because there are rewards for other qualities, such as courage and inventiveness, with which the newcomer may be well equipped. Horizons are broadened with the acquisition of new friends drawn from all classes. "Dense feelings of inferiority are diluted; conceptions of belonging develop, and a new national memory takes its shape."

Bar-On likes to tell of Nissim, an Egyptian-born reservist whose tank came under withering fire in the Sinai in 1956. Nissim started to pull back in panic, then caught himself up angrily ("Nissim, what are you doing?") and moved forward to help take the enemy stronghold. "The inner voice he heard was not that of instinct," says Bar-On. "It was the voice of his new ego, of the shame developed in his new social environment."

Orientals are not yet zooming up to the highest ranks of the army, where educational requirements are stringent. But they do emerge from Bar-On's pressure cooker with a clear awareness of the difference between freedom and license, and "a profound commitment" to the state "as the supreme embodiment of each individual's personal sovereignty."

After the army, Naftali took his new-found maturity in several directions. Instead of waiting for a job, he went out and landed one as a buyer-checker for a prefabricated-housing company.

Then he came to grips with an issue that had plagued him since boyhood: the influence exerted in the Yemenite community by extremely orthodox religious leaders. In his teens, out of consideration for his parents, he had attended the synagogue regularly on Friday nights and Saturdays. Now "a person claiming to represent religion but who actually cheated in the name of the Bible" dragged his family into a scandal. Naftali intervened and exposed the fraud. From then on he was opposed to formal religion, and "especially those who proclaim themselves teachers of religion." His own children, he says, will not be "kept in ignorance" but will have the alternatives about religious observance explained to them, and then be allowed to make their own choice.

The prospect of marriage and children is still another consequence of Naftali's recent self-sufficiency. Esther is the kind of girl he would have shied away from in his restless pre-army days: soft, delicately made, obviously raised by her Yemenite parents to run a household. Naftali had been seeing her casually at folk-dance evenings for months. It was only when she began keeping company with another boy, closer in age to her own eighteen years, that he realized the extent of his involvement.

By then, the war crisis was in the air. He hesitated to commit himself, for fear of the effect on Esther if he became a battle casualty. The night Naftali was called up, his beloved was out with his rival.

As soon as he was discharged from the hospital, Naftali took Esther to a café and declared himself. As he had been assuring himself—not quite successfully—for weeks, Esther was neither startled nor dismayed. It turned out that she had decided the other boy could not match Naftali in purposefulness; she had refrained from visiting her soldier in the hospital only out of fear of being thought forward.

Since that memorable evening, Naftali has abandoned pickups at the discotheques and become a "good boy." He does not plan to run the family with old-fashioned Oriental autocracy: "On basic decisions, a wife should defer to her husband. But generally I consider women the equal of men, and in some ways superior."

Naftali looks to the future eagerly, although with some misgivings. He feels he is operating far below his potential, without any means of obtaining the education necessary to develop his ideas. He would like to study mechanical engineering and learn how to build bridges. He yearns for a house of his own, a car, and "many, many children." But, remembering the war, he hopes to marry Esther within the year, for "who knows about tomorrow?"

DAWN: THE NURSE

THE price paid for Ammunition Hill was high. It would have been far higher except for a tiny, Italian-born nurse who had no business being anywhere near the scene. That she came anyway was a blessing never to be forgotten by scores of battle-weary paratroopers.

At thirty, Esther Arditi Zalinger was clearly exempt from the reservist call-up. Although she had spent two years in the Air Force and had been the central figure in a spectacular plane rescue, she was in June, 1967, a working mother, responsible for two young children.

Actually it was the children who sent her to war. They were convinced by their mother's past exploits that no harm could come to her. Their ingenuous faith was severely tested at Mandelbaum Gate and the Police School, where Esther treated wounded paratroopers all through the night under a rain of fire from rifles, mortars and machine guns. Men beside her were struck, a shell fragment dented her borrowed helmet; but Esther remained, as her children insisted, indestructible.

She hardly looks it. Trimly designed, with an upturned nose and curly chestnut hair that could grace a Broadway musical, Esther is a volatile package of exactly a hundred pounds.

In 1948, already a veteran of Nazi occupation horrors, she defied her elders in a determined campaign to reach the Jewish homeland. Afterward, still in her teens, she plunged into a burning military plane to drag out two unconscious officers.

Esther's initial acquaintance with violence came early. She was not yet seven when her mother and baby brother were slaughtered by Nazi soldiers before her eyes.

The year was 1943, and Italy was rapidly succumbing to German occupation. Milan, where the Arditis had lived for generations, was swarming with Nazi troops. Her father was a prosperous merchant who considered himself more Italian than Jewish. It was her Bulgarian-born mother who kept the Judaic flame alive in the family. Small and sweet-faced, speaking a warm Ladino, the Spanish-Hebrew dialect of Sephardic Jews, Mrs. Arditi lit Friday evening candles, went to synagogue services, and named her children after biblical figures—first Isaac, and then twelve years later, Esther.

To the Nazis they were all Jews. Esther's father took his wife and children, now including an infant son, southward to the wine-growing Tuscany region, a long-time Socialist stronghold that had become a center of the Resistance. They settled in a farming village about halfway between Pisa and Florence.

In the autumn, Esther's father was caught listening to the B.B.C. Brought to German military headquarters for questioning, he broke loose and escaped to the woods, where 18-year-old Isaac was already serving with the partisans.

A local Fascist informer betrayed him. Seized once more, he was pressed by the Nazis for full information on Jews as well as Resistance fighters hiding in the neighborhood. When he defied them, they beat him savagely, then went through the village house by house looking for his family.

From a hillside farmhouse, Esther's mother saw the uniformed figures approach. With her were Esther, then a fragile hazel-eyed child of six, and her baby boy.

Terrified, Mrs. Arditi cast about for a hiding place. Her eye fell on the huge, old-fashioned oven in the kitchen. She swung the door open and, pushing the children before her, took refuge behind the bricks.

Heavy boots thumped along the stone path outside. Esther, trembling against her mother's skirt, heard the front door flung open and then harsh, bantering men's voices as the Nazis scattered through the cottage.

Esther threw an appealing glance to her mother in the semi-light from an overhead grate. "I shall never forget that moment. My mother was frightened, so frightened. . . . She stood as if paralyzed, simply shivering from head to toe, clinging to my little brother and me. Instead of encouraging her children, giving them moral support, she revealed her own fear. I shall never do that to my children, or forgive her for doing it."

Abruptly the door was tugged open. The little group stumbled out, and Mrs. Arditi began a desperate plea for the lives of her children.

It was never finished. A German soldier tore the little boy from her arms and with a violent upward thrust dashed the child's head against the ceiling.

Mrs. Arditi screamed and threw herself furiously upon the German, clawing, kicking and biting.

A pistol shot rang out, then another. Mrs. Arditi crumpled to the floor.

Esther flew toward the open door. In the moment before the Nazis could collect themselves, she was able to reach the woods behind the house, a tiny quarry, hardly worth pursuing. For the rest of her life she was to carry a bitterness about her mother's failure to resist sooner: "If you die, you should die *for* something; not wait in hiding for death to come to you."

Esther was six years old and friendless, in a countryside overrun by killers. "But I had grown up in wartime; I understood a great deal." Unwilling to trust herself to strangers, she wandered alone, living on what she could find in the forest: berries and nuts, herbs, roots, an occasional bird's egg. Quickly—and painfully—she learned what was digestible.

Time became blurred, as one day rolled into the next. Now the nights were turning colder, and the foraging grew more difficult. What saved her was a little lamb that she ran into one afternoon. "It seemed as lost as I was. That lamb became my family and my sustenance." Esther called the lamb Biancina, "little white one." "We walked together, I talked to it and poured out my heart. Looking into Biancina's eyes, I felt she understood. At night, we slept in caves or tree hollows, and I nestled against the lamb for warmth. Somehow I got through the winter."

Early one morning, as Esther was sifting through a copse in search of food, two bearded men came to the forest. Biancina was nibbling at dead leaves a few yards away. Automatically Esther dropped out of sight behind a tree stump. She lifted her head cautiously. To her horror, she saw one of the men raise a rifle to his shoulder and with a single shot send the lamb tumbling into the leaves.

Forgetful of her own safety, Esther raced out into the open and flung herself across the animal's body, sobbing.

Powerful arms pulled her up. "I thought I was going to be killed, but I didn't care. My friend was gone; nothing else mattered."

She became aware that someone was crying out her name. It was the man holding her. She twisted her head and looked up into the fierce, black-bearded face. She did not dare to believe her eyes. It was her older brother.

Now a partisan commander, seeking food for his troops, Isaac had heard of the murders in the farmhouse and never expected to see his sister alive again. He brought her back to camp, to the protection of his guerrilla comrades.

The partisans were hunted men, never sure of their next meal or their next round of ammunition. But they had faith in their cause, and unfailing mutual loyalty. They lived off the bounty of local farmers, supplemented by audacious raids against German camps.

Whenever the guerrillas struck, Esther stayed behind in a cave hideout, terrified. Soon she noticed that the men came back from these desperate adventures, usually unharmed. She concluded that human beings had an extraordinary capacity for self-preservation, and that those who pursued their duty with good conscience would somehow be protected. She began to feel more at ease among the partisans.

They in turn adopted Esther. She became to them what Biancina had been to her: a mascot, symbolizing the normal world left behind and the values they were fighting for.

In the postwar spring of 1945, the partisans came down from the hills. Esther and her brother went back to a house the family had occupied for a time in Leghorn on the Mediterranean coast. It was a mass of rubble. Poking among the ruins for her old toys, Esther saw a thin, bent figure weeping under the trees, wrapped in a shawl that she remembered as having belonged to her mother. She was puzzled: who could the wizened ancient be? Approaching, she saw ugly scars on his face—and with a stab of pain, recognized her father.

The remnant family resumed living together—but hardly as before. Esther's father was a broken man, plagued with guilt over his "abandonment" of his wife and infant; unable to function, he was reduced to a welfare pension. Her twenty-one-year-old brother was preoccupied with postwar politics. The little girl, with no feminine influence in her life, longed for a mother's touch on her hair, a fluffy nightdress. Instead, she wistfully kicked a football with the boys down the road.

At nine, she was admitted to a local Catholic school. She already felt that Jews were different, unwanted; here those feelings were reinforced. She began "dreaming of a land where Jews could be free." She created fantasies about a country settled only by Jews, without knowing it had any existence in reality.

In 1946, she heard over the radio that Jews in the Middle East were fighting against the British mandatory power for the right to establish a state of their own. "I became terribly excited. When we heard about the proclamation of statehood in 1948, and the Arab invasions, I was eager for all of us to go and fight there."

The Arditi men did not take seriously these enthusiasms of an eleven-year-old. Her brother had already committed himself to the Italian Left; her father had turned his back altogether on politics. He clung to life only to look after Esther, who resembled her mother. He certainly had no desire to see his daughter pitched into struggles overseas.

To her eager inquiries about the "Jewish partisans," he made sour replies. Yes, the Jews were trying to build a state, but the project was doomed. They were already fighting among themselves, had permitted the murder of Count Bernadotte, were obviously as self-seeking as the rest of mankind.

Esther was not to be put off. The more he attacked her dream, the more she clung to it. Nobody could tell her about underground fighters; she had lived among them.

Obtaining a set of maps, she charted herself a course across the ocean. She had heard that boats for Israel departed from Naples; that meant, she assumed, that all boats leaving Naples went to Israel.

Late one evening she broke into her piggy bank, crept out of her bedroom window, and took the midnight train south from Leghorn, leaving behind a note: "My place is in Israel, fighting for freedom."

Finding the letter in the morning, her father notified the Naples police. A three-hour search of the docks turned up the stowaway, in a nest of cables on a freighter bound for East Africa.

Esther had lost a battle, but not her war. Her father now realized the intensity of her feelings. He offered a deal: she could go to Israel, if she first completed her high-school education.

"From that day on, I never knew a day's vacation. All I did was apply myself to studies, so that I could leave at the earliest possible minute." Esther skipped two years and finished high school at sixteen.

She had already enrolled in the Hachalutz ("spearhead") pioneer movement in Leghorn, which prepared Europeans for kibbutz life. Her fiery enthusiasm aroused the curiosity of her brother, who dropped in casually at a few meetings, then astonished both Esther and his father by announcing he would go with her to Israel.

They arrived late in 1953. "I ran ashore, shouting over and over, 'I'm a Jew,' luxuriating in the knowledge that here I could proclaim it freely, without fear of reprisal."

The group from Italy was sent to Kibbutz Amir in the upper Galilee. For most of them, disillusion set in quickly. Frontier life in the reclaimed swampland was a far cry from the dolce vita. Esther found herself almost alone in defending the Jewish homeland.

A letter came from her father, urging his two children to return. Once again Esther went A.W.O.L. from family jurisdiction, hitchhiking into Tel Aviv. She wandered down the seacoast to old Jaffa, where an army induction center—and an Italian-speaking officer—presented her with a solution. Although two years underage, she became an Israeli private. "The morning I put on my uniform was the happiest day of my life."

Her brother, hot on her trail, came to fetch her back to Italy. "I told him he was too late. I was a soldier of Israel, and no force on earth could make me leave."

Which branch of service to choose was a problem. Her Hebrew was sketchy, she had no office skills. But nursing—that was something needed by every army, a way to prove worthy of the uniform.

After training, Esther was assigned in January of 1955 to an Air Force base in the south. It was a typical Israeli installation, relaxed and informal. She was therefore both surprised and humiliated when, passing a hangar one afternoon, she was brought up short by an officer inside: "What's the matter, soldier, didn't they teach you how to salute?"

Yaacov Salmon was a squadron leader, a large man whose heavy features seem at first glance to be fixed in a permanent scowl. On closer view, this impression is revealed as an accident of facial topography, attributable mainly to thick brows and an enormous cavalry mustache; the real man is visible in his sensitive brown eyes.

But Esther didn't stop for a close look. She snapped up her hand nervously and scurried away. Thereafter, whenever she saw Major Salmon, she ducked.

Because of constant activity at the airfield, nurses were posted in the control tower around the clock. Weekend and evening assignments were understandably unpopular. But Esther had neither family nor friends to fill her social life; so she was constantly volunteering to take over and set some colleague free for an urgent date.

She was on such replacement duty one midnight when a sudden desert squall erupted. Bursts of lightning, accompanied by high winds and heavy rain, ripped across the sky. A training flight of four American-built Mosquito fighters, with a full complement of guns, bombs and ammunition, was on the way in.

As the flight commander at the controls of the lead plane was descending to touchdown, a violent thunderbolt plunged the airfield into total darkness. The Mosquito thudded into a field beside the runway, instantly bursting into flame.

Esther sped to the scene. Her ambulance, like the fire trucks, bogged down at the edge of the muddy field. From the plane came muffled cries for help. Esther jumped down and started running, dimly aware of a shouted warning that the Mosquito's bomb load would explode at any moment. Her shoes sank in the mire; she kicked them off.

The next few minutes were a nightmare of crackling flames, spitting machine-gun bullets triggered by the shock of the landing, and burning flesh. Somehow Esther pulled free first the navigator and then the burly pilot, unconscious and still bound to his blazing ejection seat. She had dragged them about twenty yards clear of the plane when it went up with a shattering roar.

On the way to the hospital, Esther gave the two men emergency treatment. It was then, cleaning a machine-gun wound on the pilot's forehead, that she recognized her erstwhile tormentor, Major Salmon.

The rescued navigator survived for only sixty days, but Major Salmon made a full recovery. Esther herself was hospitalized for two weeks with severe burns on the arms, hands and head, then haled ceremonially to army headquarters for a personal citation by

Moshe Dayan, then Chief of Staff. Dayan surveyed the five-foot flyweight heroine disbelievingly. "What?" He demanded. "Is that all there is?"

The airfield drama had more far-reaching rewards. Major Salmon's parents were eager to express their gratitude personally. So was the pilot, a family man with several children, as soon as he was sufficiently restored to understand what had happened. He made inquiries about Esther at the base, but she dodged all approaches until he framed an invitation in the form of a direct order: she was to come to his parents' home in Jerusalem on the approaching holiday weekend.

Even then, Esther hung back. The Salomons (the major dropped the first "o" from the name) occupy a large, old-fashioned apartment in the quiet Sanhedria district at the northern end of Jerusalem. When Esther had not arrived by midafternoon, one of the family's several boys was dispatched to scout for her. He found the little nurse wandering around the central bus station on Jaffa Street, unable to face a houseful of strangers. Although girl soldiers normally couldn't wait to change into civvies for a long weekend, she was in uniform.

The Salomons soon found out why. Delivered safely to Sanhedria, Esther was shown to a pleasant bedroom and urged to hang up her things. The "things" in her suitcase, it turned out, were a bra and two pairs of stockings. She had no dresses, no make-up.

Mrs. Salomon, a plump, vivacious woman who at fifty had already been a grandmother for eleven years, bustled her guest into the family car to embark on the first shopping spree Esther had ever known: blouses and skirts and dainty shoes, topped off by the extravagant unnecessaries that women cherish most . . . fragrant bath salts, a formal evening bag. Both women had a wonderful time.

Over the evening meal—strictly kosher and superlatively prepared—the Salomons learned of Esther's solitary existence, and the absence from her life of even an aunt. Before coffee, they had reached their conclusion: "Let this be your house."

Esther was too overwhelmed to act on the invitation. But the Salomons followed it up with unhurried persistence. Within eight months, Matithia and Breyndel Salomon were "Pa" and "Ma" to her.

She could not have landed in a more solid environment. The six

Salomon children—the major was the oldest of four boys—were seventh-generation sabras, with friends all over the country. The head of the house was a construction project manager in the Department of Public Works. Esther sensed the silent strength and deep humanity behind his gruff manner. She took her most serious problems to him unhesitatingly.

With Breyndel, her relationship was more chatty and intimate. Mrs. Salomon was one of those spontaneously generous women who make most masculine exploits look a little boyish. For ten years, unknown to her own children, she had helped an immigrant family in the nearby Beit Israel district, not only with weekly food and money but by getting down on her knees to scrub the floors.

She also had no lack of spirit—another point of contact with Esther. When her third son, Moshe, enlisted in the paratroops, a neighbor shuddered disapprovingly. "I'd never let *my* boy—"

"What's so special about your boy, that he's better than mine?" Breyndel snapped. "If he's qualified, and we need paratroopers, that's what he should be!" Then, turning to Moshe: "Just don't ever tell me you're jumping tomorrow. Tell me you jumped yesterday."

The Salomons were firmly orthodox, and Esther was innocent of religious instruction, but there was no friction over the issue. If Breyndel would touch nothing but water in Esther's highly secular kitchen, she nonetheless insisted there was more than one path to paradise; that a place could be earned, as the rabbinical sages said, "in a single moment, with a single act." Esther is terribly proud of this acceptance: "My parents understand that my religion consists of helping God; I don't think of God as a being who solves everybody's problems for them, but as one who should be helped by people. They even think God has set aside a special place in paradise for me."

Even the ultra-orthodox Grandpa Chaim Salomon became attached to Esther, partly because Yaacov, whom she saved, had been named for Chaim's father. The venerable retired builder would let Esther get away with anything, even outrageous remarks like "Ah, Grandpa, if you could only once taste the joy of a ham sandwich with milk. . . ."

Her new status as a daughter had immediate repercussions for Esther's social life. With a place to come home to, she was no longer the forlorn Cinderella of the air base. Now her past unselfishness brought unexpected dividends: girls for whom she had filled in on many a long weekend were glad of a chance to return the favor. She began riding into town every Friday afternoon with the carefree, leave-bound office workers and maintenance crewmen.

Soon the Salomons' old apartment was busy every weekend, blazing with lights and swarming with young people. One of Yaacov's younger brothers, returning home on army furlough, was startled to be greeted at the door of his home by a smiling stranger in white blouse and trim blue shorts. She had acquired a new personality. She also acquired admirers: an aircraft mechanic, a young law student, a designer of medical research instruments for Hadassah Hospital. No longer a friendless waif, she actually began to sing in the shower.

Lightning had quite literally struck in Esther's life. The bolt that had sent Yaacov Salmon's airplane into a wheat field had also opened a door for his rescuer.

Esther's military award was still reverberating in the Israeli press when she finished army duty in 1956. She took a hospital job in the mountainous Galilee. The day she started work, the driver of her bus up from Tiberias, a rugged, sandy-haired youth named Zalinger, was haranguing his passengers on the nobility of the little army nurse in the south. Esther listened quietly.

After she got off at Safad, one of the other passengers revealed her identity. The driver promptly put his bus in reverse and careened back along the corkscrew road to launch his courtship. Within a month they were married.

Esther had a son in 1958, a daughter two years later—and problems with her husband's overattentive family almost from the start. After several years of quarrels and reconciliations, the couple separated in Jerusalem in 1963.

The children stayed with their mother. Noorit, seven, is a rosy-cheeked, round-faced little girl, a model of pig-tailed innocence. Her brother Elan, nine, is lanky and more serious. Both have flaming red hair. As a friend remarked, "The character of the mother is manifested in the hair of the children."

From infancy, the children inherited (and were inherited by) the Salomon family. The children's greatest pleasure has always been a visit to "Grandma Breyndel," cornucopia of table goodies and boundless affection.

Esther was badly upset by her domestic difficulties. But she still had her children, her "parents"—and Israel.

In the spring of 1967, after several years as a nurse and ambulance driver, she enrolled in a course for tourist guides. A week before the outbreak of fighting, she was conducting first-aid courses for women volunteers at Hadassah Hospital when a letter from Italy arrived. Her brother was urging her to take refuge with him.

"For myself, there was never any question. But I did consider sending the children."

Both refused indignantly. "Even *we*," Elan reminded her, "can carry messages." And when the paratroop tanks clanked through the streets of their Beit Hakarem district late Monday afternoon, Elan said: "Mother, why don't you go and help the soldiers?" After all, Noorit pointed out, "Nothing bad can happen. A good angel watches over you."

Esther asked Noorit's teacher to look after the children, packed a first-aid kit and left the house. Outside the door she paused to contemplate her next move.

Could she really make a contribution? Or was it enough that she had saved Yaacov Salmon, who had earned his colonel's wings and had now become manager of Lod Airport?

No, it was not enough. She had to play her own role.

Esther set out for the nearby Red Mogen David (Jewish Star) first-aid station, where she had previously worked for two years as an ambulance driver. "Many volunteers were already there, but I had the advantage of an ambulance-driving license. I was assigned to transport civilians wounded by the Jordanian shelling."

She was pleased to find the old ambulance she had used, with its specially designed chair for 'enabling her short legs to reach the foot pedals.

A little before midnight, driving back from Shaari Zedek Hospital, Esther passed a concentration of paratroopers. "I learned they were about to reunite Jerusalem. I was burning to help."

Two hours later, she got her chance. A Jordanian mortar shell had been lobbed squarely into the middle of an Israeli headquarters company, killing and wounding dozens of men including a number of doctors and medical orderlies. A soldier raced up to the Mogen David station to request an ambulance.

In the momentary confusion, Esther leaped into the breach. "I pulled the soldier up into my ambulance and said, 'Come on, let's go.'"

They drove eastward toward the front lines in an increasing hail of artillery and small-arms fire. Near the Mandelbaum Gate, the old crossing-point between Jewish and Arab Jerusalem, the casualties had been gathered. "There were many men, on stretchers and on the ground. Blood was pouring from untended wounds. I saw that the immediate problem was first aid; there were others who could handle the ambulance."

Esther hopped down and went to work with bandages, burn treatment, morphine to relieve pain—and, perhaps most important, simple encouragement. Sometimes what wounded men needed most was a warm smile, a cool hand, a friendly word; anything that reassured them against the fear of being abandoned.

After several minutes of furious activity, she found a sharp-nosed, bespectacled medical officer at her elbow. "You must leave at once," he told Esther emphatically.

"Not while there are wounded men here," she replied.

The officer—Major Jack King, from South Africa—reiterated that she was out of bounds on the battlefield. Esther simply continued with the injection she was administering. King watched for a moment, brown eyes narrowing. He nodded his approval in spite of himself. Grudgingly he handed Esther a helmet. "Wear this."

The huge headgear was useless; it smothered her face completely. An officer being lifted onto a stretcher nearby with a sniper's bullet in his chest motioned Esther closer. "Take mine," he whispered. "Where I'm going, I won't need it."

This helmet was a better fit. Esther barely had it fixed in place when she felt something crash against the metal over her ear. "I looked down, and there was a piece of shrapnel."

A few hundred yards away, the battle for Ammunition Hill was now in full swing. Noah's platoons were suffering severe losses in their advance, but because of a breakdown in communications the medical unit at Mandelbaum Gate did not know it. Major King took his army team to another sector farther south. He left Esther behind.

It was just as well. Within minutes, a blood-smeared sergeant drove up in a half-track to report that medical assistance was urgently needed at the police building. Esther grabbed an armful of supplies and swung up beside him.

This time, below Ammunition Hill, it was full-fledged war. "Fire was flashing all around us. Men were strewn everywhere, and orderlies were bringing more—on stretchers, limping, supporting each other. A boy standing right next to me suddenly went down. Blood spattered over my shoes.

"For just an instant I felt a strangling sensation. I fought it back; I didn't want to be sent away. After that, there was no feeling, no desire to escape or hide. I thought only of helping as many men as possible before I too was hit."

Esther began counting to herself to see how many soldiers she could treat. "Twenty-seven, twenty-eight, blood flowing all over me, and still I wasn't touched. The thought went through my head, 'The children are right. There is an angel who watches over me.'

"The silence of the wounded was something eerie. Only the murmured word 'mother,' which the hardiest soldier will lapse into when hurt, becoming a boy again in his delirium. They called me 'mother' in a dozen languages, and I tried to be one . . . not providing just nursing care, but adding a few words of comfort, a caress on the forehead, an encouraging smile."

One of her patients was a tall blond youth stretched out immobile on the steps of the police building. "A bullet had torn through his neck, laying the spinal cord open. He wanted to know why he couldn't move. He had a new baby boy, it had been announced on the radio the day before, he had to live to see the boy.

"I told him he would be all right, that he was numb only on account of the morphine. I didn't tell him he was paralyzed."

Another wounded soldier winked at Esther as he was being lifted into a jeep. "Look," he told his companions. "As long as there's a girl around, the situation can't be too bad."

Esther was at the front for more than homeland. "Every soldier was fighting for *my* children. We all had the same dream of a future where all the children of the world could live happily, and no Jewish child in particular would ever have to suffer as I did."

To Esther, Israel encompasses everything worth living for. "I wouldn't change places with anyone in the world. Just to walk through the streets here is a wonderful thing. I feel that everybody I pass is a relative."

Back in Italy two years ago for her father's funeral, she had the feeling each person there was isolated, living for himself—"like the inhabitants of a ghetto, or of the gentile world. Among such people, fear spreads quickly. Here, no one was afraid; we reinforced each other. Our whole past, the six million destroyed, drove us forward; what else could make men rush toward death with positive enthusiasm?"

When the evacuation of casualties was completed, Esther was helped up onto a half-track and carried forward toward the Old City. Snipers were contesting every street from hallways and rooftops. She felt no fear; only a dim stirring of memory, an echo of partisans and Tuscany. "Oddly, I felt more secure moving forward with the soldiers than I would have been waiting under shell-fire at home."

But she was still a woman. As they advanced, she was horrified to see decapitated heads wearing Israeli helmets lying in the road. "Prisoners," one of the boys told her grimly. "The Jordanians tied them behind their armored vehicles. Those who couldn't keep up had their heads cut off."

The Israelis were thirsting for vengeance. Rounding a corner, they came upon an Arab woman of about thirty, carrying a wounded baby in her arms. One of the men in the half-track started to raise his rifle. Esther confronted him passionately: "If you're going to kill her, kill me too."

She jumped down and ran toward the Arab woman. "The baby was a little boy about a year old, unconscious and pale from loss of blood. At that moment I forgot that the woman was an enemy, that her relatives had probably killed and wounded our soldiers."

Esther took the child from the startled woman's arms, and stanched the wounds in its head and neck. Looking around the street, she saw a monastery a few doors away. "I brought the child there and handed him over to two priests."

Running to catch up with her half-track, she passed an Arab boy who spat at her violently. "For some reason, that gave me my only moment of fear."

A moment later, she heard footsteps behind her. She quickened her stride. A voice called out, hoarse but not threatening. Esther turned to see a venerable bearded Arab approaching. He carried in his hands a huge rectangle of candy wrapped in colored string. By gestures, he conveyed that this was a gift of thanks for treating the baby. Esther took the candy and ran on.

Through all of Tuesday, Esther stayed with the paratroopers as they closed in on the Old City. By nightfall she had acquired field equipment, battlefield mementos . . . and a legendary aura. What she had done, and was yet to do, would earn her a place in Colonel Gur's official account of the struggle.

POST-DAWN: KIBBUTZ DAN

ISRAEL'S most explosive border in 1967 was with her implacable enemy Syria in the northeast, where the heavily fortified Golani mountain range rose like a cresting tidal wave above the dozen settlements of the Jordan Basin. A thousand-foot escarpment crowned by strong artillery positions ran for forty miles, from Lebanon southward past the stunning vistas of the Sea of Galilee. And for nineteen years no Israeli among the thousands living below had been able to walk, work, eat or sleep in safety.

So cruelly placed was the overhanging balcony that a grenade casually dropped from the fortress of Tel Azaziat in the far north would land—and often did—on Israeli soil. Tiers of Soviet-made fieldpieces, dug deep into the black volcanic stone of the Golani Plateau, periodically raked the valley. Syrian machine gunners, snug in their concrete eyries, amused themselves by picking off unarmed farmers half a mile away.

Particularly vulnerable were Israeli tractor drivers. But children's buildings also were shelled; water towers blown up and settlers kidnapped by marauders who slipped through the barbed wire under cover of darkness.

Life in the kibbutzim went on, because it had to. But around the corner of consciousness in every mind was the awareness that death might slash down, without warning or provocation, at any moment. The most commonplace act was carried out in the shadow of potential disaster, with a cumulative effect that the human nervous system was not built to withstand.

Yet the tormented settler could not strike back. The Syrians lashed out from impregnable strong points impervious even to bombing. For the pioneer with his rifle and machine gun, standing over his exposed acres, the attacks were a scourge simply to be endured, in a contest of wills where all the visible resources were on the other side.

The settlements took what steps they could. Tin-roofed, brush-camouflaged machine-gun posts were strung through the woods, to be manned in emergency by small Home Guard units. Underground bomb shelters—long concrete tombs equipped with food, cots, blackboards and games—swallowed up children and older members whenever a barrage became intense.

But it was an unequal contest. Every kibbutz—Tel Katzir in the south, Noah's Gonen in the center, Kfar Szold in the north, had its own history of devastated fields, frightened children, wrecked infirmaries, and its own tales of young men who day after day took unarmed tractors into the fields, knowing that survival hinged on the whim of a bored and possibly envious Syrian sentry assiduously raised on a crash diet of hatred for Israelis. Like movie cameramen trailing far-off horsemen in a western, the Syrian regulars could with a flick of the finger swivel their weapons to keep the Israeli drivers within their narrow gunsights.

At the extreme tip of the Galilee, halfway between Tiberias and the Syrian capital of Damascus, lay the Kibbutz Dan, Israel's most northern outpost (biblical Palestine is described in Judges as extending "from Dan to Beersheba"). Planted in a slender arrowhead of land near the three-way junction of Lebanon, Syria and Israel, as a barrier against invasion from either Arab neighbor, Dan was probably the most exposed position in the entire country.

The kibbutz was founded in 1939 by pioneers from Hungary, Rumania, Poland and Belgium, along with a few Germans. Arriving in Israel as refugees in the early thirties, they had worked for seven years as orange pickers and building laborers outside Tel Aviv, collecting wages and yearning for land of their own.

When the call for migration finally came, it took them to a distant, undeveloped area still being reclaimed from swampy marshland. The early settlers lived eight to a room, bartering their first dairy produce for apricots and eggs from the Syrians—then still friendly—in the surrounding hills.

With the enthusiasm of Florida real-estate entrepreneurs, the pioneers at Dan mapped out in the boggy wilderness a collective village to be grouped around a north-south spine known as Central Avenue. East of the Avenue would be the "business district," comprising an industrial area and the various elements of farming. The other side of the dividing line would be residential. Community buildings—dining hall, school, infirmary—would be clustered in the middle of the settlement. Reflecting the vaguely Marxist leanings of the founders, there were no plans for a synagogue.

Today, Dan is spread out over 3000 acres, a flourishing community of 400 souls producing 1300 tons of apples and pears yearly, maintaining 1000 chickens and 500 beehives. Beef and dairy cattle, goats and kids roam its meadows. It is planted with corn, wheat and avocado; oranges and grapefruits; neat columns of poplar and eucalyptus; groves of shimmering olive and bursting-purple jacaranda. Its modest plastics factory has burgeoned into the manufacture of bicycles and tractor parts.

At the northern end of Central Avenue, like a local *arc de triomphe,* stands the handsome stone front of the Huleh Valley Institute for Natural History, an archaeological and scientific museum. Its soaring arches frame a magnificent view of the Golani Mountains.

The forging of Kibbutz Dan has not been quick or easy. Its fields and vineyards roll to the edge of the United Nations—marked border. Twice a year, during the spring sowing and the fall harvest, Syrian harassment has regularly reached peaks of venom. In the decade before 1967, fourteen tractors working the fields at Dan were blown up by Syrian-planted land mines.

An unprecedentedly savage artillery bombardment on November 13, 1964, hurled down five hundred shells in ninety minutes, killing livestock wholesale and wiping out the settlement's experimental agriculture station. Projectiles damaged the dining room, the dental clinic, the silo tower and the museum; another emptied the swimming pool. A dozen infants were carried out of the Children's Home minutes before a shell crashed through its roof.

After that experience, irreplaceable museum exhibits were transferred to the building's cellar. Electrical and telephone circuits for the shelters were shifted underground.

Dan has six subterranean shelters, linked through a network of deep, narrow trenches snaking all through the kibbutz grounds. Some fifteen steps lead down to cool, whitewashed rooms with roofs and walls of concrete three feet thick, buttressed by several more feet of hard-packed earth. Double layers of bunks run along a dormitory wall. Other sections are allocated to provisions, communications and recreation, with special facilities for children.

The shelters at Dan offer one of the world's oddest and most moving art exhibitions: a permanent, rotating display of misshapen airplanes and fog-shrouded mountains drawn, while shelling raged overhead, by the small children of the kibbutz.

The hazy outlines of the hills are accurately observed. The Upper Galilee ranges, unlike those of wild Judea, frequently have an unreal, dreamy quality. In the early hours of morning, wrapped in soft mist, they melt one into the other in endless, overlapping folds.

At 5:30 A.M. on Tuesday, June 6, Josi Levari was standing patrol duty on the northeast fringes of Kibbutz Dan. A high-domed, reddish-haired sabra of thirty-one, he was in charge of defenses at the most vulnerable approach to the kibbutz. Under Israeli security doctrine, static protection of borders is left mainly to frontiersmen guarding their own settlements, leaving regular units mobile. In event of enemy penetration, the kibbutz forces are expected to stop supplies and reinforcements from pouring through, until army troops arrive to plug the gap.

Behind Josi the settlement stirred in muted activity. Although Dan had gone into "defensive formation" twenty-four hours earlier, with the transfer of children and other noncombatants to the shelters, some functions could not be suspended.

Josi's watch had been for the most part quiet, with the eerie serenity peculiar to a kibbutz: something more than silence, where the contentment of the settlers themselves seems to trickle out of houses and cabins to hang adrift over the night. But just before dawn, with the tentative twittering of birds and the lowing of cattle, had come other sounds from the direction of Baniyas, a Syrian mountain village close to the demilitarized zone. Josi thought the sounds might be tanks. He had radioed his hunch to a regional army base, and an Israeli observation plane had just flown over to report that there were indeed Syrian armored forces in the area, but that they were apparently ranged for defense.

Josi wasn't so sure. The Syrians had for several years been the most belligerent of Israel's neighbors, flooding the Arab world with caricatures of pasty-faced Jews dangling from Syrian bayonets, challenging Nasser to match them in ferocity. Having goaded the Egyptians and a reluctant Hussein into hostilities, how long could the loudmouths in Damascus get away with mere shelling of settlements? Sooner or later, Josi reasoned, they would be impelled to stream down from their concrete hideaways to deliver the long-promised death blow.

Josi scuffed at the turf with the toe of his old army boot. A stone tumbled over, and a small brownish creature with glistening hide popped up from the dusty soil, then scurried away. A glass lizard, Josi noted to himself mechanically. The creature turned up frequently on both sides of the tortured border; animal life was singularly indifferent to the quarrels of humanity.

Josi snapped his mind back to attention. Next week or next month, with luck, he would be back on the job collecting research specimens—fish fossils, reptiles, birds' eggs—for the Natural History Institute, and unfolding the wonders of biology for fourteen-year-olds at the kibbutz. Today, his job was to see that by next month there would still *be* a kibbutz.

Josi was an experienced soldier, a paratroop veteran of the Sinai campaign. Later, as a sergeant, he had taken part in reprisal actions in the north under Colonel Mota Gur, a former neighbor in Josi's home town of Rehovoth.

And he had the most compelling personal reasons to fight: a slim, blonde, Chilean-born wife and two small boys huddled in a shelter less than half a mile away. Even closer to the potential front, behind a screen of tall poplars, was the Levari cottage, a neat frame house set among pepper trees and evergreens, overflowing with books, records and pleasant memories. Josi had come to Dan in 1955, after Pioneer Youth service in the army. Rachel had arrived from Santiago three years before him, a pig-tailed girl of fifteen. Within a year, sabra and South American were married.

Normally the children of Dan lived in youth quarters, frolicking with their parents only on weekends and from 4 to 8 p.m. each day. But this was hardly a normal week. Josi carried in his pocket a crayon drawing handed to him the previous evening by his younger son, with the grave assurance, "This will protect you, Daddy." It showed a smiling angel hovering over a blockhouse.

Bespectacled and methodical, Josi was a man of quiet tastes. He reveled in exploring the micro-world of nature: fish ponds and mossy banks, anthills and tiny fossils. He was free to roam anywhere in Galilee. As he often told his friends, "If I learn something, I learn it for myself—not for some stuffy school examiner." Every so often he could indulge in his most cherished thrill: to create and bring to completion a totally original study.

Josi asked nothing more of life than to enjoy his family, his Van Gogh reproductions and his Vivaldi LP's; his solo excursions into the forests and streams of Galilee, a source of fascination since adolescent days; and his High Seminar classes, where there was always the unexpected delight of discovering a lively new pupil.

He relished peace, but—as he was quick to point out—he was no pacifist. He had fought in 1956 to heave Nasser's terrorism from Israel's back, and he would do so again to keep his own kibbutz alive.

Politically, too, he made a clear distinction between the desirable and the actual. Josi was an idealist whose Polish-born parents had preached Socialist equality. In the Shomer Hatzir youth movement, he had learned to "relate to every man," Arabs included. He had expected the Soviet Union, the supposed mother country of Socialism, to "teach the Arabs to respect creative Jewry, and to aid us in making contact with the Arabs, who would become more progressive."

But he had not blinked his eyes at the bitter reality that had unfolded over the years. The Soviets had repeatedly demonstrated their disinterest in anything but their own big-power fortunes. The shells that blasted the cottages of Dan, and the land mines that killed and maimed its young men, invariably bore Russian markings. Josi was thoroughly disenchanted with Moscow, and more than a little outraged.

Accustomed as a scientist to systematic procedures, he had organized his military position carefully. He crouched in the easternmost of several machine-gun posts facing the rugged Golani range, which started a few miles to the north and swung around southwestward as if to envelop the kibbutz. Directly ahead, across a patch of stubbly wheat fields, was a narrow wadi or gully. Beyond that was a mined area, ringed with barbed wire. Dimly in the distance, a Syrian village nestled at the foot of the mountains.

A road running northward past his position dissolved after a few hundred yards into a dirt trail curving eastward up the mountain. Down that trail, according to the reasoning of the Israeli General Staff, the Syrians would sooner or later come, if only because they were protected on their right flank by the Lebanese border.

Josi was worried on two counts: ammunition, which was extremely limited, and reserves. The kibbutz could muster about a company of men, practically all of them over or under military age. A reinforcing unit of army conscripts had been promised, but had not yet materialized.

Meanwhile, Josi made the most of his own meager resources. He had a cluster of enclosed stone blockhouses under his command, built over the past ten years and certainly no secret to the Syrian gunners. On the premise that these would be the first targets of any pre-invasion shelling, he had them evacuated and stripped of weapons. They could serve as decoys; the actual defense would be carried out from new earthwork positions dug only two days before and much harder to detect. Josi had spaced these posts, heavily sandbagged, to provide maximum fields of fire, and manned them with Home Guard members of varying age and experience, mostly a good deal older than himself.

Scattered around him were some eight men equipped with three German-made machine guns, a bazooka, rifles, and a light two-inch mortar. A longer-range 8 mm. mortar was stationed with the headquarters force behind him in the kibbutz, ready to provide artillery support. Also held in the rear, until the direction of any Syrian thrust was clear, was a tiny reserve of weapons, ammunition, and willing but untrained teen-age boys.

To accompany him in the forward post, as loader on the first machine gun, Josi had chosen a wiry, leather-skinned little kibbutznik of fifty-odd years named Davidke. Davidke was a good man, Josi felt: modest without being servile, sufficiently confident of his own powers to fulfill without fuss any mission assigned to him. He could be trusted to hang on firmly till the last apple had been harvested, the last political motion passed, the last Syrian accounted for.

Davidke sat at his machine gun, red-necked, gold-toothed and balding, patient confidence shining in his tight, closely-webbed face. He had stood guard here before, practically on this very spot, when

the Syrians bombarded the settlement during the War of Independence in 1948. Davidke had been younger and stronger then, barely
past Josi's age. But he was still tough, he knew; tough enough to
wear out the other old-timers during the apple harvest, and to keep
even the young volunteers hopping, the enthusiastic *shegitz* visitors
from Stockholm and London and San Francisco.

Davidke was proud of other things: his skill in handling the bipod-
mounted machine gun; his kibbutz; and above all, his country. A
man was never alone in Israel. One could be sure of friends, companions, support in times of illness or danger. It was not like Poland,
where both his parents had been killed in World War II. Here, since
arriving in late 1939, he had raised five children and been blessed
with a grandson. A brother had emigrated to the United States;
Davidke had preferred to help build a Jewish homeland.

He was deeply grateful to Israel for the gift of personal dignity; as
long as the land existed, he existed as a full human being, too. How
better to keep faith with those who preceded him here than to
defend it with his life? He counted not on God to protect him, nor
on the good will of the Soviets, but on the bravery of his friends.

Davidke knew well the life of the citizen-by-forbearance, and he
wanted no part of it. For the tenth time, he raised his eyes to scan
the silent mountain, and rechecked his ammunition.

At 5:50 A.M.—Josi had just checked the time—a gun roared from
the Syrian battlements, and a mortar shell sailed overhead, whomp-
ing down into the vineyards near the Natural History Museum.
Seconds later the whole mountaintop burst into action, with puffs of
smoke sweeping the range as tier upon tier of field guns, short-
muzzled howitzers, Katyushka rockets and 122 mm. mortars opened
up. The shells "came down like rain." Josi told his men to take cover,
and got on the radio to his people back in the kibbutz.

In over-all charge of defenses at Dan was Israel Ronen, industrial
manager at the plastics factory, a thirty-one-year-old reserve lieutenant with a smooth, round face and thick black hair falling in a
Napoleonic forelock. Ronen had to decide whether the Syrian barrage was a random display of force, a feint to cover an attack
elsewhere, or the genuine prelude to a ground attack. He checked
quickly with his communications man, Rogani Meyer, who reported
that Kibbutz Gadot two-thirds of the way down the valley had been
under tremendous pounding for the past hour, reducing its main

buildings to a shambles.

Meyer added another ominous note: over short wave, he had intercepted artillery instructions to the Syrian gunners. The messages were in Russian.

Ronen decided that the Syrians, or their Russian "advisers," or both, probably meant business. By 6:30, there was still no sign of the army reinforcements supposedly on the way. Ronen alerted the dozen adolescents he was holding in reserve for Josi, allocating his last weapons among them.

At 6:45, Josi signaled Ronen to send everything and everyone he could spare. The biologist, adding up the nighttime clues and the mounting concentration of fire against the Israeli forward areas, was convinced the Syrians were going to try to smash through on the ground.

The first team of youngsters in the kibbutz, four boys carrying a brace of machine guns, sprinted forward from the shelter. A shell burst a hundred feet away, shredding a knot of olive trees, and for an instant they hesitated. Then they charged forward again, toward the line of poplars screening the north-south road.

Behind them came four more boys, fuzzy-faced sixteen-year-olds, struggling with a load of ammunition. They followed the trail of the gun carriers, hustling across the shrapnel-splattered open ground between the shelter and the protective poplars. Then the two teams moved forward in little spurts. Bony, green-eyed Joshua, hefting the second forty-pound machine gun, had been scared in the initial moments; "then I became too busy."

The youngsters tumbled en masse into Josi's dugout, breathless but triumphant. The last stretch of the dash had been along unsheltered road where no calculations would help; it was a case of run, duck—and pray, if you were so inclined.

These boys, on the whole, were not. Typical of them was seventeen-year-old Moshe, hair pale and brittle as straw, splotchy skin of adolescence in near-comic contrast with a doughty little mustache. Moshe was a cattle hand—a Galilee cowboy—with a mind as sinewy as his sun-browned forearms. He was "sorry for" the Syrians but he felt they were "bred to hate," so he was obliged in turn to hate them.

Moshe had hopes of going to the United States one day, but only to study agriculture. He was convinced that America was hopelessly materialistic; Jews there and everywhere else outside of Israel were "more concerned with making money than with hard work." In his kibbutz he could fulfill himself, become "not a money-making machine, but whatever I am capable of being." Any prospective mate who balked at coming to Dan—which is not every bride's dream in terms of comfort and security—would have to find herself another husband.

Josi spread out the newcomers for balance. He comforted himself with the thought that even if the soldiers of the tardy army unit had arrived, they would only have been a couple of years older than Moshe's group, and here at least he knew each boy's capacities. A couple were good rifle shots; others could help as loaders.

At 8:00 A.M. on Tuesday, the ground war in Syria began. It had been preceded by an abrupt—and to Josi, ominous—lull. The sudden silence was as unnerving as the previous two hours of roaring guns.

From the northeast, like the subdued opening of an electronic symphony, came the distant clank of tank treads. A Soviet-built T-34 lurched over the crest of the plateau and started down the hillside. Two others rolled in its wake.

The Israelis held their fire—and their collective breath. They had no weapon with sufficient range to stir a breeze within the neighborhood of the Syrians more than two miles away, and conversation was superfluous. The confrontation was now—whether the Syrians were lunging into Israel with three tanks or three hundred.

The immediate number turned out to be six. The second formation of three tanks hung back until the first was nearly at the bottom of the slope, then rumbled rapidly forward.

Now the cannonading, which had resumed erratically after the appearance of the tanks, whipped up to a furious peak, with fire from the emplaced field guns joined by low-trajectory rounds from the tanks.

By good fortune or bad marksmanship, no direct hits were scored on Josi's advanced positions, although one of the decoy blockhouses was demolished and smoke billowed over the whole area. Farther back in the kibbutz, shells were undoubtedly landing; Josi could only hope that the long and careful planning put into the underground shelters was paying off.

After fifteen minutes of "hellish fire," Josi heard excited shouts in

Arabic. A company of Syrian infantry, some wearing gas masks, scrambled up over a low mound half a mile to the southeast. They were supported by a platoon of heavy machine guns and a number of bazookas. Josi still held his fire. Although the Syrians were within range of his machine guns and bazooka, he was light on ammunition; the enemy would make better targets as they approached.

The lead squad of the Syrians, about a dozen men, ripped through the Israeli barbed wire with bangalore torpedoes and advanced to a position in a grove of trees about 300 yards away. Now Josi opened up. At this distance even the Israeli Uzzis and rifles, in the hands of hardy ex-soldiers, could be deadly.

Davidke, stretched out flat beside the gun, grabbed Josi's arm and pointed northeast. The three lead tanks were crossing the fields, bearing down toward the wadi a quarter of a mile away. Josi quickly worked out his coordinates and radioed the kibbutz to come in against the T-34's with its three-inch mortar. His own smaller mortar piece joined in.

To his right, the Syrian infantrymen were setting up a row of heavy machine guns at 200 yards. A second company came into view behind them. Ahead of the guns, the vanguard unit was advancing through waist-high wheat 150 yards away. Josi ordered all machine guns and small arms to be concentrated against them.

He led the attack himself, hitting two men with his opening burst. "When I saw them fall, I thought 'That's two less to deal with,' but I felt no joy."

Within seconds, under intensive and accurate Israeli fire, most of the dozen Syrians were put out of action. The remaining two men were trapped by a swath of flame at their backs as the wheat fields, parched under the summer sun, flashed ablaze.

The fortuitous tactic was too good not to be repeated. While Davidke reloaded the ammunition belt of the No. 1 machine gun, Josi shouted to the men in the next pit to burn up the fields all around the Syrians.

The mortars were doing as well or better. The very first shell from the kibbutz caught the lead tank in the engine, toppling it to the bottom of the wadi. The other two hurriedly closed their turrets, but the Israelis had the range: a second tank was disabled, its crew tumbling out and running for cover. The third tank turned tail and lumbered back up the mountain, where the second group of T-34's was already in retreat.

The Syrian infantry made two more stabs toward the Israeli lines, both times reeling back before the precise fire of Josi's superannuated and schoolboy sharpshooters.

By 8:30, the clash was over. The kibbutz suffered great loss of animal life, including eight cows and three thousand baby chicks; but, thanks to good luck and good organization, there were no dead among the settlers and only one wounded. The fleeing Syrians left behind a score of bodies and an imposing collection of weapons bearing the red star of the Soviet Union: bazookas, antitank guns, machine guns and rifles.

Half an hour later, the Zahal unit arrived to take over. Josi, back in his cottage for a wash and a rest, took a long, deep breath. It had been a close thing, much closer than the people of the kibbutz knew. Had the Syrians made one more determined charge—or sustained any of their earlier ones—Dan would almost certainly have been overrun. Ammunition was all but exhausted: one machine gun had had to stop firing, Uzzi magazines were empty, the bazooka was down to its last two shells.

But the Syrians, irresistible in their radio broadcasts (by Tuesday, they had "captured" Nazareth thirty miles inside Israel), bloodthirsty in combat against unarmed tractors and helpless prisoners, were less ferocious when there was somebody to shoot back at them. They fired boldly at farmhouses from behind their thick-walled fortresses; and flushing them out of their steel-and-concrete caves might be another, tougher story; but in ground attack, their rampaging tanks fell into ditches.

For the moment, the Syrian mountain guns could be endured. Those operating from the upper reaches of Jordan could not.

Along with the Monday bombardment of Jerusalem's New City, Jordanian batteries in the Jenin area had been laying down an artillery barrage from the west bank that threatened to put out of commission an Israeli air base in the north. To silence them, two columns of American Sherman tanks modified for Israeli use sliced across the border toward Jenin late Monday afternoon.

By Tuesday morning, after an all-night seesaw battle, Jordanian Pattons were falling back before the Shermans. On the outskirts of

Jenin, an Israeli convoy pushed toward the city through a thick barrier of mine fields.

Crouched over the wheel of a forward Intelligence jeep, his snub-nosed oval face smudged by flying gravel, was a slim green-eyed private named Harry Gordon. Harry had been driving steadily for the better part of twenty hours, racing over shell-pocked mountain ridges, hurtling along six-foot ledges to avoid burning enemy trucks. His single brief break came during the night, most of which he spent on guard duty fighting off Arab patrols.

Now he ducked and braked as a loud explosion sounded, and a hail of stones cracked his windshield. For a moment he thought he had struck a land mine; but it was the truck ahead that was the victim, its two rear wheels demolished. Harry swerved and pulled out ahead of the stalled vehicle, fully aware that there might be more mines alongside. In a convoy one didn't stop.

It was a rough initiation for an eighteen-year-old with less than a year of military training, but Harry had never felt better. It wasn't that he relished bloodshed: his first sight of wounded, from both sides, had nearly made him ill. But the war was revealing to Harry Gordon an elusive phantom: himself.

Private Gordon was a highly uncommon Israeli. To begin with, he looked like a soldier. On the streets of Tel Aviv, his departure from the Zahal tradition of untidiness was most glaring. Generally, Israeli soldiers on leave look like civilian campers, nature lovers out on a hike—tough, but vaguely irregular. Not Harry. Jaunty and erect, he flipped his cigarette butt to the curb with crisp precision, and offered opinions in tones that were clipped and self-assured.

Even here at the front, where his officer-passenger was grimy and bedraggled, Harry was relatively immaculate, his fair hair neatly combed, his smile enhanced by the slight engaging jut of his two front teeth. Definitely, there was something different about Harry.

The something was an American upbringing. Harry had spent almost his entire life in New York. He had been raised on cornflakes and Radio City Music Hall, snowball fights along Riverside Drive, tennis in Central Park. Vaguely interested since boyhood in commercial art, he had grown up assuming that one day, with a proper word from his businessman father, he would land in an office on Madison Avenue. It was a prospect that neither depressed nor entranced him. He was on the face of things a glib, fairly typical

American boy with fairly typical interests.

He was also, however, a sabra.

In 1946 Maury Gordon, a Jewish artillery lieutenant in the British Army, had been posted to Palestine. Gordon liked the country, married a girl who had come there from Poland, and got into the business of importing crates for orange shipments. This took him into soft lumber from Scandinavia. Within a few years he had a brisk international business, a pleasant apartment in Tel Aviv, and a son born there in 1949.

In 1953, when Harry was four, his father shifted his headquarters to the United States. As Harry grew up, his sole contact with the land of his birth was through Sunday school, where he learned Hebrew well, but was not intrigued by Judaism. As projected by his semi-orthodox teachers, it struck him as rather smug and self-righteous.

By all logic, Harry in the summer of 1967 should have been watching the U.N. Security Council discuss Israel's war on television. He was fighting it, instead, because of a visit to the Holy Land when he was fifteen.

He had been invited by an aunt who lived in Jerusalem. Mildly curious, he accepted. He wandered the country, swimming in the icy springs of the Galilee, mingling with the shirt-sleeved crowds in Tel Aviv's Dizengoff Square. He saw boys of his own age on the streets, listened to their raillery—and felt strange stirrings. As he explained later to his father, "It was as if part of me had always been back there, and never left when I went away."

Returning to the states after four weeks, Harry was restless. After a year of brooding conflict, he unburdened himself to his parents. Home for him, he suspected, was Israel. His mother, spontaneous and emotional, embraced him delightedly. British-bred Maury Gordon showed more reserve. But behind his dry monosyllables, Harry sensed a deep satisfaction.

If Harry was to opt for Israeli citizenship, he would have to be on hand for army service before his eighteenth birthday. He was a little over seventeen the day he left New York for Lod Airport.

He found the Israeli Army a drastically different world, whose first dividend was self-sufficiency. Alone in the Negev at 3:00 a.m., with your jeep broken down and Bedouins all around you, you learned fast how to make repairs.

He was astonished at the maturity of his fellow recruits. Unlike most of his American friends, they were usually perfectly clear about what they wanted to do, where they would live, sometimes even whom they would marry.

That was another shock: the intimate quality of personal relationships. In Israel you didn't make love to strangers. Boys and girls took the trouble to know one another. Parents, too, were closer to children. The result was a richness of human exchange, an openness between fellow Jews, such as Harry had never experienced. Within months he wrote home that he was "feeling more Jewish," and was beginning to think in terms of "giving something to the army" rather than taking from it.

Still, he had occasional uncertainties and misgivings. A random remark about front-wheel drive would take him back to the American scene, as if he were suddenly tuned to a different wave length. He wondered sometimes about his commercial art career, and how his parents would react to the Tunisian girl he had met in the army . . . graceful, bosomy, and brown as a Virgin Islander.

Then Nasser let out his first belligerent bellow, and for Harry, listening to the radio, everything came into focus. His random yearnings were fused into a single desire: that something be asked of him personally, a demand be made that only he could fulfill. He knew he would not have felt quite the same way about going to Vietnam.

Tuesday night, bone-weary after another day of furious driving under fire, Harry Gordon pulled into a bivouac along the mountain highway to Nablus. Stretched out on the stony ground, he dined with gusto on canned beef and orange juice. Then he put his feelings together in a few scribbled lines for his parents, to be mailed when the opportunity came: "We are advancing and I am well. I consider myself extremely lucky to have been on the scene when the war broke out. Here, in the Judean Hills, I realize that this is what I have been waiting for all my life: to give myself totally to a tangible, constructive cause."

He folded the note and put it in his knapsack. Then he crawled into his sleeping bag, contented. Here in Israel, Harry Gordon was not a wanderer, an international floater forever on the periphery of things. Here his presence counted.

The Third Day

THE OLD CITY

ON medieval maps the Old City of Jerusalem glows red, center of the world. For Jews, it has never relinquished that status. Moslems rank it behind Mecca and Medina as the goal of glorious pilgrimage; Christians bracket it as a holy site with Bethlehem and Catholic Rome. But Jews look only and eternally to Jerusalem, "the place," according to Deuteronomy, "where Yahweh chose to dwell"; city of David, Solomon and Isaiah; home of the original Temple, marked today by the remnant western wall; survivor over the centuries of countless sieges and bombardments by civilizations now buried in layers beneath its cobbled alleys.

Jerusalem is so old that its very name is lost in antiquity; so rich in mystic overtones that it has nourished the legends of three great religions. It is pre-eminently a mood, an atmosphere compounded of memories, dreams and aspirations, not confined to the old walled area but hovering as well over the Jewish New City built up to the west since 1860. Something in the rare, dry air, the tawny golden stones, the inverted-custard hills with their ancient terraces carved out by farmers long, long dead, pushes judgment aside in favor of feeling; slows the pulse and quickens the senses. A steady under-current flows beneath the surface like a deep, sustained pedal point on the organ. Few places on earth resound to so many and such distant echoes.

The heart of Jerusalem is the Old City, seized by Jordan in 1948 after the U.N. had proposed to place both it and the Jewish New City under international jurisdiction. Less than a square mile in area, it is enclosed by a jagged rectangle of Turkish battlements thirty-eight feet high and ten feet thick, replete with romantic turrets and menacing archery loopholes. Ten gates give entry to the city, many of them framed by majestic pillars and flanked by crenelated walls, atop which blocks of roundheaded stones march in long files like paired chess pawns. This is of course not the original masonry of Jerusalem. The city claims some forty centuries; the Ottoman conquest by Suleiman the Magnificent dates back a mere 450 years.

Inside Suleiman's walls is an incredible jumble of mosques and monasteries, rambling alleyways, long cool tunnels lined with medieval shops; ravaged synagogues and deserted pools. Squat iron doors with Crusader markings open onto vast unexpected courtyards; unfinished Mameluke arches overlay Greek remains.

Originally laid out on two undulating hills and the hollow between, Old Jerusalem still has long, meandering passageways broken by an infinity of steps and stairways that take the traveler back in time to the days of plodding donkeys and foot-weary pilgrims. The donkeys, lineal descendants of the biblical originals, still crowd the narrow alleys, patient past servitors of Bronze Age Canaanite and monotheistic Hebrew, Babylonian merchant and Roman centurion, dissident Christian, scimitared Moslem and mailed French Crusader.

Although its major arteries can be traced back to the Aelia Capitolina built by the Romans in A.D. 135, in the minor circulatory streams that create its character Old Jerusalem obeys no laws of logic. It sprawls and strays in response to the dictates, not of any architectural concept, but of life itself. No single mind could have fashioned its magnificent confusion of styles, its winding tunnels of fantasy. The city had to grow, accumulating its scars and its triumphs, evolving like the human psyche into a one-of-its-kind patchwork mingling past and present.

The noisy market district below Damascus Gate is a frieze from the Middle Ages. Coppersmiths beat out shining platters; leather craftsmen cut sandals to patterns first laid down in the Roman forum. The aroma of a hundred fruits and spices in open stalls mingles with others less endearing (the animal population is large, its habits casual).

Everything is for sale here, from sheep to nuts. A street vendor clashes brass cymbals to advertise his wares, evoking brays of alarm from a fly-bitten donkey, stumbling along under a huge, mustached Bedouin who carries, mysteriously, a mattress on his back. As the babble of voices rises in a score of languages, from monk and tourist, student and peddler, soldier and ubiquitous street urchin, a Syrian money-changer surveys the scene shrewdly, puffing with infinite calm on his nargileh (water pipe).

Meticulous in preserving the past, Jerusalem refuses to be overwhelmed by it. With splendid unconcern, it plants a mod-style barber shop directly across from a sixth-century hospice and its white-robed nuns. A sign within the shadow of pre-Christian ruins briskly identifies the "Herod's Gate Grocery"; just around the bend, a café poster advises that "Uncle Moustache Welcomes Beatniks."

The dwelling places of the Old City are like no others: rooftop living rooms open to the stars; doorways scrawled with primitive drawings and hieroglyphics to ward off evil spirits; barred windows where poppies sprout from a battered oil can.

A typical apartment at St. John in Crypt lacks a street number or any other public hint of its existence. A waist-high, oak-and-iron door, built by the Crusaders to keep out avenging Moslems, creaks open before a heavy key. The local citizen stumbles through a short, unlighted tunnel to emerge into spacious convent grounds. To his right, a four-story spiral of apartments and courtyards culminates in his top-floor flat, a converted chapel whose domed roof and graceful archways would be a sensation in any bohemia. For the Jerusalem touch of timelessness, a TV set sits cosily in a niche designed for saintly statuary.

The Old City is the perfect kaleidoscope, never presenting the same scene twice. In its bewildering fusion of past and present, it is more than merely "cosmopolitan" like New York or Paris; it is a miniature cosmos unto itself, a "father's house" sheltering all the children of Western man.

Yet it is the religious image that still dominates Jerusalem. Perhaps the most celebrated thoroughfare in the Christian world is the steep, twisting Via Dolorosa, whose fourteen Stations of the Cross trace the path followed by Jesus on the way to His crucifixion. The last five stations are at the Church of the Holy Sepulcher, twice destroyed, seven times renovated, on the site near the center of the Old City where the True Cross was assertedly found. All along this route, and on the same east-west axis starting from the top of the Mount of Olives, are churches and shrines commemorating events in the lives of Jesus, St. Mary and St. Anne.

Of rival significance is Mount Moriah or the Temple Mount in the southeast corner, where David reconsecrated the sacrificial altar of Abraham, and Solomon built his glorious temple to house the ark of the covenant. Here, from the same rock where Abraham prepared to slay Isaac, Moslem tradition says Mohammed was borne to heaven on a winged mare, a miracle glitteringly celebrated in the 1275-year-old Dome of the Rock.

Over the centuries, the Old City has become bejeweled with lofty-spired churches, stately synagogues, dazzling mosques. Each day in the life of Jerusalem has been welcomed in and ushered out with an uproar of holy sound: ringing catheral bells, tremulous muezzin cries, the lusty singing of pious Hasidic Jews.

But in spring of 1967, the Jewish voices had for nineteen years been stilled. The most beautiful of the synagogues lay in ruins, the habitat of wandering goats. And the western wall of Solomon's Temple—to which access had been promised under the armistice agreement with Jordan, but was never granted—was hopelessly out of reach. Nowhere on the horizon was there anything to suggest that history had a dramatic reversal up her sleeve—or the kind of commander who could carry it out.

The mild April sun splashed across the lawn at suburban Afeka outside Tel Aviv. In the canvas camp chair, the burly red-haired man paused for breath. The little knot of children gathered around him leaned forward, eyes shining expectantly, hands clasped in excitement. Their host waited, prolonging the exquisite moment of suspense.

"It was a difficult situation," he resumed finally in his deep rumbling voice. "But Aza—the little dog named Courage—never hesitated. He had delivered his message and done his duty. Now, as the jeep came racing down the road, he ran up to the roof of the barn, made a flying leap, and landed right on the hood of the jeep, safe and sound!"

The children crowed their delight. Two little girls applauded, and a six-year-old boy turned triumphantly to his companion. "See, Moshe? I told you he'd get out all right."

"Aw, I wasn't really worried. Not after the way he brought back those two lost kids, last time."

The big man stood up, and the children clustered around him. What kind of adventure was in store for Aza next week? Would the little dog be helping the lonely young doctor in a border kibbutz again (favored by the girls)—or joining the dauntless crew of a rescue helicopter (overwhelming choice of the boys)? The rival campaigners pressed around their friend, wheedling, stroking his brawny arms.

The Saturday afternoon scene was commonplace enough except for a single detail: the popular storyteller was one of Israel's toughest professional soldiers. That he should also have been, in the words of a harassed and envious housewife, a "natural-born kindergarten teacher," was typical of the unorthodox paratroop Colonel Mota Gur, whose brigade two months later was to take Ammunition Hill and clear the northern approaches to Jerusalem. On his shoulders would fall the most prized and delicate mission of the war: to capture the Old City without doing violence to its shrines.

At thirty-eight, Mota Gur is a rugged 190-pounder who looks as though he could still boot a ball the length of a soccer field. His forearms are meaty; his reddish curly hair spills down to a neck corded with muscle. Mixed with this is an unexpected small-boy earnestness, manifest in his intense brown eyes and reinforced by the center gap between his teeth.

Women find Mota "cute"—a term that most men would hesitate to apply to anyone of the colonel's proportions. They respond, among other things, to a rich, resonant voice used with what frequently seems to be conscious splendor.

Women are also taken with his breezy, faintly impudent manner—a trait which some colleagues find disconcerting. Mota has been accused of being impulsive, theatrical, not altogether "serious." Ironically, other senior officers regard him as *too* serious, too determined to impose an intellectual stamp on the army. A few wonder aloud if he is not excessively ambitious (ambition being a characteristic that somehow always turns up in other people).

Certainly Mota is an amalgam of paradoxes: an ex-Lothario converted into a model family man; fierce enough in battle to lead a guerrilla night attack on a police fortress, and sensitive enough to weep at the sight of his wounded; a stern disciplinarian and a subtly gracious host; equally at home on a nursery floor or in the council halls of the United Nations; willing to grapple barehanded with an Egyptian machine gun in the Sinai, or with the obscurities of French absurdist playwrights like Beckett; a veteran of three wars and countless reprisal raids against the Arabs, who will not permit abuse of conquered property, indignity to prisoners, or even a contemptuous reference to the foe. These contradictions are blended into a cohesive surface with no visible fissures: in the showdown on the battlefield, Mota evokes total loyalty. His communication with the paratroopers is as sure and steady as with the small fry of suburban Afeka.

Like Israel Tal, Mota is that unique Israeli phenomenon, the soldier-intellectual. Less methodical and analytical than the Armored Forces Chief, he has more personal flair. His mind is flexible and imaginative, operating often with the intuitive leap of the creative artist. One senses that where Tal is attuned to the broad sweep of history, Mota is especially alive to the present moment, and his place in it.

Mota's forebears came from Russia. His father was thirteen and his mother twelve when they arrived in Israel from the Ukraine, part of the same wave of immigration that brought Premier Levi Eshkol. The two adolescents met while working in the orange groves—a propitious-enough setting for romance. They married young.

When the first World War broke out, Mota's father volunteered for Britain's Jewish Brigade, serving as a sergeant. One of the men in his platoon was Yizhak Ben-Zvi, current President of Israel.

Mota was born in Jersualem in 1930. Two older boys preceded him—a fact undoubtedly important in his development. The influence of older brothers, and especially the first son, is much greater in Israel than in the United States. Throughout his youth, Mota was the youngest and smallest of three vigorous, athletic, socially active boys modeling themselves after an aggressive father. Mota had to stretch hard to keep up—and he did. The habit of straining to get out front, of charging into the heart of the action, never left him.

When Mota was twelve, his family moved to Rehovoth on the coast south of Tel Aviv, where he followed his brothers into secondary school—and onto the soccer team. He was a stubborn and plucky contender. Life in the small-town milieu was more friendly and closely-knit, but Mota never lost his affection for the grandeur and mystery of Jerusalem.

Adolescence was a free and happy time, shared with the bigger boys and a sister, various companions on the athletic field, a rapidly widening circle of girl friends, and comrades in the Haganah. At school, Mota was an attentive student—"nobody could distract me for a minute during class"—but homework was another story. There were too many competing attractions.

A major one was the Haganah, the underground People's Army of the Jews in British-administered Palestine. In Jerusalem, Mota had, like his brothers, gone into the Scout movement. Upon the shift to Rehovoth, the older boys were ready for Haganah; Mota, although barely turned twelve, tagged along. "It was the thing to do, part of the atmosphere all around us. My parents knew it and approved."

The dominant issue among the Jews of Palestine in the early 1940's was Britain's anti-immigration policy and how militantly it should be opposed. Haganah was ready enough to defy the law, but balked at the terrorist tactics favored by the Irgun Zva'i Leumi, or "Etzel." In the bitter factionalism that split the settlers, many Jewish youngsters—with the approval of their parents—cut their military eyeteeth on each other. Mota was about fifteen, enjoying an evening tête-à-tête with his girl friend of the moment, when there was a rapping at her door.

"It was my father. He took a stick out from under his coat and said, 'Go home, the Etzel are looking for you.'

"There was bad blood between Etzel and Haganah at the time, and a bunch of them had come around to beat me up.

"Well, I took the stick and raced on home. There, near my house, was a group of five boys standing in the street. We all knew each other. I went up to them with the stick in my hand and I told them, 'Okay, you have your opportunity—go ahead.' They turned away. I told them, 'Okay, you don't want to fight, I'm going home.' So I did. They hung around outside for twenty minutes or so, then drifted away."

Already Mota had the self-confidence of his sabra generation. At eighteen, Mota reached a crossroads. In spite of his distaste for homework, he was one of two boys from his high school to be awarded a university scholarship in Great Britain. He was already fluent in English, and his high-school principal was sure he would make a brilliant teacher. His father, on the other hand, strongly recommended a career in law. "He didn't insist—here, nobody insists—but he felt I had the mind for it.

"Both ideas were out of the question—because the year was 1948. I was then commanding the Haganah youth movement in Rehovoth. With a military crisis shaping up, I felt my place was in the regular army.

"My father made no objection. He was a man who placed national duty first, and he himself had liked army life."

The apparent contrast between a teaching career and military leadership has always struck Mota as exaggerated. "Except when an army is in active combat, what are you doing? Educating, teaching. In some of the more mechanical branches, the instruction is largely technical. But with the paratroops, the main thing is the men themselves. They run, they jump, they fight with light weapons. It's the way the individual character is formed that makes the difference. And that's a question of education, very much like in a school. You'll find that a great many officers in our army, when they reach retirement, turn instinctively to teaching."

Education was to be a recurrent motif in Mota's life. But some hard soldiering came first. In the 1948 struggle he enlisted in the jeep-riding 9th Raider Battalion of the Palmach, the "Wild Beasts of the Negev" who bedeviled and finally routed the invading Egyptian armor. After the war, he switched to Nahal, the farming-fighting garrisons posted to critical border areas.

In 1951, assigned to a junior staff post with the Jerusalem Brigade, he signed up for a degree in Middle Eastern Studies at the Hebrew University. The three-year course included twelve hours of political science, and a broad review of Islamic religion as well as the history, archaeology, economy and sociology of the region. "They were trying to provide a general picture; no single subject was really explored to the proper depth."

Halfway through his finals in spring of 1954, Mota learned that his beefy friend Ariel "Arik" Sharon, organizer of the night-fighting

"Unit 101" commandos, was taking his elite unit into the paratroopers. Sharon aimed to counter a widely acknowledged and highly alarming postwar decline in army morale.

Mota dropped his books for a day and drove out to Sharon's camp, leaving word that he wanted to join the paratroopers. The next day he was appointed a company commander. He still had one major exam to finish, slated for June; Sharon wanted him to start in May. The degree, like the scholarship to England, went begging.

Mota embarked on a training program of a toughness and intensity unprecedented in Israel, in some respects more demanding than even that of the U.S. Marines. The band of men around Sharon were determined to slough off what they regarded as the softening influence of western European army procedures, and restore the original Israeli concept of daring improvisation. With the change in tactics would come a renewed spirit of total commitment to country and comrades, expressed in a reckless valor that would make obsolete such terms as "retreat," "too weary," and "too few."

The paratroopers had a chance to demonstrate their theories when the government ordered a series of reprisal raids against the mounting terrorism being carried out along Israel's frontiers. Mota fought in half a dozen penetrations of Egyptian bases in and around the Gaza Strip. Riding at the head of his company in a retaliatory raid at Khan Yunis, he was badly wounded in the leg by fire from the police station. He wound up with a citation for leadership—and six months in a hospital bed.

It seemed, if nothing else, an ideal place for catching up on his bachelor's degree. But the leg was not yet healed when Mota was called back to staff duty; a paratroop landing at the Tiran Strait was being planned. In succeeding weeks, as the pre-Sinai tension increased, he saw sharp action across the border in Syria and then at the Arab Legion police station in Kalkilia, after Jordanians murdered and mutilated two Israeli workers in an orange grove.

In 1956 came Sinai, and a celebrated seven-hour struggle at the Mitla Pass bottleneck near the western edge of the peninsula. Sharon's paratroopers took the pass, but at heavy cost. Moshe Dayan later publicly questioned the necessity for the action, as well as the prudence of Sharon's troop alignment; at the same time, Dayan paid tribute to the bravery of the paratroopers in the hand-to-hand combat that drove Egyptian gunners from their mountain caves: "No other Israeli unit would have fought as they did."

Mota, as a sidekick of Sharon's and one of his company commanders, was intimately identified with the brickbats as well as the applause. Dayan's comment provided ammunition for both schools of thought about the dashing paratroop commanders: that they were incredibly audacious . . . and somewhat capricious.

In the business of combat leadership, Mota is conceded to have few peers. According to a staff aide, he has "an instinct for knowing what men will respond to at a given time; how to talk to them in the fever of battle; when to be light, and when to be serious."

Up to this point, he had demonstrated an equally sure touch with women. Mota of the broad shoulders, the slumbrous voice and the rakish eye cut an appealing figure before the eighteen-year-old girl recruits in the army—not to mention their older sisters. He had the charm frequently cultivated by younger sons who might otherwise go unnoticed. His successes in the boudoir threatened to rival those on the battlefield.

After Sinai, he was promoted to major and sent to London with Arik Sharon and several other senior paratroopers for specialized military studies. They were a cocky, self-assured crew who succeeded in antagonizing a number of lesser members of the mission. But Mota, as usual, captured at least one secretarial heart in a spectacular romance that inspired a good deal of cocktail conversation.

In midsummer of 1957 he returned to Israel, and ran into one of the most drastic changes of his life. Her name was Rita: a dark and vivid beauty with black eyes, gleaming white teeth and a delicately chiseled nose. Daughter of a jewel merchant, Rita had emigrated from Poland at the age of six. She was in her early twenties, several years younger than Mota.

The doughty paratrooper capitulated, almost without firing a shot. What's more, he became as dedicated a husband as he had been a gadabout. When children arrived—Ruthie in 1962; a son, Ori, two years later; and Tami, a second girl, in 1966—the conversion was complete. Mota is a family man who cheerfully does the dishes, mows the lawn, and brings out the drinks for friends visiting their comfortable California-style ranch house.

With children he is unbelievable. He drops to his knees to become a bucking bronco; rolls over and plays sick to be doctored; sails boats for neighborhood moppets in a plastic swimming pool on the lawn; and is of course celebrated as the chronicler of the little-dog-named-Courage. He came in one evening when Rita and two other young matrons were struggling tearfully with a swarm of brawling five-year-olds. In a matter of seconds he had restored order (that's when he was nominated for the kindergarten post). Locally, his identification with children is such that when his promotion to brigade commander of paratroops was announced, one thirteen-year-old girl flatly refused to believe it: "You mean Mota, the one who's always playing with the *babbies?*"

Shortly after his marriage, Mota was sent to Paris for eighteen months of military studies. Rita enrolled at the Sorbonne in a special French-orientation course for visitors, and the two plunged enthusiastically into a lively intellectual ambience whose very existence came as a surprise. "The level of cultural life in France gives you a shock. It's so pervasive a force that you smell it, feel it, everywhere . . . in the newspapers, the streets, the theater . . . and also in the smallest things."

Because of his active liaison with French officers, Mota had the obligation—and the opportunity—to master the language quickly. "I had to participate, to exchange ideas, so I picked up a good practical vocabulary. Rita moved ahead faster on the literary front."

But Mota came close behind. French movies were a pleasurable form of instruction; the Gurs floated happily on the first currents of the New Wave. Increasingly at home in the Paris milieu, Mota ventured beyond Molière and Rousseau, dipping into the whirlpool of perennial controversy surrounding such contemporary literary figures as Jean Paul Sartre, Albert Camus, Samuel Beckett, and their followers. He was profoundly intrigued by existentialism, that protean philosophy of a hundred quarreling disciples, partly because of its striking parallels with principles already evolved in Israel . . . not in university lecture halls, but under pressure of military circumstance.

Existentialism, for all of its subdivisions, ramifications, and offshoots into religion and psychology, exalts above all the individual will, making a responsible choice in a concrete situation. It holds that nothing is predetermined; there is no fixed order imposed by theological, economic or historical forces that cannot be overturned by courageous action. Man is the being who by the exercise of choice within a free society, has the possibility of "going beyond his situation," of himself creating history.

Existentialism, like pioneering in a border kibbutz, thrusts a man back upon his own resources. It puts its confidence in personal commitment rather than statistical probabilities. There could hardly be a doctrine more appealing to a reflective military leader in a small nation constantly being urged to abandon its impossible dream.

On a social level, the French experience was less gratifying. "We had few invitations to people's homes; they were not very cordial. I don't pretend to know how they live. No French officer ever told me about his love affairs, even in Vietnam, though it was obvious from their smiles that they had them—and lots of them. Our relations were simply not that close."

Toward the end of his stay in France, Mota attended courses in nuclear physics. He promptly began to wonder if he shouldn't be concentrating on that field. As Rita explains, "He can't stand being on the sidelines. He has to be in the center, wherever the most important thing is happening. Once, right after Sinai, we were traveling near the Syrian border. A man was working on a tractor, right at the frontier. Mota said, 'I should probably be plowing that land, like him. What am I doing wasting my time in the army?' And after he found out what people were doing in advanced physics, he went through the same self-questioning: 'If I should be anything, it's a nuclear scientist.'"

Upon returning to Israel, Mota was summoned by the Chief of Staff, Major General Tsur. "I want you to take command of the Golani Brigade. Inoculate them with the spirit of the paratroopers."

Mota protested. He had no yearning to leave his home. His friends were all in the paratroopers.

"In the paratroopers," replied Tsur, "the job is already done. We need to create the same atmosphere in the Golani Brigade."

Mota grumbled. But he knew exactly what Tsur was talking about. He remembered an incident in Algiers, when he and Rita were visiting a French colonel's home there. The colonel had a batman, a corporal who shined his shoes and did the marketing. Rita had asked the colonel's wife if the batman would not be embarrassed when he returned home and somebody asked what he did in the army.

"Embarrassed?" The colonel's wife was puzzled. "Why should

he be? Everybody would envy him, he stayed at the colonel's house. . . ."

This was not exactly the paratrooper spirit of eagerness to be first on the firing line, a spirit derived primarily, Mota thinks, from pre-battle convictions: "The motivational factor comes early, before you move in. Whatever else happens, the state must survive. Once you are actually in the line, you have to behave. You react in a way that reflects your entire past education. You don't know exactly what you are doing or why--you just do it . . . out of friendship, loyalty, personal need, training, all the things you have experienced."

In taking over Golani, Mota faced two contrasting personnel problems: the many conscripts of Oriental origin, whose education was limited and whose background in the Moslem countries had been anything but militant; and, at the other pole, political sophisticates from the kibbutzim.

The Golani driver assigned to bring Mota to his new post was astonished to find the commander busy scrubbing down his living-room floor. Leaning on a mop, the colonel chatted amiably with the Moroccan-born private.

The private—and the brigade—quickly discovered that Mota's informal manner was not to be confused with slack standards of discipline. Soon after he took over, there was foot-dragging among members of a unit assigned to a reprisal operation. The commander of the group reported to Mota that a number of soldiers were questioning the desirability of the attack, demanding of him, "What did the Syrians ever do to you?"

Mota called the unit together.

"Anybody who doesn't wish to be here—leave. We don't need the unwilling.

"But you must understand this. A decision was made by the highest authorities of the country that a military operation must be undertaken against Syria.

"The only question now is, do you want to carry it out yourselves —or leave the job for someone else to do?

"You're in the army for two and a half years. You have to realize that if there's something to be done, we're going to request and make any effort necessary to achieve it.

"If you don't like it, go home. Here, your job is to fight."

The word got through. During Mota's two-year stewardship in the north, there was a shift in the Golani attitude from a reluctant "Why me?" to the proud "Why not me?" of the paratroopers. In fact, the brigade decided there was no reason it could not outdo the paratroopers in aggressive *élan,* and before Mota departed it had beaten them out for the coveted assignment of a punitive raid against the Jordanian village of Nukeib on the Sea of Galilee, whose snipers had been taking potshots at unarmed Israeli fishermen.

Mota had a dual reward. He was given his own brigade of paratroopers to command. But since it was a reservist unit, he was delegated also to superintend the army's "private university," the Staff and Command School.

He ran the brigade with his customary disregard for ceremony. Salutes were rare, confined to early-morning greetings. The term "Sir" doesn't even exist in Hebrew. To an occasional awed recruit, Mota was *Hamefaked,* "the Commander"; otherwise he was simply "Mota." Junior officers could always be sure of his ear, on personal as well as military problems, and of his intervention if some overzealous martinet was using the rule book instead of common sense.

And he ran the Command School with a vigor and originality that were unprecedented. Once a month, he brought in a prominent poet, playwright, historian or other intellectual layman to lead the officers and their wives in an evening of discussion. Each of the students was obliged to write a number of extensive essays on leadership, military history and similar broad themes. And Mota himself turned out a highly controversial paper defining the Israeli Army officer as "the intellectual fighter."

Many disagreed. Mota conceded that his training standard was not an easy one to meet, but he felt that it paid off in the superior fighting qualities of the officer who understood the value of every act, and could adapt rapidly to changing circumstances.

His administration at Staff and Command became known as the "Cultural Revolution," a term applied by skeptical colleagues with mingled irony and respect. Yitzchak Rabin, who had by then taken over as Chief of Staff, always greeted Mota with the dry query, "How goes the Cultural Revolution?" But he backed Mota's innovations.

From his experience at the Command School and in the field, Mota developed some unconventionally frank and dogmatic views about Orientals in the army. "They can do their jobs wonderfully.

Under proper leadership, they will serve bravely and unquestioningly in the most difficult circumstances.

"But as of today, they are not officer material. We have some junior officers and a handful at the field-grade level, but with very few exceptions they are not among our best. The Oriental majors will do their work, but they have to be pushed.

"I think this situation will continue for at least the next twenty years; that was our conclusion from research conducted at the Command School. It is not merely a question of introducing a new generation; you have to rebuild the entire home life of the Oriental newcomers, their whole culture. Even those living here for decades have often remained untouched because they didn't mix in Western society. Now things are moving faster, but it will still be a very difficult process for them to blend in."

Mota emphasizes that no soldier of Oriental origin has any complaint. "They know they get a fair chance, that in fact we extend ourselves to make opportunities for them. Still, when you see them coming up year after year, and there are no majors, no colonels— well, you keep telling yourself maybe the shock will come one day, but finally you can't ignore the reality. The one thing we are never permitted to do is lower our standards of officer performance."

This is a position well understood—and accepted—in the Oriental community. Although there is frequent "reverse discrimination" practiced in Israeli civilian life—that is, deliberate preference given to Oriental applicants in civil service and some businesses—there are no cries for such a policy in the army. The feeling is that "in matters of security one doesn't take chances; the army is sacred." And the army is generally acknowledged to have made greater strides in integrating the newcomers than have civilian authorities, to the point where public-school officials have approached senior staff officers for guidance.

As for the general quality of Israeli society, Mota hesitates to make an appraisal: "Rita tells me I have a very limited view of what is going on in the country, and that's probably true. The army constitutes a special society in Israel, much more Zionistic; I mean, things that for other people are part of the past, are for us the present and future."

He feels a national culture blended of diverse elements is still in the process of crystallizing. "If someone should ask me why to come,

I can say, 'Because here you have only Jews, here you feel yourself free.'"

He wants to preserve that freedom for his children, hopefully with peace. A few days before the outbreak of the fighting, Mota and Rita sat in the garden with a few of their closest friends: a psychiatrist and his chemist wife, an economist and his film-producer daughter.

Rita was gloomy about the future. When Mota pointed out that there were many countries where people lived under worse conditions, she refused to be consoled. "Show me a place in the world," she said, "where for three generations we can live in peace—my parents, my children and I—and I will go there."

"The far future," Mota replied, "nobody can foresee. All one can hope to affect is what is immediately ahead. If I am fighting next week, it will not be for us but for Ori. He is only three. I don't want him to see war."

Mota Gur is no superman. But, like the leaders of the American colonial revolutionaries, he is most emphatically a man, capable of independent thought and action. In the seventh decade of the twentieth century, afflicted by nuclear and economic anxiety, massive sloganeering and rampant conformity, that is not such a commonplace quality. It was enough to make quite a difference at the Old City.

Dawn came Wednesday to a Jerusalem eerily silent. A single jeep sped through Saladin Street in the American Colony, dodging past wrecked vehicles and rubble in the road. Paratroop Brigade headquarters had been established farther east at the captured Archaeological Museum, popularly known as the Rockefeller Museum because its construction in 1933 was financed by John D. Rockefeller, Jr. A small Israeli patrol, circling back to the command post, hugged the building line for protection against sniper fire. Across Jericho Road from them, on the northeast wall of the Old City, Arab Legion sentries rubbed their eyes sleepily and stared at the newly established paratrooper positions in the museum tower.

It had been a long night of talking and planning for Mota Gur and his staff, mainly because junior commanders were so unfamiliar with the terrain around the Holy City. The paratroopers had cleared all of the built-up area north of the walls; they now faced the

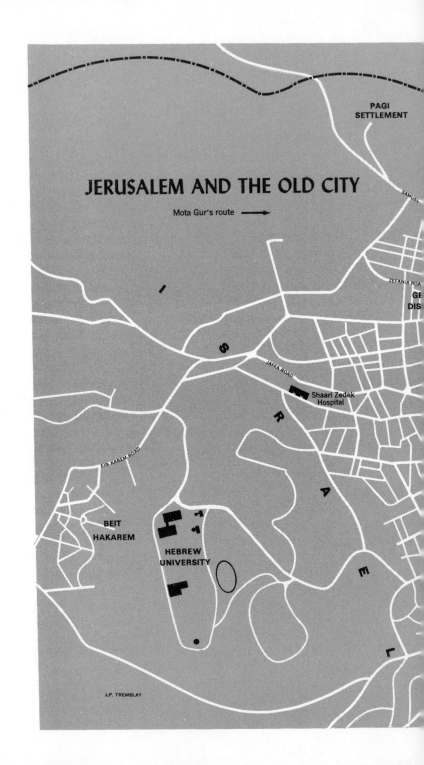

JERUSALEM AND THE OLD CITY

Mota Gur's route ⟶

PAGI
SETTLEMENT

SAMUEL

ZEFANIA ROAD

GE
DIS

JAFFA ROAD

Shaari Zedek
Hospital

EIN KAREM ROAD

BEIT
HAKAREM

HEBREW
UNIVERSITY

I S R A E L

J.P. TREMBLAY

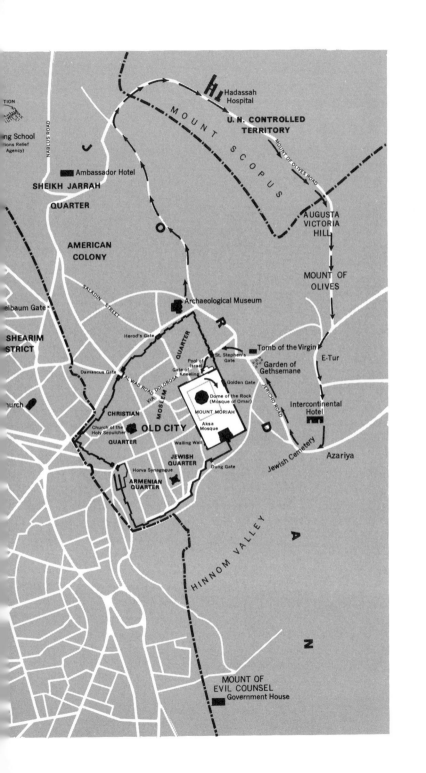

climactic task of investing and capturing, with a minimum of damage, the Old City itself.

The attack was not slated to resume until an hour before noon. But at 5:00 A.M. a call came through from Chaim Bar-Lev, the imperturbable Yugoslav-born Deputy Chief of Staff, warning that pressure for a cease-fire was mounting rapidly. Mota would have to hit as soon—and as hard—as he possibly could.

Ten minutes later, Mota led his group across the broad courtyard of the museum to an adjoining house whose porch offered a clear view of the mountains to the east. While the Russian-born lady of the place bustled over coffee in the kitchen, the planners spread their maps and reconnaissance photos in a second-floor study.

Two scouts were already en route up to the Israeli detachment on Mount Scopus, to get intelligence regarding the strong Jordanian artillery positions directly south of there on the ridge at Augusta Victoria Hill. Mota was anxious to avoid a repetition of the previous evening's disaster, when a headquarters directive had obliged him to send an armored force eastward without adequate preparation. In the absence of aerial photos, the striking force took a wrong turn on the road and wound up trapped on a highway bridge in plain sight of Legion gunners on the eastern wall. Withering crossfire from the wall and the lower slopes of the Mount of Olives cost the lives of five scouts and two tankmen; eighteen others were injured.

Mota had firm ideas about his tactical approach. "Every senior commander always had in the back of his mind the possibility that one day we might be fighting again for Jerusalem. My problem was the limited time we had for bringing reserve officers into the picture."

As the paratroop commanders huddled over their maps, there was a commotion overhead. Down the stairs trooped a quartet of Israeli soldiers, shepherding between them seven Arab Legion regulars. The Jordanians, fully armed and uninjured, had spent the night hiding in the tiny upstairs attic. Evidently paralyzed with fear, they had not opened fire when the Israelis entered the building, but crouched for an hour, grenades untouched in their belts, within ten feet of Mota and the rest of the unsuspecting command staff.

At 6:00 A.M., Mota crystallized his plans. Key targets, as prelude to the descent onto the Old City, would be the heights dominating it to the east: Augusta Victoria, the village of E-Tur farther south, and below that the crossroads of Azariya, named for a king of Judah of the eighth century B.C.

The first of his three battalions, victors at Ammunition Hill, would move in a sweeping northeastern hook up to and through the Israeli positions on Mount Scopus, advancing southward toward Augusta Victoria. The same position would be attacked frontally by the Second Battalion, moving directly eastward across the valley from the Rockefeller Museum. This would involve a daylight assault exposed to fire from the Old City walls, but Mota felt "there was little choice, whatever the cost." The Third Battalion would push along the northern wall eastward from Herod's Gate, turn the corner southward and break through somehow into the Old City.

Pointing out that the paratroopers were fighting "both the enemy and the clock," Mota underlined the stakes: "Our tanks are at the Canal. The Egyptians have been smashed. We cannot have a less decisive outcome where the Old City is concerned."

Looking down the table, Mota caught the eye of Josi, the kibbutznik commander of his First Battalion. Josi sat in silent misery, inconsolable over his unit's losses of the morning before.

For a moment, Mota felt a wave of pure fury toward the Arabs. Never before had he hated the enemy. He had always been scrupulously correct in victory, even forbidding his soldiers to use the mild slang pejorative "Araboush" (roughly translatable as "nothing but an Arab," or "a mere Arab"). But this war of 1967 was essentially so absurd, so unnecessary a slaughter on both sides. The Arab peoples, bedraggled by the dust of centuries, had everything to gain from the progressive society of Israel; instead, their leaders preferred to wage a grandiloquent "war of annihilation" against the Jews.

In this they would not succeed; he was confident of that. Army training—the intangible creation of atmosphere—would pay off. "We really believe in education. If you talk all the time about bravery, obligation to comrades, tradition—well, when the time comes, you get the proper response. After all, it's just a moment that we're pointing toward—a moment of decision. It is clear from talking to section commanders who were at Ammunition Hill that everybody was scared to death there. Still they went forward."

For himself, Mota had special plans, only dimly formulated in his mind. But they definitely involved Sergeant Moshe Ben-Tsur.

Ben-Tsur was a driver, a 210-pound Jewish Falstaff whose light-green eyes crinkled at the corners with every sally. Ample-bellied and quick-witted, he had luxuriant brown hair sweeping upward from a full beard and vast mustache to a tumbling Niagara of sun-bleached curls on top. Dimples lurked in the far reaches of his round hearty face. His girth was deceptive, obscuring powerful arms and the quick reflexes of a veteran paratrooper.

Ben-Tsur was a thirty-three-year-old reservist, married and the father of two children. In civilian life he was a tourist guide who over a fifteen-year period behind the wheels of tractors, cars and buses had never had an accident.

He first met Mota Gur in 1955 when Mota, then a company commander, came to his village to pay a consolation call on the family of a reservist killed in the Gaza Strip. A decade later, during his own month of brush-up training, he served under Mota in the Negev Desert as regimental noncom in charge of transport. The two became very friendly. Ben-Tsur found the colonel "warm, approachable, a human being"; Mota was impressed by the big fellow's genial reliability. The two had in common a penchant for the bantering phrase; a light manner combined with solid underpinning.

Mota's opinion of Ben-Tsur had been soundly reinforced by the sergeant's performance during the Tuesday fighting. Returning to the Rockefeller Museum with several Intelligence people after delivering a Jordanian officer to rear headquarters for questioning, Ben-Tsur's Land-Rover came under heavy sniper fire from the Old City wall near Herod's Gate. A bazooka missile smashed the leg of a captain in the party. For more than six hours, Ben-Tsur covered the injured man with his body, while wriggling under fire to the protective entrance pillars of the Rivoli Hotel. Later, defying a storm of machine-gun bullets that killed a second officer, he carried the captain to safety on an improvised stretcher.

Back at the museum Tuesday evening, Ben-Tsur was summoned to Mota on the darkened courtyard steps. "I want you next to me," the brigade commander said. "You stay here." Mota's half-track rumbled into view, and a young corporal scrambled down from the driver's seat. Mota's deputy pointed to the command half-track. "You're handling this," he told Ben-Tsur. "Stand by for Mota's orders."

At eight o'clock Wednesday morning, Israeli aircraft and artillery started blasting the Jordanian mountain positions. Half an hour later the ground attack exploded. The depleted northernmost battalion, including Noah's forces, rode up the slopes of Mount Scopus jammed into bright-blue civilian buses behind a spearhead of tanks and jeeps. Another small tank unit, followed by a battery of recoilless guns, led the head-on charge of the Second Battalion against Augusta Victoria. The Third Battalion waited momentarily, poised to strike into the Old City either through Herod's Gate or around the corner to the east.

Resistance on the ridge was astonishingly light. A company commander from Battalion Two was killed on the approaches to Augusta Victoria, and a couple of tanks were damaged by mines; but there was no serious Legion attempt to defend the fortress-like hospital building dominating the height.

Mota, accompanying the battalion, left the main force to hold the position and continued southward with a reconnaissance column along the Mount of Olives Road running parallel to the eastern wall of the Old City. With him in the command half-track were Ben-Tsur at the wheel; his Operations officer, Major Amos, a hefty, slow-spoken sabra to whom there clings a subtle suggestion of the countryside; a signals crew and a couple of Intelligence officers. They carried a light machine gun and some hand grenades.

At a sparsely settled crossroads below Augusta Victoria, Mota's force encountered some Legion stragglers who tried unsuccessfully to escape. "We knew there were tanks further up and also south, in the direction of E-Tur village and Azariya Junction, so we turned our column left along the ridge and swept it with fire." Then Mota raced on, past the silent one-story stone houses and occasional stores of E-Tur, to a point just below the sumptuous new Hotel Intercontinental. Here, with the Old City spread at his feet below, he stopped the half-track and got out. It was not quite nine o'clock.

His military position was remarkably like that of the Roman general Titus, who in A.D. 70 assembled four crack legions against Jerusalem after the upstart Jews there had wiped out first a Roman-occupied garrison and then a force sent up from Caesarea to punish them. Titus, like Mota, had one legion camped on Mount Scopus, and another farther south on the Mount of Olives. His third troop of fifteen thousand men was north of the city, and a fourth was in reserve. The Roman commander, for all of his battering rams and stone-hurling catapults, needed four months to subdue the city.

Mota did not intend to take that long.

Before him, shimmering in the light morning mist, lay an incomparable panorama of religious history. Northward, to the right, the bell-shaped blue spires of the Russian Church rose over the closely packed dark-green cypresses of the Garden of Gethsemane. Farther west and north stood the fifth-century Tomb of the Blessed Virgin. Diagonally across from the tomb was St. Stephen's Gate, named for the steadfast early Christian who, as described in the New Testament, was denounced for blasphemy and taken out of the city to be stoned. This entrance was known also as Lions' Gate after the bas-relief lions placed on either side by Suleiman the Magnificent, who was said to have dreamed he would be torn to pieces by lions if he failed to build a wall around the Holy City.

Through this portal Christ walked to His trial and crucifixion. A hundred-odd yards to the south, massive stones sealed off the Golden Gate, where Christ made his first triumphal entry into Jerusalem on what is now celebrated as Palm Sunday.

Beyond the gate stretched all the glory of Jerusalem, Old City and New, Christian and Jewish and Moslem, an unbroken wave of sparkling towers, domes, spires and minarets sharply etched against the pale blue sky. For Mota, who could still smell the spices of his boyhood wanderings in the Old City, there was no sight in the world like it.

Two mighty domes out-glittered the rest: the silvery cap of the Church of the Holy Sepulcher, near the center of Old Jerusalem; and the great golden roof crowning the Moslem Dome of the Rock in the southeast. The third leg of what was for long a magnificent triangle, the lordly Horva Synagogue near the southern wall, had been demolished by the Jordanians. But between the gold and silver domes there still gleamed a hoary patch of pink-gray stone dearer yet to Jewish hearts: the top of the western or Wailing Wall.

Last remnant of the temples built by Solomon and Herod, the wall abutted on the spacious rectangle of the Temple Mount, important to Christian tradition as Mount Moriah but even more significant to Islam and Judaism. Here Moslems believe Mohammed ascended to heaven, leaving behind a footprint in the hallowed stone. To enshrine the event, a seventh-century caliph built one of the architectural splendors of the world, the Dome of the Rock or

Mosque of Omar, a dazzling octagon of iridescent marbles and mosaics.

Jewish tradition has sanctified the area even longer. Here, according to legend, Adam lies buried, near the Foundation Stone which was the beginning of the world, and from which prayers ascend directly along the path of Jacob's Ladder to the "very gate of Heaven." It is here that Elijah is to signal the coming of the Messiah by blowing a shofar made from the curved horn of Abraham's sacrificial ram. Scholars claim that David deliberately purchased the site, used as a threshing-floor by the last Jebusite king, in order to reinstitute there the ancient altar of Adam and Abraham.

Certain it is that David's son, Solomon, built the First Temple there some three thousand years ago to house the Holy of Holies. Solomon's Temple was ravaged by Nebuchadnezzar in 586 B.C., but was rebuilt seventy years later, then enlarged and beautified by Herod in 10 B.C., lasting until the invasion by Titus of Rome in A.D. 70.

Orthodox Jews believe that the *Shekinah,* or Divine Presence, hovers permanently over the Temple Mount, at the heart of the city which has nine of the "ten measures of beauty" adorning the world: "To pray in Jerusalem is equivalent to standing before the throne of God."

Mota brought up his field glasses and scanned the scene again, this time as a military man, for a long moment, concentrating on the firing posts and gun slits running the length of the eastern wall. What he saw strengthened the hunch taking shape in his mind.

He went back to the half-track and signaled Mount Scopus, where General Bar-Lev had arrived to provide on-the-scene representation for headquarters. In view of the time factor, Mota asked for permission to charge the Old City directly, instead of enveloping it gradually and forcing a surrender. He felt the Jordanians were sufficiently demoralized to yield the prize with negligible damage before a bold attack.

Bar-Lev told him to wait; the change would have to be cleared with Rabin. After a few moments the Deputy Chief of Staff was back on the air: permission granted.

Exhilarated, Mota leaped into the front seat of the half-track and slapped Ben-Tsur on the shoulder. They swung back onto the road, shooting past several vehicles. Mota picked up his transmitter to address the battalion commanders, when he had a sudden change of mind. For once, he wanted to be ceremonial. The occasion demanded a flourish. Orders of this weight should not be delivered hastily from a careening half-track; they required a proper setting, nothing less than the most stupendous view available.

Mota told Ben-Tsur to go back toward the hotel. One of the young Intelligence officers laughed nervously at the gesture, but the brigade chief was not to be put off. Once again confronting the Temple Mount, he picked up the transmitter and flicked on the switch:

"To commanders of all regiments, Paratroop Brigade. We stand today at the gates of the Old City, where so many of our dreams lie. Now we are going up to the Old City—the Temple Mount—the Wailing Wall. The order of battle is as follows: Battalion One will go directly down the slope from Augusta Victoria. . . ."

He knew that the designation of actual unit numbers in an *en clair* radio transmission was, theroretically at least, "an awful breach of security"; but Mota Gur, flamboyant partisan of the soldier-intellectual, had no intention of altering the map of the Middle East in secrecy.

His radio message confirmed plans previously laid out for the other two battalions. The men on Mount Scopus would likewise charge down, while the third force would advance toward St. Stephen's Gate along the Old City wall; all units would have covering fire from tanks in forward positions. It would be a free-for-all race to burst through the city walls: "whoever arrives first will be the winner."

The slightest of quavers broke through Mota's normally even voice. "For thousands of years the Jewish people has prayed for this moment. Israel is awaiting our victory. Good luck."

Mota turned back to Ben-Tsur, and the half-track roared south again, quickly overtaking a tank and a group of jeeps in the advance column. The hillside below and to the right was covered with a very old Jewish burial ground. Mota had a brief, bitter impression of toppled headstones. The Jordanians were consistent; they did not desecrate only synagogues.

It was a few minutes after nine when they reached Azariya Junction. Here a right fork swung away from Bethlehem and doubled back along the Jericho Road toward the Old City. An Israeli tank force, halted at the turn, was pouring thunderous fire against the mortar-spouting wall of the Moslem Quarter. The huge rampart rattled; several stones were dislodged and crashed to the ground. But all the shelling was to the north of St. Stephen's Gate; the tankists, like the artillery batteries and recoilless gun units, were under emphatic orders to avoid hitting any of the Holy Places.

Trying to thread his way through the junction, Moshe Ben-Tsur had his hands full making sure that the tanks didn't hit *him.* In the smoke, fire and turmoil at the vehicle-crowded crossroads, visibility was near zero. Confined to what he could see through the narrow strip of windshield, Ben-Tsur felt like a man driving blindfolded. He asked Mota to open the small sliding windows set at an oblique angle to the side. Through them, he spotted a clear stretch of asphalt. He made a sweeping arc to his right and was soon racing north along the Jericho Road at fifty-five miles an hour, ten miles beyond the theoretical maximum attainable by the ten-ton half-track.

Ben-Tsur was hazily aware of the thrilling landscape unfolding to his left, where the Old City was coming into closer focus across the picturesque ruins of the Jehoshaphat Valley. He grinned sideways at Mota. "For years I've been a tourist guide. Now it's my turn to make a tour. I've never been in the Old City."

Most of the reconnaissance force was now behind them, but a couple of fast-moving tanks were still out front. Over the radio, Mota urged the whole column forward. "Faster, boys, faster! You're making history!"

They were now bearing down toward the highway bridge at the low-lying intersection leading upward to St. Stephen's Gate. This was the area where Mota's scouts had been pinned down twelve hours before; a charred Israeli tank and three bodies still lay in the far corner. From the bridge, a sharply-angled incline to the left climbed three hundred yards in a straight, precipitous line to the battlement-crowned gate.

The rapid dip, abrupt turn and steep rise made heavy going for the tank drivers. While one struggled to maneuver forward, the other pulled over to the side and opened close-range cannon fire against the gate above.

Mota squinted up at the formidable slope. Fiery impetus was all very well, but . . . "It was tricky. A good deal of our fuel was carried on the outside of the half-track, easily inflammable, and there were burning vehicles farther up the road. Also, the angle was so bad that our tanks couldn't take it."

The brigade commander turned and looked into the bearded face of his driver. "Can we make it, Ben-Tsur?"

For answer, the big man pressed down carefully on the gas pedal. The half-track faltered, shuddered, then began crawling upward as the heavy truck tires of its front section bit into the pavement. Gradually, its 160-horsepower engine straining to the limit, the vehicle picked up speed.

Mota and his command force were all alone now: before them, snipers on the gun-mounted Old City walls; behind, shells from their own tanks whistling over their heads.

The great battlements of St. Stephen's came into view, sixty feet high, split through the middle by a Gothic arch surmounting a pair of eighteen-foot steel doors. To the right of the entrance, a shell-struck civilian bus was blazing furiously, its flames singeing the cheeks of the approaching paratroopers.

The famous bas-relief lions were clearly visible, facing each other in profile across the main arch. So were several abandoned bazookas on top of the gate. Less certain was the situation in five firing niches scattered around the opening. Any or all of them might conceal Legionnaires who had only to drop a grenade onto the open half-track as it passed beneath.

The left door, a tightly packed mass of knobby steel plates, stood slightly ajar. It was eight feet wide, a few inches broader than the onrushing half-track, and nearly a foot thick. Driver and commander exchanged glances.

"Go, Ben-Tsur, go!"

Ben-Tsur went, hurtling into the steel with an impact that tore the huge door from its hinges. The half-track squeezed through, crunching over loosened stones that clattered down from the shell-gashed pillars.

A single, startled Arab soldier stood just inside the entrance, where an archway opened to a courtyard on the left. Would he toss the grenade that could wipe out the whole party? Mota decided the man was too dazed to act. The Israelis rolled forward, holding their fire.

Ten feet farther on, the narrow walls of the Via Dolorosa opened into a clearing wide enough to permit the half-track to turn. Ben-Tsur swung left along a gravel path into the ancient Pool of Israel area, now a dry and dusty rectangle covered with a scattering of donkey stalls.

At 9:50 A.M. Mota was firmly inside the Old City, the first man to storm it successfully in more than eight centuries, the first ever to penetrate its walls from the east. His immediate predecessor was Godfrey of Bouillon, the Crusader commander who in 1099 rammed through the Moslem defenses near Herod's Gate. Like Mota, Godfrey led the assault himself, swinging down from a siege tower and crossing a ramp to breach the parapet.

In this as in most of the other countless battles over Jerusalem, the people most concerned—the Jews—had been victims or spectators. Jewish conquerors composed a brief if illustrious list: David, the Maccabees, Simon Bar-Kokba . . . and now a sabra who had made an existentialist decision. While the great powers, presumed makers of universal destiny, glared at each other across wider barricades, Mota was writing his own history.

But he had not yet reached the Temple Mount. A small wall to the south blocked the way. Ben-Tsur slashed across a cobbled path toward the arched doorway of the Gate of Kneeling. Just before the thick wooden doors a motor bike lay in the path, perfect setting for a booby trap.

Once again, Ben-Tsur looked into his colonel's eyes. Mota nodded curtly. The half-track crashed forward, over the bike and through the door, into the ancient quarter-mile compound of Jerusalem most sacred to Jews and Arabs.

During the sweep down from the Mount of Olives, the half-track's machine gun had fired a few bursts. Now Mota ordered it silenced. "We were in a Holy Place."

They faced a large pine grove surrounded by barbed wire. Beyond the trees, majestic staircases led up to a vast paved plateau some two hundred yards square, the grand plaza of the Dome of the Rock. A diagonal gravel path knifed through the grove to the northern steps; Turkish flagstones, skirting the trees southward, gave access from the east. Ben-Tsur took the old Turkish road.

Seconds later the paratroopers were bounding up the spacious steps, passing beneath the superbly graceful pillared arches known as El-Mawazeen or "the Scales," where Moslems believe the deeds of men will be weighed on the Day of Judgment.

To their right was the tiny mosque known as Kaba el Baraq, where Mohammed is said to have tied up his noble horse Baraq before mounting it again for the flight to heaven. On their left was the silver-topped Aksa Mosque, third holiest in Islam, built in A.D. 693 by the Caliph Abd-el-Malik on the site of Solomon's Palace of the Cedars of Lebanon.

And directly before them was the Caliph's masterpiece, the all-but-incredible Dome of the Rock, an anachronism of medieval sensuousness in a dull technological world. Soaring arches, multicolored columns of precious marble, and a fireworks display of mosaics—blue, gold, mother-of-pearl, green—blazed brilliantly under the great golden helmet of the Dome.

Shots rang out from unseen rifles. Undeterred, Mota ran forward across the square. Beside him sprinted a senior aide who scrambled up the side of the building, climbed an iron railing and planted the Star of David above the gleaming golden cupola. At a little before 10:00 A.M. on June 7, 1967, the Jews had returned to the Temple Mount of Solomon.

Two Arab civilians, one of them in turban and trailing robes, emerged from the Aksa Mosque on Mota's left and moved slowly toward the Israeli colonel. Mota recognized the Governor and the Kadi, or chief religious judge, of the Old City. He greeted them in Arabic.

The Governor proffered a formal surrender. Organized Arab Legion units had withdrawn from the city, he told Mota. He could not speak for isolated "bandits," but as far as he was concerned, there would be no further resistance.

Mota replied that he would like to consolidate his positions without further bloodshed. However, if the mopping up ran into trouble, "we will know how to take care of ourselves. Tell your people the paratroopers are here."

Mota's Second Battalion was now piling through St. Stephen's Gate. He radioed orders for them to continue directly west, clearing snipers out of the Via Dolorosa, and then swing north to occupy the Damascus Gate. Herod's Gate was to be taken by the Third Battalion, while the First Battalion circled around the southeast wall to join units of the Jerusalem Brigade at the Dung Gate.

Meanwhile elements of the scouting force, having followed Mota onto the Temple Mount, were looking eagerly for the western wall (the traditional "Wailing Wall"), where no Jew had set foot prior to the 1948 war.

Ducking through a low opening in the southwest corner of the compound, they found themselves in a musty alley, hemmed in by tall buildings. A white-clad Arab emerged from a doorway. In reply to a shouted query, he beckoned them forward to another narrow aperture. Scrambling through after him, the paratroopers entered a paved, crooked passageway designated by a street sign as Al-Afdel-iyyeh Road ("Road of the Better One"). Two Legionnaires in a guardhouse beside the entryway threw up their hands; the excited Israelis ignored them.

Running forward, they dodged under a low stone archway, then another. A small doorway to the right was sealed with loose rocks. A sergeant smashed them aside with the butt of his Uzzi. Below, a worn and slippery stairway wound down to the base of a high gray enclosure. "The Wailing Wall!" screamed the sergeant. "I can see it!" The men tumbled down the steps after him.

Elsewhere in the Old City, Israeli forces advanced carefully, doorway to doorway, against holdout opposition from rooftops and windows. Small dramas flared across every dark alleyway. Near the Damascus Gate, an English-speaking Arab who volunteered assistance led three paratroopers into an ambush. Two were killed by hand grenades; the third, a former jeweler in London's Carnaby Street, suffered a broken leg. Half a mile to the south, an Israeli rifleman came around a bend in a market arcade to confront an armed Arab. Each reached for his trigger, when in the half-light the Israeli recognized a boyhood friend from Jaffa. "Abdullah!" he shouted, and the two embraced.

Mota continued to direct operations from the Mount, amid a wild hubbub of congratulations and interviews. While fighting continued, he had work to do.

At his elbow, a young officer with a bandage around his head talked with a newspaperman. "She treated dozens of us," he was saying. "Nobody knew who she was, how she got to Ammunition Hill—or why she stayed there. Some of the boys actually thought she wasn't flesh and blood, but a visitation from heaven, sent in our time of need. Our 'angel in white,' they called her."

Mota turned. This was not the first word he had heard of the paratroopers' "angel." Who *was* the girl? he demanded. And would somebody please find her, so he could communicate his respects?

Several men shrugged. One thought he had caught a glimpse of the volunteer nurse in the early moments of breakthrough into the city, getting down from a half-track on the Via Dolorosa; but he felt that in all the joyous tumult he might have been mistaken.

He wasn't. Esther had spent all of Tuesday with paratroopers in the field, helping to bring up medical supplies and organize the transport of wounded to the rear. Wearing a white nurse's robe with a blue ribbon arm band, she identified herself to commanders simply as "Dr. King's nurse." Early Wednesday morning, after a few hours of sleep at the Police School, she joined a vanguard unit of the Second Battalion moving toward the Old City.

Just inside St. Stephen's Gate, two men in her half-track were felled by sniper fire. Esther treated them with the American medical kit she had picked up early Tuesday morning at Mandelbaum Gate: morphine, burn-dressing and plasma. After they were evacuated, she went forward in a jeep to the Temple Mount, then made her way on foot, through alleyways jammed with excited soldiers, to the Wailing Wall.

Esther had no idea what to expect. She had never seen even a picture of the wall, and had only the sketchiest notion of its history. Suddenly she stood before it, five feet of girl facing sixty feet of great unmortared slabs cracked and battered by time, each as wide as the height of a man. Shrubbery sprouted like green beards from between chinks in the hoary stone, blue-gray in the lower rows, warming to golden pink in the slanting sunshine. And paratroopers were crushing forward to weep and pray and join their hands to the timeless granite, touching, caressing, banging it with their fists in irrational ecstasy. One orthodox trooper, yarmulka on his head, wore a cartridge belt around his neck in place of a prayer shawl.

This was the wall from which, legend said, Roman wrecking-crews had fallen back in confusion and dismay 1900 years before, unable to execute their orders. These stones had assertedly been laid by the poor, in line with the ancient practice of apportioning construction tasks among different elements of the population. Roman Legionnaires approaching them, after tearing down the other three segments of the temple wall, found angels hovering overhead who declared, "This wall built by the poor shall remain."

A Roman general who defied them was struck dead on the spot. When Titus himself raised a sledge hammer, his right hand withered. According to the story, six angels then came and seated themselves on top of the wall, weeping tears that seeped down and hardened into cement, binding the stones together for all time.

Legend aside, archaeologists have no doubt of the authenticity of the wall, although many doubt that it dates back to the First Temple.

Herodian embellishment or relic of Solomon, the wall gripped Esther Zalinger with overwhelming power. "It was a live force, speaking directly to something hidden inside me . . . unfamiliar, and yet remembered. I ran forward with the others and laid my head against the stones and cried . . . for the blood that had been shed, for our victory, for my mother's death and the suffering of all the Jews through the ages."

Esther stayed at the wall for several minutes, a tiny figure among the burly helmeted paratroopers. Drained of tears at last, she felt a "wonderful sense of inner tranquillity."

She heard singing around her, the hoarse breathless voices of exhausted men: "*Yerushalayim shel zahav, veshel nechoshet veshel or: Halo lechol shiraych ani kinor. . . .*" ("Jerusalem of gold, of copper and light; Let me be a violin for all your songs. . . .")

A hand reached out to her from the milling crowd. She smiled up at Major Jack King, the battalion medical officer whom she had not seen since the Mandelbaum Gate. Esther was still carrying the huge multilayered slab of candy given to her in the Sheikh Jarrah district for saving an Arab child. She thrust it at the doctor, begging him to distribute it among the troops. One thing she held back: the red-and-yellow string, as "a souvenir for my daughter."

Her mind was returning now to her family, but there was one more task to perform. She circulated among the troopers picking up messages for relay: a phone number to call or a greeting to put in the mail, scribbled on the back of an envelope, a candy wrapper, even a military diagram. When she had collected sixty-three names, she turned her steps back toward Israeli Jerusalem.

Her first stop was at the Salomons. Holed up through the night in a bomb shelter, they were unaware of the paratrooper victory, and at first could not believe it when Esther reported, "I kissed the

Wailing Wall in your names." Marveling, Mrs. Salomon agreed with her husband that their "daughter" had earned the rare privilege.

From there Esther hitchhiked home, to organize the task of relaying greetings from sons, husbands, brothers, sweethearts . . . the priceless word that the sender was still alive. To recipients who had no telephones, she would mail out the precious scrawled memos—sometimes no more than a word or two in a dearly loved hand.

But first she went to the shelter where a teacher friend was looking after Noorit and Elan. "I'm back," she cried excitedly. "Your mother is back alive!"

Noorit looked up calmly, pigtails dangling. "Of course you're back," she said. "We knew you would be." Then she threw her arms around Esther's neck.

Elan, awaiting his turn, reminded his mother that a special angel watched over her. "Do you think," he asked reasonably, "that we would have let you go otherwise?"

At the western wall, an Israeli flag had been run up—the same crude ensign smuggled out of the Old City in 1948. Blood now spattered the lower steps of the old staircase, where a corporal had been cut down by a last bitter sniper firing from a minaret.

A quavering blast from the shofar announced the presence of the army's Chief Chaplain, Brigadier General Shlomo Goren, never far behind the combat troops at critical moments in the war. A stocky, bemedaled figure conspicuous for his bushy beard and thick glasses, Goren clung to the small blue-sheathed Torah that he had carried into battle earlier in 1948 and 1956. He conducted services at the wall, opening with a whispered Yizkor, or prayer for the dead, in memory of those who had fallen along the way.

Goren pledged to the non-Jewish world that the Israelis would care scrupulously for "the holy places of all religions." But, "from here we do not move. Never. Never."

As the day wore on, national dignitaries arrived to share in the mystical reunion with the past, to hear within themselves a distant "Shma Yisroel" echoing down the centuries of exile and grief and longing. David Ben-Gurion, hurrying down the steps, grasped the dust-caked hands of the paratroopers, thanking Noah and his comrades on behalf of the generation that created the new Israel. Yitzchak Rabin made a short, emotion-charged speech. And Moshe Dayan, violet wildflowers in his buttonhole, honored an ancient custom by slipping a handwritten Hebrew prayer between the stones. It read, *"Lu yehi shalom al kol Israel"*—"May there be peace upon all Israel."

In every corner of the land, the people rejoiced—with fervent tears, solemn prayers, wild Oriental dancing. The tide of feeling reached out to embrace the most hardened Socialist skeptics. As Dr. Falk Schlesinger, director of Shaari Zedek Hospital, said: "A corner of their hearts that had been sleeping suddenly came alive."

Air Force Chief Mordechai Hod, a nonreligious kibbutznik, broke out a bottle of Scotch. "Hard liquor was strictly forbidden during the war. But this was too much to resist—the wall in our own hands for the first time since the days of the House of Lords in Jerusalem!"

Radios of every description, in kibbutz dining halls, hospital wards, Sinai encampments, blared out Mota Gur's story. "Of course this is a special day for me, for all of us," the deep voice was rumbling. "There isn't a man in the paratroopers who hasn't dreamed for years of coming back to the Old City—to be in Jerusalem, to fight in Jerusalem, even to die in Jerusalem. We have had many battles, but this was something more. This is history."

Did Colonel Gur think, a reporter asked, that the victory had special significance for the orthodox?

"The Temple Mount is for everybody—to me, it's even more than the Wailing Wall. But as for the orthodox . . . I don't interfere in their life, I don't want them to interfere in my life, but one thing I can tell you: they are wonderful soldiers, very brave. For them there is never a moment of hesitation: Israel is our country."

"Are you happy today, Colonel?"

"Happy? No. How can I be happy after so much suffering by my boys?"

Mota was tired; tired of the questioning, the celebrities, the noise and the crowd. Increasingly his thoughts were of his troops, of the boys who would never again till the fields of their kibbutzim, or stroll the streets of Tel Aviv with their girls. He suspected that, for all the talk of glory and tradition, the men of his own generation, like Yitzchak Rabin, were thinking more of the terrible price of victory, and of the comrades lost before the capital in 1948.

A wry thought crossed his mind. Mota turned to Rabbi Goren. "Imagine when I go home and tell my daughter about this morning. She loves to hear stories: for her, the classic heroes are very real.

When she finds out that her father liberated Jerusalem . . ."

The weaver of fantastic tales for children had created one of his own, to endure in the pages of Jewish history beside those of David, Bar-Kokba and the Maccabees. Neither Mota, nor anyone who heard him on that morning of June 7, would ever forget the tremendous moment when he was able to seize his transmitter and say, "The Temple Mount is in our hands. Repeat: the Temple Mount is in our hands."

The Fourth Day

THE TANK CREW

GUNPOWDER and spices. A strange combination of smells, Karni Bilu thought—yet symbolic of Jerusalem. Early Thursday, less than twenty-four hours after the capture of the Old City, Karni was walking through the ancient market place below Damascus Gate. A buxom twenty-one-year-old with a Jeanmaire hairdo, she wore khaki blouse and miniskirt, and the silver bars of a first lieutenant in the paratroops. Her high Slavic cheekbones and full sensuous lips were underscored by dramatic make-up that gave her face the patina of a semi-Oriental mask.

Zahal is an army of both sexes. In 1948 the women of Israel, like those of the American pioneers, frequently fought beside their men. By 1967, although still subject to two years of training that included the use of light weapons for defense, they were serving behind the lines in administration, communications, nursing, transport and ordnance, releasing large numbers of men for duty at the front.

First Lieutenant Bilu was commanding officer for the group of girls, mostly clerical workers, attached to Mota Gur's brigade. Less officially, she was aide-de-camp to the colonel, undertaking special assignments and serving as his escort on ceremonial occasions. As a reservist, she had been recalled a few weeks before from language studies at the Hebrew University.

133

Karni swung along, past the shuttered stalls and shop fronts, up and down the cobbled stairways, anxious to absorb all that she could on this momentous first visit. Her wide gray eyes reflected her excitement. She was in Old Jerusalem, the city of longing and dreams for her parents and generations before them, the city whose legends had colored her childhood since infancy.

It was almost unfair that after all the yearning by her elders the privilege of this return should be hers. But the brigade had earned the honor, and she could claim a small part. Her assignment had been to identify and report casualties, maintaining a round-the-clock vigil at hospitals and receiving stations so that higher command always had a clear picture of the brigade's manpower situation. Early Tuesday, she had come under shellfire in Jerusalem; for forty-eight hours afterward she had endured the far more painful experience of recording the dead and wounded among her intimate friends.

As she later explained to her parents, "to look at a boy you have known well who has a single bullet drilled through the center of his forehead . . . to hear their shocking cynicism about their injuries, their careless gallantry . . . I would rather fight. Of course, I would always be afraid, and if I had to shoot my way forward in an advance I would be very, very terrified. But standing guard duty would be better than standing in a hospital corridor, and hearing the scream of the approaching siren, and wondering who it was going to be this time, which of your friends they would bring in. . . ."

Military duty for women in Israel is less rigidly enforced than for men. In Karni's case, the desire to serve was built in from infancy. She had her baptism of fire at the age of two, strapped to her mother's back amid the flying bullets at the 1948 Battle of Jaffa; Mrs. Bilu thought her child would be "safest" there. Both parents were officers in the aggressive underground organization Irgun Zva'i Leumi, which unlike the essentially defensive Haganah did not shrink from terrorist tactics to break the British ban on immigration. The name "Karni" was originally one of her mother's underground pseudonyms. Her father was jailed by the British two weeks after his daughter was born.

At ten, on a visit to South Africa, Karni learned to shoot a pistol.

Eight years later she entered the army, to emerge at twenty with her officer's bars. The award ceremony was the emotional high point of her life. When she ran across the parade ground afterward to receive her father's kiss, it was not only a filial blessing but a bestowal —and acceptance—of the underground torch.

Now, a year later, she was walking in a restored Jewish Jerusalem. It was hard to believe. Karni entered a cool, dim arcade, probably a fruit market but now silent behind steel shutters. As she emerged into the sunlight, she caught a glimpse of a small face at a barred window. Instantly a hand came into view, snatching the child away.

They're scared of us, Karni thought. They needn't be. We don't make war on women and children.

She wondered whether an Arab army would have been equally forbearing in victory. No, she concluded; not after the propaganda that had been saturating the Arab countries for years.

An instinctively generous, motherly girl, quick to set the coffee brewing or to sew on the errant button, Karni wrestled endlessly with her conflicting feelings about Israel's neighbors. As she had put it in many a late-night discussion with intellectual comrades in Tel Aviv, "Yes, I know—they're people, too. But they're people who endanger my life. I know the Egyptian fellah is untutored, that he may not realize what he is doing; but it's enough for him to get a bulletin, or hear Nasser talking on the wireless, and he comes to shoot me. I can't—I simply can't—develop any affection for that kind of person."

Whenever she spoke of the Syrians in particular, her voice grew thick with indignation. "Look at their behavior, slaughtering unarmed farmers! They are simply blind, they don't see reality. They don't fight just soldiers. Tell them to shoot, and they will shoot anyone."

Still, Karni had always insisted that "potentially, I love every human being in the world." She was a girl seething with contradictions, drawn both to the Spartan austerity of her parents' generation, and to the frivolity of Paris fashions; to the blunt honesty of Israeli men, and to the glossy polish of those from overseas. She admired the simple comradeship of the kibbutzim, while questioning the effects of regimentation on personal growth. Pleased with her country's rapid industrialization, she was fearful that somewhere in the process its special essence might get lost. She oscillated between pride in her own firm idealism, and rueful contemplation of its cost in lost opportunities.

Karni dwelt in a more reflective world than most of her contemporaries. Her father was a Tel Aviv city official; her mother and seventeen-year-old brother both liked to paint. She had read Aldous Huxley and Jean Paul Sartre in the original, was a regular concert-goer, and missed few of the plays staged by the Habima Theater.

With women "changing a lot in Israel," she also found herself increasingly intrigued with fashion design and make-up. "Now that there is no longer such a need for pioneering, for roughing it in men's clothes, women here are more conscious of styles. They want to be perfumed and feminine." Karni always made it clear she wasn't talking about hippie beads and knee-length tresses, extravagances "natural in other parts of the world, where the youth have no challenge to meet. Here we have no time to be self-centered and get depressed."

Confident of her own female capacities, Karni looked forward to administering a large household. She had no taste for the pill: "Any contraceptive device is a kind of murder. That one in particular upsets the balance of the sexes. The world has been created in a certain way; you can't change things around just for the convenience of people." She intended to have as many children as she could afford.

Just who was to father this brood, Karni had not yet figured out. Israeli men generally aroused mixed feelings in her. She liked their alertness, their relatively rapid maturing, and their political idealism. Acutely feminine, she was less happy with their brusque, sometimes imperious manners: "I'm sensitive about small courtesies."

Karni had dated boys of Oriental background a number of times during army service, mostly kitchen workers from Morocco or Tunisia. She found them as a rule "less stimulating" because of their limited education. And they were liable to react furiously to insults, real or fancied.

Karni shied away from such unrelieved intensity. The man for her would have to balance his seriousness with humor. "He must be so sure of himself that he has no fear of sometimes being childish. Only a man with a strong personal sense of security can make me feel secure."

Unhappily for Karni, the kind of man to whom she gravitated—worldly, poised, with a wide range of interests—was precisely the type shipped out of the country on diplomatic and educational missions. As she once complained to her mother, "Every time I find a really superior man, he leaves two weeks later for a seminar in Geneva or our consulate in Buenos Aires."

Karni was reconciled to a leisurely search; Israelis married too young, anyway. "That's the main reason for our high divorce rate." She considered her private frustrations little enough sacrifice for the blessings of living in a Jewish homeland: "I didn't fully appreciate our freedom until I saw the life of the blacks in South Africa. I couldn't possibly live like that. We must not become too much like others, or we will lose our special meaning. People who come here look for something different, and we must preserve the difference."

A good deal of that difference was conveyed in a 1966 letter that Karni wrote to a family friend, a commander whose unit had suffered severe casualties in a border ambush:

I wanted to call out to you at the funeral service, "Don't merely weep; scream aloud and cover up their groans with your scream."

I wanted to stand at attention and lower my head; to salute and cry out "Heroes!"

But I cried, I only cried.

I had no brother there, nor son or friend.

But they were all my brothers, my sons and friends.

I wanted you to know that I ache and it hurts so; that you are not alone. . . .

I only wanted you to know.

The walk through Old Jerusalem was not an unalloyed delight. At an intersection off the Via Dolorosa, where an Israeli guard stood shouldering an Uzzi, the remains of a Jordanian wooden barricade were scattered in the street. Stooping, Karni picked up a blood-smeared eyeglass case with Hebrew lettering.

Too many young men had shed their blood in this unwanted war, and not only from "her" brigade. She thought of her musician friend Dudu Sela, Dudu the irrepressible. He had been badly wounded in the Sinai, according to a surgeon from Beersheba whom she had run into at Hadassah Hospital. She wondered if Dudu was still alive.

Far to the south, at the Beersheba hospital in the Negev, Dudu stirred groggily after an interminable and near-sleepless night. All through the dark hours, he had been refighting the battle of the coastal highway . . . hearing the roar and crackle of guns, feeling his finger on the trigger and the soft gummy Sinai sand under his thick paratroop boots . . . and seeing what he did not want ever to see again, and yet seemed unable to escape: his cousin Giora, one moment tall and erect in the neighboring half-track, the next instant toppling forward with terrible finality.

Other details of the nightmare shifted and blurred. The rifle cradled under his arm became a bazooka—or was it a cello? The face of his driver became that of a long-forgotten history teacher from high-school days. But one image, constantly thrust away, kept returning: the awful sight of Giora being shot down.

He became aware of murmuring voices, and opened his eyes. His mother stood above him, with his young surgeon, Dr. Irving Kaplan. Mrs. Sela reached forward and touched the top of his head, very lightly, very carefully.

His body was mummylike under layers of white wrapping, his face bearded and disfigured by raw red splotches. Held above him in traction were bandage-swathed forearms and hands. Dudu had been in surgery constantly since arriving at the hospital at midnight Monday, after a long and harrowing trip from the front. Evacuation helicopters had not been able to operate because of the bypassed pockets of Egyptian resistance, so for several hours he had been carried forward on a stretcher, left by the side of the road whenever there was a fire fight, to tremble helplessly as tanks rumbled by a few feet away.

The hospital doctors found internal bleeding, cracked ribs, a seam of shrapnel along his left leg, and painful burns all over the body. As for playing the cello again—the only thing that seemed to concern Dudu—they looked grim. They were not even sure he would survive.

A series of operations removed Dudu's spleen, set his ribs, eliminated the chunks of shrapnel, and gave preliminary treatment to his many burns. Later, with luck, patches of new skin might be grafted onto his hands and face. For the moment, the doctors could do little but hope—and wait.

Waiting with them was Mrs. Sela. Dudu's mother had awakened from sleep just before midnight Monday, suddenly convinced that her son had been hurt. Telephone inquiry confirmed her fears. By the time Dudu emerged from his first operation, she was at his bedside. She had been there ever since, feeding him encouragement, and ready, as soon as medical permission was granted, to administer hot homemade soup.

Dudu's father had come, but not for long. Unable to bear the cruel sight, he had turned away in tears. So had several young friends. Mrs. Sela alone remained, bucked up by her friend and ally, Dr. Kaplan.

The doctor, subdued in manner but intensely alert to his responsibilities, was a plastics specialist in his thirties who had immigrated to Israel from Rhodesia five years before. He did not know Dudu, but was in the hospital's snack bar with several other surgeons late Monday night when a nurse ran in, weeping and distraught. She told them about the paratroop lieutenant who had just been brought in, a boy she had known from youth movement days, who was a talented musician, an exceptional person: "This boy you've *got* to save!"

Kaplan threw himself into the task. He formed a team of four surgeons, and he himself was on hand a dozen times a day, from 5:00 A.M. to midnight, checking fever chart, medication, dressings—and simply chatting. Kaplan's interest was more than professional. He was responding to a raw determination such as he had never seen.

For Dudu refused to give up. Not only would he recover and live, he told the doctor, but given any kind of chance, any semi-restoration of the power in his fingers, he would perform again. From the moment of his arrival in the hospital, even as he was being prepared for surgery, he had begged nurses and attendants to move his fingers, stretch them, preserve what suppleness was left in the flame-shriveled skin. Afterward, his hands numb under bandages, he asked his mother to get him a hard rubber ball. He would need it for squeezing exercises to strengthen his fingers as soon as the bandages were removed.

Meanwhile, he endured what could not be helped. His blackest thoughts were not of himself but of his cousin Giora. When a C.B.S. television unit came to interview patients at the hospital, Dudu told them of the long walk he had taken with Giora in the Negev on the Sunday evening before the war. "We talked about all the situation, and we asked only for peace, to live in this wonderful country in peace. And we had to fight, and we had to kill; and we saw that when you have a good aim, and you have something to protect, you are cunning and brave. I was shooting; and it is so cruel, it is awful." He described the shock of Giora's death: "If Nasser starts another war, I won't go into the army. I'll go to Egypt personally and kill him."

The newsman asked Dudu how he felt about the blow to his own career. Dudu looked over at the rubber ball on his bed table, not yet usable but perhaps a bridge to the future. Through swollen lips he forced out his answer: "I shall play again."

On the face of it, the prediction seemed unrealizable. But so had the military victories that were carrying his comrades deep into the Sinai.

The Sinai Desert is a vast primeval expanse of stone and sand, as chilling to contemplate as it is broiling to endure. Ruggedly heart-shaped, it sprawls under eternally blazing skies between the northeast shoulder of Africa and southwestern Asia, separating the Mediterranean from the Red Sea by some of the most forbidding—and inspiring—scenery in the world. This is the biblical wilderness in which the Children of Israel wandered for forty years; crossing it today in modern vehicles, one can only marvel at their fortitude.

The Sinai, baking in summer under Death Valley temperatures of 100-130 degrees, is four times the size of prewar Israel: 37,500 square miles of loose wind-swept sand dunes, picturesque hills of iron-red or turquoise-blue, and barren eroded plateaus. In the deep south of the peninsula, the stony massifs rise into fierce, jagged peaks. One of these naked spires, thrusting its 7400-foot crest heavenward in violent splendor, is Gebel Musa or Mount Moses, legendary site of the Ten Commandments.

A short flight from the Mount, at the southeast tip of the Sinai, lies the Strait of Tiran, where Nasser set up the blockade that in

Israeli eyes was an act of war. Running along the western edge of the desert is the Suez Canal, starting at Port Said in the north and terminating ninety miles away just beyond the town of Suez. East of Suez City is the key mountain gap that provides the only entry to, or escape from, the center of the peninsula: the celebrated Mitla Pass. It was along this arid fourteen-mile defile that Mota Gur's paratroopers had blasted Egyptian gunners out of overhanging cave positions in 1956.

All through the fourth day of the war, as Egyptian positions collapsed in the eastern desert, a flood of enemy armor and troop carriers had been pouring toward the Mitla escape hatch. (A map of the Sinai Peninsula appears on page 24.) Israeli flyers roamed over the narrow corridor, pummeling the retreating phalanxes and leaving the sandy road strewn with wrecked vehicles. But thus far no Israeli force had penetrated westward through the pass to establish an Israeli presence at both ends. This was essential not only to capture the canal bank beyond, but also to discourage a rally by the still-formidable Egyptian force trapped between the mountains.

In the waning hours of Thursday afternoon, a British-built Centurion rumbled up from the east, bellwether of an Israeli tank force that had already swept some 125 miles in a nonstop southwest diagonal across the heart of the desert. Its four-man crew was headed by a last-minute replacement, a mathematics student. Second Lieutenant Azgad Yellin was at twenty-two the youngest man in the quartet and the junior member of the entire three-tank reservist platoon under his command. Azgad's crew had been fighting without a break for sixty-five hours, having led their battalion across the border at Nitzana thirty .miles below the coast just before dawn Tuesday to open a new phase of the desert campaign.

Tal had already broken through in the north. So had Brigadier General Arik Sharon in the central Um-Kattef–Abu Agheila area. The Centurions were part of the third and last Israeli armored division, under Brigadier General Avraham Yoffe. An earlier Yoffe force had already threaded through "impassable" dunes to block Egyptian reinforcements from moving against Tal; Azgad's unit was attached to Yoffe's second brigade, whose job was to exploit Sharon's victory in the center by cutting off enemy paths of retreat and racing for the far-off banks of the Suez Canal.

Both objectives rested on the Israeli ability to paralyze and demoralize the enemy by the sheer speed and fury of their advance, a technique that made heavy demands on the "qualitative superiority" so prized by Tal. It meant nonstop pressure, driving and fighting night and day without pause for food or rest, without concession to the blistering, energy-draining sun—pushing to the last limits of human nerve and muscle.

Azgad, his face layered with dust where it was not covered by goggles or communications gear, rode Israeli-style in the open turret of his Centurion, a medium tank distinguishable from the American Patton by its squarish rather than curved turret. The tradition of the tank commander riding into battle with head and upper body exposed is a matter of morale with the Israelis—like that of the Scottish bagpiper who marches unarmed and defiant at the head of his regiment. It also has its practical side: a tank commander can make a 360-degree sweep of the horizon more rapidly with his binoculars or the naked eye than he can by using the nine periscopes available to him under a closed turret.

Azgad had acquired his command responsibilities through a typically Israeli series of improvisations. On May 21 at 7:30 A.M. he was lying abed, brooding over whether to continue in higher mathematics at the Hebrew University of Jerusalem or switch to industrial applications, when the telephone rang. He was urgently wanted at a tank base—not his own.

Reporting, he discovered that the base, already mobilized, was concerned about the difficulties of rounding up reservist commanders living in the north, where communications and transport were often erratic. An Egyptian attack was considered a momentary possibility, so the base had put out an emergency call for qualified tank officers from the Tel Aviv area.

Azgad was sent to help organize a tank company. The company's commander had been operating without a deputy; now, with war threatening, he felt he needed one. He chose one of his platoon commanders—which left that platoon leaderless. Azgad was drafted for the job. Although he had never been in charge of more than one tank before, he had been an instructor in the Tank Officers' School and therefore knew tactical theory. The practical problems of handling a dozen strangers, all of them from earlier reservist classes and therefore older, would have to be met as they came up.

Below Azgad and to his right sat his gunner, a twenty-four-year-old sergeant named Evik Ben-Bassat. Evik's main responsibility was to operate the giant tank cannon, a twelve-foot piece with a 360-degree swivel and free up-and-down movement. Although the tank commander had master control of the cannon, and frequently lined up the target in rough fashion, it was Evik who had to make the swift and precise aiming calculations before loosing his twenty-five-pound shell. He also operated a small machine gun below the cannon, observing his results with both through a periscope.

To the left below Azgad was his gun-loader and radioman, Corporal Yaacov Basil. Yaacov, working on his feet in a narrow compartment, fed the guns by hand from an ammunition bin on his right and a cache of shells under the floor. No matter how rapid the firing, he had to keep Evik fully supplied at all times. He was twenty-three.

Between Evik and Yaacov, deep in the belly of the fifty-two-ton monster, was the driver, Sergeant Dani Tal. At twenty-five, Dani was the old man of the crew. Although his space allotment was relatively lavish—five feet by five—his breathing arrangements were not. With temperatures outside boiling up to 130 degrees, Dani worked in a virtually airless hotbox. He also had to cope with seven speeds, a pair of periscopes that limited his vision to some ten yards on either side of the road, a tricky stop-and-go steering mechanism, blinding sandstorms and mountainous dunes. Fortunately, the Centurion could hold its own in desert terrain.

The four-man crew was a fairly typical mixed bag of sabra youth. Dani the driver and Evik the gunner were kibbutzniks. Yaacov, like Naftali Cohen of Ammunition Hill, was an Oriental of Yemenite descent. Azgad was the most Westernized, a product of the prosperous suburbs. If the crew was weighted numerically toward the kibbutzim, that was because of the dominant role in defense staked out for themselves by the settlements since the earliest days of Zionism.

There are four major kibbutz movements in Israel, each associated with a political grouping. Reading politically from right to left, they belong to the religious parties; to Mapai, the dominant center originally led by David Ben-Gurion; to the Socialist-Labor Achdut Ha'avodah; and to the Far-Left Mapam, which has traditionally had pro-Soviet leanings. Together, the kibbutzim contain only 4 or 5 percent of the country's population; but they contribute a far higher proportion of key personnel to the defense forces.

Dani and Evik were both from Mapam settlements. Dani, married and the father of two children, was a slender, silent boy. Wispy corn-colored hair and pale blue eyes contributed to an impression of almost painful self-containment, merely accented by an incongruously ferocious Balkan mustache.

Dani was a student of agricultural technology at Kibbutz Ramat Hashofet—"Hill of the Judge"—named at its founding in 1941 for the late Judge Julian W. Mack of the New York Federal District Court. Situated in the stony and picturesque biblical hills of Ephraim southeast of Haifa, Ramat Hashofet specializes in sheepbreeding and plum orchards.

Evik was a foreman in the plastics factory at Bet-Zera, a lushlyplanted kibbutz in the hot, flat Jordan Valley north of the Sea of Galilee. A year younger than Dani, he appeared much more sure of himself socially. His opinions were delivered almost as pronouncements, reflecting the forensic flavor of kibbutz discussions. Although his parental lineage was, oddly enough, the same as Dani's—Bulgarian and Lithuanian—the accent in Evik's case fell on the more southern heritage, if not on earlier Sephardic roots in Spain. He had the classic oval features, warm dark eyes and long sideburns of a Castilian nobleman.

Both boys were sergeants fully qualified as tank commanders. As fellow-disciples of Mapam, they had a great many other things in common. Both grew up in special children's quarters where, separated except for visiting periods from their parents, they learned unswerving loyalty to the basic tenets of the group: total democracy (cabinet members home on vacation are expected to take their turn as waiters); an antipathy to formal religion (Evik felt "like an Israeli, not a Jew"); unsentimental directness (Dani, summoned to his tank in the middle of a math exam, simply scribbled a note to his wife saying he would be away for a while); extremely close ties within the community; and a moderately sympathetic view of Russia (which turned sour for both boys, in Dani's case to something "near hatred").

The kibbutz was the lens through which Dani and Evik viewed the world. The settlements allowed no private bank accounts; members relied on the community for food, housing, medical care, even advanced education. In Mapam settlements, sexual contact between boys and girls was prohibited until they finished high school. After eighteen—if the two were "serious"—sexual freedom was encouraged on the grounds that it was "good for them to know one another."

Kibbutzniks earnestly hope that their communal form of social organization will regain its dwindling influence in Israel. To preserve that possibility, to maintain a bridgehead into a more idealistic future, they are quite willing to give their lives.

A very different history lay behind Yaacov, the Yemenite gunleader in the crew of the Centurion. Lean-limbed and cavernous of cheek, with melancholy deep-green eyes looming in a dark triangular face, Yaacov was visibly a young man grappling for a foothold in a still-bewildering world. His handshake was limp, un-European. The gestures of his long supple fingers were more expressive than his low, droning speech.

Yaacov's parents emigrated to the Promised Land fifty years ago, bringing with them some books and prayer shawls, several magnificent knitted wool jackets, a long curved nargileh that his mother still smokes (his father, at eighty, finds the pipe too much for his lungs)—and an abundance of hopes. Thrust without farm training or technical skills into a Westernized society, the Basils multiplied—Yaacov was the youngest of twelve children—but did not flourish economically. Social equality too has been a yes-and-no affair; better than their minority status in Arab Yemen, but something subtly short of total acceptance.

Twenty years ago they managed to build a small house in the Hatikvah quarter of Tel Aviv, a congested and somewhat rundown area inhabited mainly by Jews from North Africa and the Near East. Here Yaacov grew up, a dutiful boy who in his daily religious-school instruction absorbed such precepts as "honor your elders, do not beat girls or keep bad company, avoid hashish, behave as befits your surroundings."

In his teens he attended technical high school, learning metal work. As his older brothers and sisters gradually established families of their own, Yaacov was left with his parents, sharing with them the tiny upstairs apartment: six-by-ten foyer, neat, crowded kitchen, small bathroom and a bedroom some sixteen feet square, bulging with cots, wardrobes and tables. The walls were stained from winter rains; the single window offered little relief from summer heat. In Yaacov's corner were a hard cot with tattered but spotless pillow;

an unshaded lamp alongside Hebrew-language versions of Churchill's memoirs and James Jones's *From Here to Eternity;* and, on the wall, a photo of Yaacov's army unit at the start of training.

He entered the army at eighteen, and was delighted with its atmosphere of absolute democracy: "There was no prejudice whatever, and especially not against me"—a reference to the fact that once when he got into trouble for swinging at a sergeant major, he was treated with great leniency.

Less heartening was his treatment in the commercial world when he returned to civilian life at twenty. Officially, there was no discrimination; but there was an unspoken attitude that seemed to shunt him quietly aside. "If I was waiting on line at a labor exchange, and there was another applicant behind me who could speak Yiddish [the tongue of the European ghettos]—he got the job."

Yaacov's bitterness was compounded when he met an attractive girl of Greek background and, after a year of courtship, her parents blocked the marriage. Soon afterward, happily, he had better luck with a pretty kindergarten teacher in the neighborhood. It took months before she permitted him to kiss her; this, says Yaacov approvingly, "showed she was serious."

At the time he was recalled to his tank unit, Yaacov was unemployed and vaguely discontented. He had been spending a lot of time hooting at melodramas in cheap movie houses, and attending protest rallies demanding more recreational facilities for the youth of Hatikvah. Although his faith in a just God was superficially intact, it was undeniably diluted by comparison with that of his parents; "each generation," he observed, "has its own challenges and its own spokesmen."

No such reservations attended his feelings about fighting for Israel: "I knew that if we didn't fight we would be a ghetto people again. And if we lost, it would be worse than under the Nazis."

Yaacov went to war somewhat scornful of the Arabs—"they don't change, they have no education"—but hating nobody. For Israel, he wanted only peace. For himself, his deepest yearning was toward a home he could call his own, with room for family and friends and the luxury of solitude—very much the kind of home, in fact, that Azgad Yellin had enjoyed all his life.

Azgad—the name is biblical, and means "lucky-strength"—was a

Israel Information Services

Major Avihu, seen through the plexiglass dome of his plane

Brigadier General Mordechai Hod, commander of the Air Force

Brigadier General Israel Tal, Chief of Armored Forces

(Left to right) Major General Chaim Bar-Lev, Deputy Chief of Staff of the Army during the Six-Day War; Major General Yitzchak Rabin, Chief of Staff; and Brigadier General Ezer Weizmann, Army Chief of Operations and former commander of the Air Force

David "Dudu"

Robert Szereszevski in 1964 (above) and in June, 1967 (center rear)

Shaari Zedek Hospital, Jerusale
A shelter in Shaari Zedek Hospital during the Jordanian shelling of Jerusalem

K. Weiss, Jerusalem

Esther Arditi Zalinger in battle dress

At Kibbutz Dan: (above) Josi and Rachel Levari with their sons during a weekend, and (below) Davidke sorting pears

Colonel Mordecai "Mota" Gur

Moshe Ben-Tsur, Mota Gur's driver, the day after the capture of the Old City. The Dome of the Rock is in the background.

Cornell Capa, © 1968 Magnum Photos

Noah being congratulated by David Ben-Gurion on the Temple Mount,
Wednesday morning, June 7

The tank crew at the Suez Canal: gunner Evik Ben-Bassat (second from left);
Yaacov Basil, gun-loader and radioman; and driver Dani Tal

Yaacov Basil

Azgad Yellin, commander of the

Fighting in the Sinai, near Abu Agheila.
This photograph was taken by Yaacov Basil.

Sargeant Yaacov Handleman of the Golani Brigade

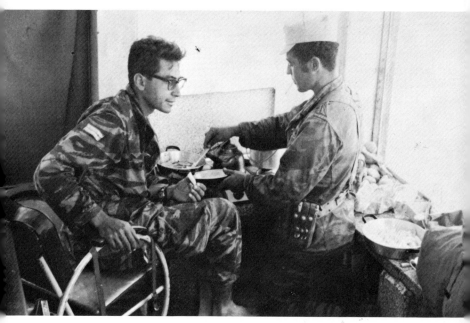

"The Professor," William "Moshe" Horn (left)

Jacqueline Ochayon

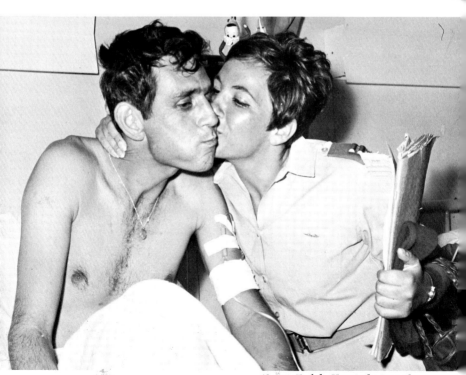

Shaari Zedek Hospital, Jerusalem

Karni Bilu on rounds at Hadassah Hospital. Her friend is
the first man from Mota Gur's brigade to be wounded.

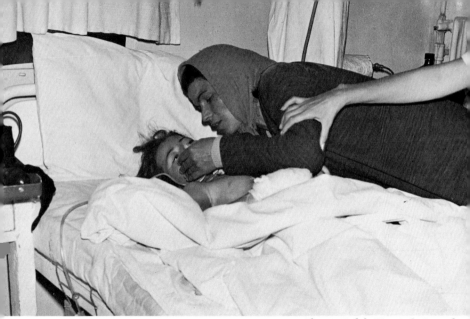

Shaari Zedek Hospital, Jerusalem

Arab mother who believed that her daughter was dead sees that she is alive. Nurse at Shaari Zedek Hospital tries to keep the mother from disturbing the child's tracheal pipe.

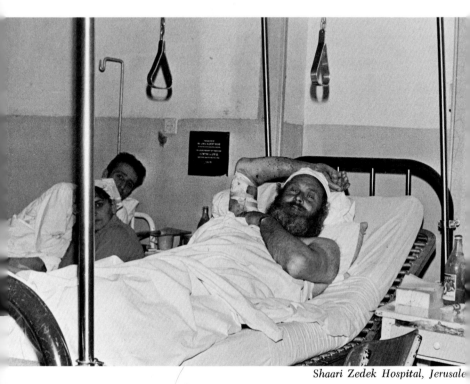

Shaari Zedek Hospital, Jerusale

Eliezer Eckstein recuperating in Shaari Zedek Hospital

fifth-generation sabra whose great-grandfather founded the country's educational system. His father, a militant Haganah fighter jailed for several years by the British, later became one of the leading plant managers in Israel, supervising a thousand employees at a factory in Ashkelon. In recent years, the Yellens have occupied a spacious modern villa in Zahala, a Westchester-like suburb of Tel Aviv popular among senior army officers, past and present.

Azgad, like Dudu Sela, had a tempestuous boyhood, clashing constantly with school authorities and with his quiet, studious older brother David. At seven, he would throw "anything in sight"; lowering his head, he would bull fearlessly into ten-year-old David. Azgad's father ended their brawls by hiring a boxing instructor; obliged to fight "properly," Azgad became bored.

He was a brilliant mathematics student, but resisted efforts to make him work harder in the humanities. The high-school principal who tried to push him in this direction complained, "The boy looks at me as if he could kill—but he says nothing." Azgad got by in history and languages through enforced briefings by his literary-minded mother. His main pleasure came from tinkering with machinery and building models.

At seventeen, the simmering-down process was under way. He had an intense romance but dropped it when the girl urged marriage; he felt he had to find his own direction first. A year later he was in the army. Like his father and older brother, he became a reservist tank officer.

Azgad went to war determined to make it "the last one for Israel, to win such a smashing victory that the enemy would understand it does not pay to attack us." He was a stocky boy. His round face, snub nose and light curly hair gave him the appearance of a surly cherub—till he started to speak, when an abrupt decisiveness emerged.

Reporting to his platoon in the Negev, Azgad needed all the assets he could bring to bear. Even if he had been ten years older, his job would not have been easy. For one thing, there were his antecedents. Kibbutzniks like Dani and Evik tended to look upon city-bred boys as soft, spoiled, vaguely incompetent. The fact that Azgad's family lived in a plush upper-bracket suburb hardly made him more endearing.

Then there were the desert conditions, nibbling away at morale during the long, dragging wait for a political decision. Negev summers are as fierce as those of the neighboring Sinai. From early morning to late afternoon there was no refuge from the searing sun. Some days brought the khamsin, a stifling wind-blown blanket of hot, motionless air. The only visitors to the encampment were gnats, flies and mosquitoes.

The other tankists had at least the advantage of mutual familiarity. The social framework was the company, whose various platoons had trained together for two and a half years, spent their leaves together, and in many cases formed lasting friendships. As reservists, they often saw each other on vacations; they knew each other's tastes and habits.

Azgad had a helpful briefing from the commander he was replacing. And, during the first couple of days, Dani acted as a bridge to the other men.

Then Evik joined the crew. Already annoyed because his mobilization had been delayed by a technical slip-up, proud of his reputation as a tankist "sniper" able to pinpoint his long-range cannon fire, Evik did not take kindly to new supervision. Soon he had swung his fellow kibbutznik, Dani, to his side, and Azgad was locked in a subtle tug of war with his crew. His main concern was his own short temper; loss of control would be disastrous.

The duel ended, curiously enough, after he dealt successfully with a recalcitrant elsewhere in the platoon. Another of his reservist gunners, a lawyer, had been clamoring for action—until the news of Egyptian concentrations on the border became really ominous. The lawyer suddenly developed crises that "required" his presence at home. Turned down, he went on strike. Azgad was boiling, but refused to be drawn into a shouting match. Finally the lawyer resorted to the extreme provocation of ignoring a direct order, but Azgad kept his peace and quietly referred the matter to higher authority.

His self-possession was duly noted in the platoon. There were no other disciplinary problems.

Gradually Azgad's crew came to know and respect him. The scrupulously equal sharing, whether of tedious housekeeping duties or of the occasional much-welcomed food package from home, was a binding force.

Still, the daily strain kept nerves on edge. With an Egyptian air strike a constant possibility, the men had to stick close to their camouflaged tanks, ready to move on two-minute warning. The heat was devastating; often the crew preferred to forgo a meal rather than send one man on a three hundred-yard trek to the mess tent.

The monotony paralyzed mental processes. As Azgad wrote in a letter home, "We have to think twice to remember what day in the week it is." Will power dissolved; it became harder to enforce orders against the taking off of boots than it would have been to launch a general attack.

Unexpectedly, it was Yaacov who saved the situation. Behind the heavy-lipped brooding mask of the Yemenite's face was the soul of a natural comic. Yaacov found something for agile mimicry in the eccentric slouch of the supply major, the fruity baritone of the radio announcer from Tel Aviv, even in the gnats. Suddenly self-proclaimed "cultural officer" of the platoon, he chased the doldrums with everything from acrobatics off the tank turret to torch songs.

His specialty was the meal-time prayer, delivered in the quivering quarter-tone wail of the Orient but spiced with modern twists in the text. Over a "table" set on a canvas tank cover in the middle of the desert, Yaacov would chant a blessing to precede the drinking of water, but instead of ending on the original phrase "according to God's will," he would wind up with a deadpan "let everything arrive inside my belly."

In more solemn mood, he would invoke the words of Shabadi, a famous medieval Yemenite poet, raising his voice in a high-strained wail that a listener with eyes closed would swear was coming from an Arab muezzin perched in a minaret: "Help me, my God, to overcome my enemies; help me to find victory in war."

Evik and Dani, forgetting their ingrained resistance to religious ritual, were enchanted. After a few days, they wouldn't start their meal without a blessing from Yaacov.

Thus encouraged, the Yemenite boy expanded his repertoire. Confessing that he had "always wanted to be an entertainer"—his family included a well-known café singer and "the great Suleiman," a noted campfire stroller—Yaacov launched into the wild, nasal style of Yemenite girl performers, suggestive of the free desert wind. He next held his listeners with the nimble, lively rhythms of "The Police Van," a song of underground days; then switched to a plaintive love song learned during his brief stay in army prison: "I see your hair flowing in the wind. . . ."

On the Saturday evening before the war, the platoon gathered around a campfire. "Somehow," Azgad recalls, "we sensed this would be our last chance to relax together." Yaacov, home that day on leave, had brought back a jug of wine. The men talked and harmonized, starting with old melodies of 1948 and 1956. Then they joined in new songs like "Nasser Is Waiting for Rabin," Chaim Hefer's ironic parody of a popular folk tune, in which the Egyptian dictator is assured that Israel's highest-ranking soldier will accept his invitations to battle. Once again, predicts the song, a beaten Nasser will "shout ay-ay-ay, as he did in Sinai." It was after 2:00 A.M. when Azgad, Dani, Evik and Yaacov stretched out in their sleeping bags beside the Centurion.

A day later they were at war. The command to the platoon's drivers came from Azgad at 2:30 A.M.: *"Nuah . . . nuah . . . sof!"* ("Move . . . move . . . end message!"). Azgad's lead Centurion rolled forward under a thin bright moon.

For him and his crew, there was the chill of anticipation, the relief of action at last, and something else: an awareness of the challenge laid down by the preceding generation, the veterans of 1948. Each boy expressed it differently (for Evik, it was an annoyance with "rumors" concerning the "bad reputation" of some of his peers); but all felt it keenly.

The tanks rumbled due west, in single file, along the paved highway cleared earlier by Sharon's troops. It was the coolest hour of the desert time-cycle. For Azgad at least, riding in the open turret at twenty-one miles an hour, there was a pleasant breeze.

As they approached the battered Egyptian defense area around Abu Agheila, the first pink light was beginning to spread over the desert. The tank unit fanned out, advancing over a mile-and-a-half front across the dune-covered sands alongside the road. Sharon had smashed the three-layered enemy fortifications at Um-Kattef, but nobody knew exactly how much Egyptian armor was still dispersed in the region.

The lurching of the vehicles made it difficult to focus binoculars. Dropping his glasses, Azgad peered through the dust churned up by his tank tracks. Just north of the crossroads at Abu Agheila, he saw a long gun barrel poking up behind a low hill some 130 yards away. He knew it had to be part of an enemy tank: "Big cannon don't fly around in the desert."

He knew also that the Egyptians must have spotted him, probably as much as a minute before. Enemy tanks habitually held good firing positions in this undulating terrain, bunkered hull-down, their yellowish paint blending with the sands. They had a commanding view of the Israelis advancing over the rises, heralded by billowing clouds of dust.

Azgad didn't know, or pause to meditate on, why the Egyptians hadn't opened fire. For the moment he was a sitting—or creeping —duck. He swung his gun turret rapidly toward the target, simultaneously issuing orders over the inter-com to his crew: "Gun . . . armor-piercing shell . . . four hundred meters . . . you're on it . . . fire!"

Azgad had heard reports that Evik was the best gunner in the company, but there had been no practice with live ammunition during the wait in the Negev; now he would find out.

For Evik, there was one terrible moment as he swiftly checked his range. Staring straight into the gun barrel of a now-visible T-34, he realized he was squarely in the sights of the Egyptian gunner. In western movie parlance, the enemy clearly "had the drop" on him.

Evik made his adjustments and fired. The whole process, from the time Azgad began speaking, had taken two or three seconds.

The Russian-made T-34 shuddered and spun around, nailed by a direct hit in the engine. Egyptian crewmen scrambled out. Evik, fascinated, watched the bizarre spectacle of men tearing off their boots to run more freely through the flourlike sand. A moment later the T-34's fuel tanks caught fire, and the whole vehicle was in flames.

A second Egyptian tank came into view. This time Evik had an easier job. "Now I knew the range—the problem is always the range. I just had to move a little to the left, and there he was." Once more Evik's shell caught the engine at the rear of the tank, disabling it completely. He would have preferred to hit the turret with its gun controls; "but if you miss the turret, it's not bad to hit the engine." Azgad knew he had a good gunner.

Now the tempo of battle mounted. Scattered apparently at random all through the eastern desert were Egyptian troop carriers, ammunition trucks, groups of infantry, the headless remnants of defeated brigades.

The advancing Israelis sped past clumps of enemy soldiers lying motionless on hilltops. Soon Azgad discovered that the "corpses" were letting the Israeli tanks roll by, only to snipe from behind. He brought Evik's machine gun into play. Evik fired at a patch of moving khaki two hundred yards away, and suddenly the silent mound came alive with men—firing, running, shouting. Evik picked them off one by one.

According to Azgad, the act of killing is less traumatic for a tank-ist than for a foot soldier. "I can give the order to kill a man half a mile away from me, without even seeing his face. It becomes imper-sonal, like squashing a fly."

Senior Israeli commanders, intent on trapping the splintered Egyp-tians, improvised swiftly on the battlefield. Azgad's force, shifted south of Abu Agheila, caught up with a substantial formation of enemy armor. In the brief, fierce clash—some dozen tanks on either side—Evik knocked out another T-34 at a range of nearly a mile.

Next, Azgad was sent to help block off the mouth of a canyon leading westward. Truckloads of Egyptians, heavily armed but ap-parently unable to organize an effective stand, were tumbling over each other in an attempt to squeeze through.

Sometimes, along the swirling front, it was enemy forces who suddenly held the upper hand. Late Tuesday afternoon, from a mountain trail on the way to Ismailia, an Israeli reconnaissance group flashed a radio S O S: fuel almost gone, they were hemmed in by a large formation of Egyptian armor.

An Israeli pilot, leading a ground-support mission against targets farther west, picked up the signal. Changing course, he tracked down the beleaguered unit—first on the map, then on the ground. Hiding in wait for them behind the dunes at the end of the trail were no less than thirty-five Egyptian tanks, including a number of giant Stalins.

The pilot summoned reinforcements from his squadron and swooped low, cannons blazing. In ten minutes his flight knocked out sixteen tanks. A second follow-up formation destroyed or dis-persed the rest. The pilot was the unflappable deputy squadron leader, Major Avihu.

Avihu had not seen his family since early Monday. He had been virtually living in his Mystère fighter, sharing a squadron *élan* that was irrepressible. Later in the first morning's action there had been some bad moments on return runs over the Egyptian airfields—"when you see a hail of fire streaming up at you, you *have* to be frightened." His squadron leader had been hit by a MIG exploding on the ground, and he himself had caught a shell in the right wing; but he had simply flashed a warning to his No. 2 to change course, and then kept on fighting.

So had the younger pilots, frequently in spite of injuries. Men grounded for treatment refused hospitalization, chafing at the minutes lost while they were patched up on the spot. One boy, ordered home with a severe arm wound, hid his bandages under his coveralls and tried to slip back onto the flight schedule.

By Monday afternoon, the squadron had shifted to ground-support action over the Sinai, less spectacular but more personally rewarding. Here there was tangible evidence that the pilots, even though far removed from the grime and sweat of the bearded infantrymen below, were part of the same war, an indispensable aid to their comrades. Too often combat flying had a quality of detachment, like a medieval joust; shooting down a MIG once in a reprisal raid over Syria, Avihu had peered back, hoping against himself to see his enemy bail out successfully. Perhaps one felt this kinship because aerial combat was such a lonely business, removed from higher command, on both sides.

Avihu knew also that it was flying itself that he enjoyed, not killing. His biggest thrill in the Sinai came when he soared above the wild peaks where Moses had communed with God. All he sought for Israel was "what we couldn't have for the past twenty years, or for that matter the past two thousand: a chance to develop in peace." One simply couldn't be trampled upon; perhaps if the Jews in the Spanish Inquisition or the Warsaw ghetto had been equipped with Mirages and Mystères, "the slaughter wouldn't have been so easy."

Operations continued all through Tuesday night, with hundreds of Egyptians taken prisoner. Several times, Azgad crossed paths with his older brother David, commanding another reservist platoon in the same tank battalion. "We waved to each other through the bullets."

By Wednesday morning, Azgad's battalion had driven sixty-five miles westward to Gebel Libni. The static Egyptian defenses had been cracked, but there were still enormous enemy forces spread through the central Sinai. The next Israeli move was to cut off and destroy. Down from brigade headquarters came a new order, splitting up the battalion. The vanguard tanks were to head directly for the Mitla Pass.

Azgad's task force followed the Bir Hasana–Bir el Thamada highway in a deep southwestern arc. Miles of tumbling dunes, barren hills and craggy mountains stretched between them and the entrance to the pass. From 10 A.M. to four in the afternoon, the sun was murderous. Rest was out of the question; in five minutes the men were drenched with sweat. It was easier for them to keep moving; then there was some hint of an air flow.

Early morning brought the flies; late afternoon, sandstorms. The only respite came in the cool starry night; but by then the tankists were slogging on mechanically, numbed to sensation.

They stopped only to refuel or reload. For two days, Azgad touched no food, although he drank water constantly. It was a case of drink or die. At every stop, he pitched in, carrying jerricans to the fuel tanks and loading the heavy shells: "If you left them all to one man, he'd break." As it was, the loader in his cramped compartment had a hard ride. Several times, careening over gullies, he had to ward off twenty-five pound projectiles that threatened to tumble down on his head.

The wild sprint toward the pass was less of a strain for Evik. Opposition in this area was relatively sparse, and he had a place to sit. Several times, lulled by fumes from gunpowder and fuel as well as by the onward rush of the tank, he was able to doze off.

Once, reflecting on the possibility of being killed, he diverted himself by speculating, à la Tom Sawyer, on how it would be to return to his kibbutz afterward and eavesdrop on his comrades' eulogies. But generally he felt very secure in the tank.

Dani, of course, carried the main burden. For him the pressure on eye and leg muscles, the nervous tension, the maddening racket of the engine never let up. His throat was constantly parched, his hands blistered. After a long run of driving, he had to be helped out of the cab, bent over like an aged arthritis victim into a crablike posture.

Dani longed for an hour of quiet, for the utter, peaceful quiet of the sheep-covered hills surrounding his home. Often he thought of his family: his slender black-eyed wife Maya with her saucy boyish hairdo and her quick, understanding glance, his little girl of three and his infant boy. "Whenever we stopped, or I had a stretch of straight road, I was longing for them, wanting to see them, wondering what they were doing."

Late Thursday, Azgad reached the entrance to the pass. He found an incredible melee there: a Times-Square-on-New-Year's-Eve mass of churning tanks, trucks and half-tracks; of jeeps, gun carriers, supply vehicles, everything imaginable on wheels. It was all Egyptian, with one important exception. Elements of Yoffe's First Brigade, which had left the Negev before Azgad, had arrived earlier at the mouth of the pass and were successfully blocking it from Egyptian entry.

The pass itself, however, was still a no man's land, crammed with powerful Egyptian units. The military post at Sharm el Sheikh at the other end of the peninsula had been captured the day before, breaking the blockade of the Tiran Strait. To complete the Sinai victory, Israel had to control the Mitla artery and the banks of the Canal. A cease-fire was in the wind, so the time factor was urgent.

The task force headed by Azgad's platoon paused at the entrance only long enough to confirm their mission, then charged ahead without refueling. Azgad found himself in a narrow road, with high cliffs on either side and smashed or stalled vehicles in front of him. Some were burning from Israeli air attack; some had overturned in a desperate attempt to evade air pursuit or to circumvent obstacles blocking the road. He pushed the first couple of trucks aside, using the tank as a bulldozer. "We simply climbed over them, flattening out what was left of chassis and axles."

It was slow, difficult going. Dani, his narrow field of vision further restricted by the twists in the road, was completely dependent on Azgad's directions. There was the constant danger of getting stuck or turning over, sometimes a matter of centimeters. There were Egyptian mines, open and buried, to be evaded.

Deeper into the pass, Azgad found himself alone among scores of enemy tanks, big guns thrust menacingly forward. It was impossible to tell which ones were still manned. Many were quite new, with Russian markings. But they didn't shoot. Apparently their crews were still dazed from Israeli air attacks.

Azgad was determined to keep them that way. "If they ever pulled themselves together, they could wipe us out. The important thing was to get a complete force through the pass, show the Egyptians that we were on both sides and that they were locked in, beaten, with no way out."

Evik was baffled by the passivity of the Egyptian armor. "We must have passed a hundred tanks in good working condition. With a third that number, they could have overwhelmed us."

Azgad fired only when he had to. As soon as they reached some recently-bombed troop carriers, this became quite often. Infantry soldiers were scurrying all over the canyon, trying to get away from burning trucks. They swarmed around the tank, some of them firing.

Azgad tried to let Evik answer their fire. "It's easier for a man looking through a periscope to shoot. It's like a camera lens; you don't have direct contact. Facing your enemy with the naked eye is a much rougher experience."

It was one he could not avoid. "They started coming at me, eight or ten feet away. I had to use my Uzzi, again and again. It was my life or theirs."

Once he had a vivid close-up glimpse of the man he was shooting. "He was young, we could have been playing soccer together." It was one of the hardest moments of the war for him.

Zigzagging around hairpin bends, Azgad was aware that he might plunge head-on into ambush. "Momentum was everything. If the Egyptians ever saw that Israeli tanks too could hesitate, they might take heart and rally."

Azgad was nearing the end of the canyon when, grinding around a sharp curve, he found himself looking into the muzzle of a T-34 planted farther down the road. He wheeled his gun turret around and shouted a command to Evik. A fraction of a second later, machine-gun bullets spattered into the cliffs over Azgad's head. They came from an angle to the left of the T-34. Straining his eyes, Azgad saw that the tank was empty; but soaring up behind it was a MIG-19. The Egyptian pilot had dived and missed. It had been a clever try. Stopping the Centurion on that bad turn would have tied up the whole Israeli advance.

Half an hour later, as a fiery sun dropped below the horizon, the Israeli tank force emerged from the western end of the pass. They found two companies of T-54's and T-55's waiting in ambush, commanding the final approaches to the Canal. The Egyptians held strong firing positions on either side of the road.

The Israelis spread out for battle. After an inconclusive tank exchange, Azgad radioed his battalion commander for an appraisal of the situation. He was told that a cease-fire was definitely under way; if they didn't reach the Canal within an hour, the entire operation would be a failure.

Azgad turned up his lights and charged full-tilt down the road, heading straight for the Egyptian gantlet. The other Centurions followed in single file. The enemy tanks broke formation and lumbered away.

Turning abruptly left at the Canal, Azgad made the final dash down its eastern bank and continued south along the shore of the Gulf of Suez. By 8:20 P.M. he had reached his objective, Ras el Sudar (Cape Sudr), a winter resort on the edge of major Egyptian oil fields. The last elements of the task force had scarcely disembarked from their tanks when word came that Nasser had formally quit.

At Ras el Sudar, Dani got a whole hour of sleep, his first in three days. Yaacov, who had been living on chocolate bars and water, had a hot meal. And Azgad acquired peace of mind. Since leaving the central Sinai he had heard persistent rumors that his brother David's company had been ambushed, with heavy casualties. Now David's unit pulled into camp, intact, and the brothers were reunited.

But other elements of Yoffe's two brigades had not been so lucky. His losses were considerable. Typically, 25 percent of the dead and wounded were from the kibbutzim.

A gleaming silver crescent, shiny-smooth as old sterling, hung over the blue-green waters of the gulf. Yaacov Basil slumped back against the trunk of a languidly swaying palm and kicked off his boots. He had never dreamed there could be such luxury in the simple act of removing one's shoes.

Yaacov felt wonderful, at peace with the desert night, with himself and with the past. Like the ancient Hebrew warriors, he and his comrades had fought for survival and won; in the long historical caravan of Jewry, he was a small but equal unit.

Everything was as it should be. Even his employment problem would straighten itself out. It might take a little longer than if he were a European, but ultimately he would find work.

Yaacov closed his eyes. His last waking thought was of the gentle, quietly merry girl waiting for him at home, so satisfactorily assembled, so appropriately named. She was called Tikvah, "hope."

Azgad trudged along the bank of the shimmering gulf. The white sand, stubbled with patches of grass, was pleasantly firm after the soggy footing of the desert. Azgad had just finished a two-hour reunion with his brother David, and he had many impressions to sort out.

First, there was the staggering news about Shamai Kaplan, the regular-army officer who had been his superior at the Tank Commanders' School. Although only twenty-eight, Shamai was accepted as an equal in the councils of senior army officers, a rare combination of leader and comrade for whom even Azgad had suspended his usual aversion to hero worship.

Shamai was dead, killed in the turret of his Centurion the day before by an Egyptian bullet through the heart after he had destroyed seven of thirty mammoth T-55's intercepted by his small task force.

Shamai the kindly, the wise . . . It was incredible, irrational, cruel. Shamai was a husband and father, with another child on the way. How would his young wife stand up under the shock? How could she?

For the second time that day, Azgad found himself reflecting on the possible supportive powers of religion. A few hours earlier, about to plunge into the caldron of Mitla Pass, he had suddenly thought, "How much easier this would be for a believing man, who could tell himself that God would be watching out to protect him." He had promptly dismissed the idea as irrelevant; it was perfectly plain, in the face of these flames and spitting cannon, that nothing but his own skill and courage could carry him and his crew through the canyon.

Yet, after they arrived safely at Ras el Sudar, the notion of religiosity lingered. Like most of his fellow sabras, Azgad had grown up with the feeling that religion was a needful cement in the past, when Jewry was scattered; with the establishment of Israel, the nation itself took over the binding role. Formal observance was suitable to ghettos and suffering minorities, but not to the free Israeli.

In the past year or two, however, Azgad's views had softened somewhat. He had previously ridiculed the Passover service as childish. Recently, reading it carefully for the first time, he was obliged to admit that it had its points. Perhaps he and his sabra friends, in their self-conscious rebellion against the past, were overreacting, just as they had to parental idealism.

His generation had long chafed under reminders of their privileged position and the parental sacrifices that purchased it. The young people felt vaguely, and unfairly, accused; they considered it only natural that, with statehood won, they should have less specific goals than their elders, fewer spurs to total idealism. Many reacted by jeering at overt sentimentality and "old-fashioned" nationalism. Yet in their hearts they were troubled.

Time after time before the war, Azgad had driven through Bab-el-Wad, the steep-walled canyon on the Tel Aviv–Jerusalem highway where Arab ambushers took a terrible toll of Israeli convoys in 1948. Passing the burned-out shells of old armored cars, the pathetic fading wreaths, he had felt quiet envy of an older generation who had known such challenges, and been tested under fire.

Now, treading the conquered shore of the waterway, he knew he would never have that feeling again. He recalled his sensations Tuesday morning at the sight of the Israeli tank armada sweeping like a huge cloud across the desert—"Here come the sons of the biblical warriors"—and he knew his generation had proved itself, had established that it was not inferior to its predecessor in values or performance. A misunderstanding had been wiped out, and a continuity of values restored.

The cost had been considerable, and the struggle against the Arabs was not yet ended. A people brainwashed in hatred might embroil his own sons as well. But at least he had not betrayed the standards of Shamai Kaplan; he could hold his head high in the presence of his father.

Seventy-five miles to the north, on the captured right bank of the Canal opposite Ismailia, a forty-one-year-old businessman-soldier was also reassembling his thoughts. Standing on the terrace of an abandoned villa, surrounded by night-jasmine fragrances and implausible greenery, Regimental Sergeant Major Amnon Lor was shaving by candlelight, a straight trim figure in grimy British battle dress of another era. As he scraped away at a thick tangle of beard, Lor pondered many things: man's need for physical comforts (definitely exaggerated); the waywardness of human nature (one moment brutally callous, the next overflowing with compassion); the quality of Israeli youth (appearances could be marvelously misleading).

Three weeks previously, almost to the minute, Lor had been in executive session at the quietly elegant Carlyle Hotel, favored as the New York residence of American presidents since the days of Harry Truman. Lor, a leading corporation executive in Israel whose holdings include metal and cardboard manufacture, had been in the United States for about two weeks, moving serenely through New York's loftiest financial circles. In appearance, he was the complete international businessman, indistinguishable from his American and European colleagues: tall, pleasant-looking, unchallengeably urbane in dark oxford suit with white shirt and blue tie. His black hair was closely cropped, his small reddish mustache neatly clipped above a firm smiling mouth.

On May 19, Lor met with an associate at the new Regency Hotel on Park Avenue before proceeding downtown to arrange the transfer of several millions from a Swiss bank affiliated with his group.

Twenty-four hours later, Amnon Lor was in a trench on the Israeli-Egyptian border. He had exchanged his luxurious park-view suite for a sleeping bag. Instead of parlaying with captains of industry, he was briskly relaying the orders of a twenty-four-year-old army captain.

In between, Nasser had ejected the United Nations peace-keeping force in the Sinai. Lor promptly flew home to Tel Aviv—first class, of course, as a matter of habit—to find mobilization orders waiting. Without pausing to chat with his wife or two teen-age daughters, he changed into uniform and headed for his unit in the Negev.

As a holder of the highest noncommissioned rank in the Israeli Army, Lor was directly attached to the colonel commanding his battalion. He had come by his army responsibilities the hard way. Born into an orthodox family from the ancient cabalistic center of

Safad in the Galilee, he had been an underground fighter at thirteen; a ship repairman and welder during World War II; an infantryman, M.P. instructor and improviser of armored cars during the War of Independence.

In 1956, Lor was with a field artillery unit supporting infantry. This time, his battalion handled the light AMX tank, converted into a kind of mobile artillery for the support of larger armor by removal of its turret and the mounting on its hull of a 105 mm. gun. In its Israeli version, the French-built AMX has a respectable range of nearly nine miles, but can be fired only from a stationary position because of the severe recoil.

Lor's job as Regimental Sergeant Major included going along with scouting parties to search out firing positions that would be secure from enemy counterbatteries. He then relayed the positioning orders to the AMX commanders, and continued to the rear to ensure proper delivery of ammunition, personally leading supply trucks back to the battlefield. He was also expected to make spot decisions on such matters as the evacuation of wounded and the silencing of sniper fire.

Operating in support of Tal's northern division, Lor's battalion crossed the border on Monday afternoon into the Gaza Strip, where fighting was especially bitter. They reached El Arish the next day (en route, Lor negotiated the surrender of three hundred Yugoslavs at a U.N. camp), then cut south to join the big tank battles at Bir Lahfan and Bir Gifgafa.

For three days, Lor didn't eat. For twelve, he had no contact with a razor. The immaculate industrialist had been converted into an unkempt, red-eyed figure not likely to be recognized—or welcomed —in the lobby of the Carlyle Hotel.

What startled Lor was the ease and complacency with which the transformation had been effected. Normally the most fastidious of men, who in New York or Tel Aviv would send back a plate of soup with a speck in it, he had lunched that afternoon within three feet of a blackened corpse. Lacking a fork, he had not bothered to slice his canned meat with a knife but, like the others, had dug into it with his dirty fingernails and stuffed it straight into his mouth. Then he had wiped off his hands on his trousers and started shooting again.

Fighting, Lor reflected, a man emptied his head of all thoughts. He became possessed by a single impulse: to advance, shoot, wipe out any targets in the way. Everything else was forgotten: food, drink, family . . . and centuries of culture. Lor recalled an orthodox boy in his unit, usually shy and thoughtful, the quintessence of kindness. In the Sinai, the boy had gone rampaging through the trenches, in search of snipers to shoot at.

Earlier in the evening, Lor had been discussing this behavior with his commanding colonel. "You see," he theorized, "every man has something of the beast in him. Usually, it's kept under control—by social restraints, personal inhibitions. If you're in a restaurant and the drunk at the next table becomes obnoxious, you might want to swing at him—but you don't.

"In battle, however, the small animals within you become giants. They take over. You do things you ordinarily wouldn't dream of —and not just killing. Stealing becomes commonplace, part of some instinct for survival that has been released. It's as if by owning something, you feel more secure.

"You really revert to the cave-man state—and the worst of it is, you don't mind."

Yet, the whole process could be suddenly reversed. A single stab of recognition could pierce the wall of indifference. It could never come from the sight of death: a corpse had no more impact than a burned-out tank, or a rock in the sand. But a live man, going up in flames across the hood of a half-track or writhing in agony on the ground . . .

He thought back to the second morning of the war, at the height of the struggle for El Arish. His AMX unit had just taken up firing stations in an abandoned Egyptian Army camp at the outskirts of the town. Driving out through the gate, Lor saw a young soldier lying beside a Russian rifle on the ground—evidently the enemy sentry. Lor stopped to investigate. The Egyptian was a boy of eighteen or nineteen, clean-shaven and even-featured. The phrase that flashed through Lor's mind was "sweet-looking."

Blood poured from the soldier's ears, nose and mouth. Stooping, Lor saw that he had been shot in the shoulder, lung, liver and leg; judging from the stitched pattern of the wounds, by a submachine gun. He had probably been bleeding profusely for half an hour.

The boy shuddered slightly, evidently in shock. Lor concluded that death was a matter of minutes away, and that the soldier was suffering acutely. Perhaps it would be an act of kindness to end his agony. Lor hesitated, his hand halfway toward his revolver.

At that moment, the soldier raised his head. "*Awuz doctor*," he whispered in Arabic ("I want a doctor").

The instant he spoke, everything changed for Lor. The Israeli forgot his gun, went over to the youth and lifted his head. Taking some water from his canteen, Lor moistened the Egyptian's lips with his hand; with those internal injuries, drinking was out of the question. "I'm going to get you a doctor," he promised.

Jumping back into his command car, Lor drove to the supply convoy where he found a battalion doctor. "Would you go help an enemy?"

"Are you crazy? I'm a doctor, first."

The doctor came to the fallen Egyptian with two corpsmen. They administered heart-aid injections and plasma transfusions, cleaned the multiple wounds and applied bandages. Three more aides came to help, building a temporary blanket-tent to shield the wounded man from the scorching sun. Then they transported him by helicopter to hospital in El Arish. "He'll make it," the doctor told Lor.

Summing up the incident for his colonel, Lor remarked, "It was as if somebody threw a stick into the middle of a huge revolving wheel and said, 'Stop the war; aid this boy.'"

But one gesture did not make a civilization, and he saw no immediate augury of a more brotherly future. On the contrary, immorality seemed to be flourishing on a widening international scale. He was glad Israeli armor had smashed through to the Canal; it gave his country an ace in the rude struggle for survival that lay ahead.

And he was equally glad for something else he would have been less quick to predict: the caliber of Israel's new young fighters, European and Oriental alike. Supposedly self-centered and materialistic, they had fought as bravely and as well as the soldiers of 1948. Amnon Lor had been among those most skeptical of the "discotheque generation" who had nationhood "handed to them on a silver platter." He was happy to acknowledge that the "platter" was obsolete, overshadowed by the hard steel that in the hands of Israeli youth had reasserted the nation's right to existence.

The Fifth Day

THE SYRIAN HEIGHTS

BY late Thursday evening, the Sinai was secured and the west bank silent. That left in the field only Syria, the most bitterly resented of Israel's enemies and the single hostile force that had escaped trouncing in 1948 and 1956. Most Israelis felt that Syria, more than any other country, had provoked the Six-Day War by its wanton shelling, incessant terrorism, and persistent goading of Nasser. Syrian propagandists had outstripped even Radio Cairo in their savage and intoxicating fantasies; a famous drawing in the Syrian Army publication *Al-Jundi Al-Arabi* showed a pile of skulls, each stamped with a Jewish star, heaped before the ruins of a still-smoking city. It was captioned, "The Barricade in Tel Aviv."

Now, after three days of Arab defeats, Radio Damascus was still spewing its neighborly message: "Miserable Jews, we will pluck out the other eye of your Moshe Dayan. Your army is surrendering everywhere. Jerusalem is burning, Tel Aviv is wiped out. Kill the bastard Zionists."

There was strong Israeli sentiment, in both the government and the army, for dealing decisively with the fanatics at Damascus. Until their fangs were drawn, even the victory at Jerusalem would be clouded.

164

But an attack in the north posed complex problems, political as well as military. The great powers, particularly the Russians, would react badly; nobody knew whether Moscow would be angered to the point of intervening on behalf of its protégés. And the campaign itself was hardly inviting.

Twice the Israelis had been poised to strike. On Wednesday afternoon, cloudy weather forced postponement. By Thursday, Moshe Dayan was having second thoughts about attacking at all. In spite of his reputation for impetuosity, Dayan was extremely cautious about committing men to battle. He was willing enough to gamble on the Soviet response, but not on the ponderous Syrian fortifications. He feared that any attempt to overrun them might lead to wholesale slaughter.

Yitzchak Rabin, the Army Chief of Staff, challenged the Defense Minister's view. He asserted that his men could be in Damascus in thirty-six hours; at a price, to be sure, but one that would be justified by the gain in future security to the state.

The issue engaged two strong men whose relationship was already strained. Dayan's entry into the government had relieved Rabin of intolerable nonmilitary burdens, but at the same time had altered the dominant command role of the Chief of Staff.

Before Dayan's appointment, Prime Minister Levi Eshkol had been running the Department of Defense himself. A renowned economist but inexperienced in military affairs, Eshkol had been unable to rally the cabinet behind him for a vigorous response to Nasser. For more than a week, Rabin had been obliged to shuttle between the impatient military leaders and the hesitant policymakers in Jerusalem, saddled with the responsibilities of a Defense Minister but lacking the corresponding cabinet-level authority.

National morale was sinking rapidly. A ground swell began building for Dayan, an outspoken critic of the government but unquestionably a symbol of resolute action. Eshkol, not anxious to promote the fortunes of a man pledged to topple him from office, temporized, offered Yigael Allon as a compromise candidate, and finally bowed. As Dayan remarked to an American correspondent, "It took eighty thousand Egyptian soldiers to get me back into the government."

The effect on the country was immediate and electric. On June 1, Azgad Yellin's brother David wrote home from the field: "You should have seen how the news of Dayan's appointment electrified people here. It was passed from crew to crew by tankists who heard it during the night. It reminds me of the story about Churchill's return to the Admiralty, when the ships of the British Navy flashed the signal 'Winnie is back' from one to another."

Yitzchak Rabin was free to go back to soldiering—but under new circumstances. He now operated in the shadow of a colorful Defense Minister to whom the news media flocked automatically. The Chief of Staff would have been less than human if he had not somewhat resented being thus elbowed out of the spotlight. Given Rabin's unusual personality, however, he was probably also rather relieved.

Rabin dodges public exposure, the way Dayan glories in it. He has his own kind of quiet authority. Taller and bulkier than Dayan, he is as solid and purposeful as a cathedral. With his high-crested reddish hair, unblinking blue eyes, and thick freckled farmer's forearms, Rabin projects an impression of vast inner strength held tightly in reserve. Dayan is a gleaming sword blade; Rabin a blunt mailed fist.

Like Dayan, Rabin is a nonreligious sabra of Russian stock, trained in the Palmach. He too is a loner with few intimates. But he has strong ties to his family, and no visible drive for political power.

Rabin's shyness has deep roots. The son of passionately dedicated Zionists (his mother, Rosa Cohen, was a member of the Haganah high command), he scarcely saw his parents except on Friday evenings during the early formative years. At the time of the Arab riots in 1929, when Yitzchak was seven, he and a younger sister were looked after by neighbors for weeks. They had difficulty washing at home because the bathroom was stacked with hidden arms and ammunition.

A silent but attentive student, Yitzchak qualified for the prestigious Kadoori Agricultural High School in the Galilee. Like General Douglas MacArthur at West Point, he was graduated with the highest grades ever recorded at the institution. Raised to regard material considerations as "vaguely shameful," he didn't bother to collect the ten-pound prize awarded by the British High Commissioner.

He was to enter the University of California at Berkeley in the fall, to study water engineering on a scholarship from the British mandate government. But that was the spring Hitler attacked the Low Countries; among the minor casualties were Yitzchak's plans.

Within months he had joined the Palmach. His recruiter was a twenty-four-year-old company commander named Moshe Dayan. When the British invaded Syria, Rabin slipped behind the Vichy French lines to cut communications. He remained a soldier for twenty-six years.

Rabin engineered the daring 1944 raid on the British detention camp at Athlit, ascribed in the novel *Exodus* to the fictional Ari Ben-Canaan. Later, disguised as an electrician, he reconnoitered the British Army compound at Jenin, suffering a broken leg that led to imprisonment.

After serving as deputy commander of the Palmach during the War of Independence, Rabin moved up to a variety of top staff jobs, interrupted by field command of the northern forces from 1956 to 1959. He traveled to England, France, the United States, the Far East and Africa.

Between truces in the 1948 fighting, Rabin got married. He found the ceremony more unsettling than running the blockade of Jerusalem. Ill at ease in stiff civilian clothes, Rabin agonized under the public gaze while sweating out the customary wait for the (as usual) delayed rabbi. When the cleric arrived at last and raised his voice cheerfully in booming prayer, Rabin begged him to tone down: people were looking.

Rabin has not mellowed in his attitude toward social ritual over the years. Colleagues say he falls silent before cocktail chatter, "too honest" to engage in the slightest pretense.

For such a man, Leah Rabin has been a splendid buffer. Tall, slim and dark-haired, daughter of a wealthy grain merchant from Germany, Leah radiates easy confidence. She runs an uncomplicated household in suburban Zahala, not far from Azgad Yellin's home. Laundry dangles in the spacious backyard, where a close-cropped lawn is tended by the entire family, which includes Dahlia, seventeen, and her brother Yuval, twelve.

Rabin maintains a grueling schedule, relaxing mainly with his family. He is a loving but undemonstrative father who will call home six times a day when one of the children is ill. His own lonely childhood is still very much with him; he tries to curtail his absences from home, and to share the children's interests, "so that they should not feel the way I did."

For the army, Rabin has been, in the words of the young Israeli poet Amos Ettinger:

> Father and mother for all feelings, emotions, decisions . . .
> For such a father, a young private told me,
> We are ready to excuse one more wrinkle than the
>   last day has brought upon him.

This quality of steadiness, of quiet reliability, has led some people to think of Rabin as an unimaginative plodder. This is a gross misjudgment. He has always been conspicuously daring both as soldier and tactician, with a penchant for the surprise approach and a gift for unconventional exploitation of his weaponry.

In the case of Syria, Rabin had studied the situation in elaborate detail. He was convinced that a bold, concentrated smash could produce a decisive victory before the big powers fully realized what was happening. It was a position fully consistent with his past record.

Similarly, Dayan's hesitance could raise eyebrows only among those unfamiliar with him. He has often been accused of talking from the hip—but never of shooting that way. For all of his dashing image, Dayan is a prudent, even cautious commander who estimates risks carefully before acting. Aides say "every single life" weighs heavily with him. As Defense Minister, he wrote a personal letter to the family of every man killed, but concealed the move until he had gone through the entire list, lest those who had not yet heard from him be offended.

Such warm concern for strangers is startling in a man apparently indifferent to his own family. His novelist daughter, Yael, has sketched a home life through which Moshe Dayan moves like a wraith, unexpectedly appearing and vanishing, showing little emotion except with his two grandchildren. There is a touch of poignancy in Yael's remark, recounted in her 1967 war diary, on the eve of the Sinai fighting: "I don't think anybody in the world, excluding my brother, cares whether I exist or not." Dayan has said openly that people with his kind of political dedication would do better never to marry.

At fifty-four, Dayan has become a little rounder in the face and belly. His hair is thinning; but his magic is not. He presents a combination of Mars and Puck that women find irresistible. Some claim to detect a resemblance to Yul Brynner. Dayan would not be flattered. He is not interested in resembling anyone.

The Dayan brashness, so attractive overseas, arouses mixed feelings at home. Many Israelis who admire Dayan as a soldier question his personal flamboyance; the basic sabra style is understatement. He has the flair for showmanship of a Leonard Bernstein; and, as has been known to happen with Bernstein, his genuine merits are sometimes overlooked by those who cannot forgive his mannerisms.

Dayan sails through these uncertain seas with aplomb. He makes no concessions, and asks none. The country can take him or leave him—as is.

But he can always be diverted by humor, and is quite capable of it himself. When a U.N. official was staggered by a particularly strong Dayan pronouncement, the Defense Minister sympathetically proffered a tray of pills: "Have a vitamin."

Dayan's military thinking is aggressive and original; for instance, he thinks agile little David should have been the odds-on favorite in the celebrated biblical encounter: "Goliath was nothing more than a walking fortress." For his masterminding of the 1956 Sinai campaign, Dayan acquired a global reputation; if he were a chess player, he would be ranked as an international grand master.

Dayan likes to make his own decisions, in solitude and silence. In the early stages of the Six-Day War, he was instrumental in emphasizing the priority of the Sinai front, and in shifting the Israeli objective there from the capture of geographical points to the destruction of Nasser's army. At Jerusalem, he had capitalized instantly on Hussein's truculence.

But still he balked at Syria, the more so when kibbutzim on the vulnerable northeastern border began to exert political pressure for an attack.

In the end, Dayan yielded to the judgment of the cabinet—only to run into an ironic shift by the Syrians. In the small hours between Thursday night and Friday morning, Damascus announced it was accepting the U.N. cease-fire.

The Israelis paused again; this was a new situation. The Syrians themselves obligingly resolved the dilemma. Either because of poor

communications or from sheer habit, they resumed the shelling of
Tel Katzir and two other settlements at 6:00 A.M. An hour later,
Rabin had his go-ahead to attack.

Dayan had good reason for his misgivings. Never before—not by
its Roman strongholds, Crusader towers, Turkish ramparts or British
police posts, had the siege-scarred Syrian battleground been so awe-
somely fortified.

To the natural barrier of the rugged ridge running for forty miles
along the frontier, the Syrians had added tier upon tier of elaborate
defense complexes stretching ten miles into the hinterland. Two
decades of laborious digging, much of it under Soviet supervision,
had sunk bombproof galleries and command quarters twenty and
thirty feet deep into the volcanic stone. The mountain was honey-
combed with gun emplacements, plastered with pillboxes, trenches,
miles of mine fields, and of course barbed wire. In theory, there were
three separate north-south lines extending the length of the plateau,
from Tel Azaziat in the north down to the lonely blockhouses
marking every turn in the road winding westward to the southern
tip of the Sea of Galilee; in practice, Damascus had so crowded the
terrain between the mini-Maginots with camps, launch sites and
tank traps that the entire mountaintop was like a giant plate of
prickly armor.

To cross the border from Kibbutz Gadot in the center of the line
was a voyage into desolation. U.N. observers—the only people to
make the trip before the war—climbed the rickety B'nat Ya'acov
bridge into Syria to find themselves in a bleak forest of mines,
casemates and tank obstacles: thirteen thousand fertile brown acres,
once a major breadbasket of the Mediterranean basin, now sown
only with death. The land breathed a sullen hopelessness, underlined rather than relieved by its occasional pathetic patch of corn.

The contrast with the world left behind—the tilled fields, orderly
fruit groves and glistening fisheries of Israel—was inescapable.
Below the Syrian balcony, the green plain beckoned. There in the
Galilee, the average Arab citizen could look forward to a life span of
seventy-seven years; here, a few miles to the east in Syria, he would
be lucky to reach forty.

Farther south, Syrian garrisons peered down at one of the most magnificent views known to man. The harp-shaped Sea of Galilee, actually a lake, lay serenely cradled among pine-covered foothills, like a sparkling pendant on a gracefully rounded bosom. It was a perfectly proportioned picture, inspiring even without its religious associations. Syrians saw it through a machine-gun slit.

Rimming the eastern shore of Christ's lake were mine fields, climbing up to pillboxes and strong points that continued down through the whitish limestone hills nearly to the three-way border with Jordan and Israel. Here, crossing into the lakeside kibbutzim, guns abruptly gave way to lush groves of date palms, pines and bananas.

The major Syrian citadels along the ridge followed a common pattern. Over some 150 square yards of hillside stood a fortress, an elliptical mass of steel and concrete rooted beneath the ground and sloping upward to its crowning feature, a turreted fifteen-foot gun post with walls five feet thick. Tiers of interlocking trenches, more than seven feet deep and three feet wide, lined with boulders of volcanic stone, zigzagged through the compound. Sometimes the trench walls were mortared to a smooth finish; nearly always the winding passages were protected at strategic points by overhead roofing with curved steel plates.

Each complex was surrounded by a sea of mines, enclosing a ragged perimeter of barbed wire. Directly within was either the lowest row of trenches, sandbagged every twenty feet, or a series of mortar positions behind a high earthen embankment. Camouflaged stone barracks, heavy guns, and more trenches culminated in a network of covered concrete tunnels leading up to the bombproof gun tower. This was totally sealed in, except for narrow gun slits protected against return fire by canted overhanging roofs.

Planted in and around these lethal catacombs in early June were six fully equipped brigades, the cream of Syria's regular army. They were loaded with modern armor and artillery including 350 new tanks. Nearly three hundred fieldpieces, many of them with electronic fire-direction controls, had a collective launching capacity of more than ten tons of shells per minute.

The Syrian force totaled 60,000 men. By conventional military reasoning, the Israelis would need three times that number—180,000 troops—for a successful attack. They had 20,000 available.

Dado Elazar, the slight, soft-spoken Israeli general commanding the north, weighed his possibilities. As an artillery platform and springboard for invasion, the Syrian ridge was bad enough. As a defensive system, it looked just about unbreakable. Israel had complete control of the skies, but the Syrians weren't in the sky. They were embedded beneath it. Mortar shells would bounce like gumdrops off the three-ply shields of concrete, steel and packed earth. Aerial attack might destroy some guns, but it could hardly hope to demolish the mountain. Tanks would have to tear a path almost straight upward across virgin cliffs that were continuously exposed to cannonading from above.

At his disposal remained one element not draftable in Damascus or purchasable in Moscow: men. Against the "impossible campaign" he would pit the irresistible fighter, exploiting the difference in morale between the two armies.

Acting on his long-held conviction that Arabs "give up when you get behind them," Elazar decided to risk everything on a narrow frontal attack designed to crash through into the enemy rear. He chose armored units from the west bank as the hard-ramming spike for the operation. Backing them would be infantry of the Golani Brigade, trained a few years before by Mota Gur, now rivals in toughness of the paratroopers.

The Golani outfits currently under conscription, although officered by Europeans, were predominantly Oriental in the line. Veterans of several knifelike reprisal actions against the Syrians, they were bitterly resentful of the border terrorism, the long cold winter nights they had been obliged to spend in frontier foxholes, and the Syrian goading that most Israelis felt had precipitated the war. But most importantly, the Golani Brigade was a close-knit fighting force, with a tremendous *esprit de corps* that reached down to the smallest unit.

Elazar's friend and fellow Yugoslav, General Chaim Bar-Lev—who has since succeeded Yitzchak Rabin as Chief of Staff—had a theory about the source of Israeli military strength. "It's the spirit of the unit. A man about to do something extraordinary isn't thinking about his children, or the state; he knows somebody must do it to fulfill the mission of the group, or platoon, or tank. You can have two companies that measure up equally in terms of ideology, intelligence, education—yet in one, the performance is consistently much higher. The difference is in cohesiveness—the responsibility of each man toward his comrades."

That's where Elazar was placing his bet. The general had never met Sergeant Yaacov Handleman of Tel Aviv, or even heard Handleman's name. But he knew there was a Yaacov—or two, or three —among the tents of the encamped brigade, checking a rifleman's weapon, helping a recent immigrant to compose a letter home, swapping a jest or a camera.

Handleman was a lithe, tigerish, green-eyed youth with strong overtones of Kirk Douglas: small nose, close-cropped blond hair, narrow waist rising to bulky shoulders, and even the cleft chin, the aftermath of a fist fight during early training. Although Handleman was not a particularly big man, his was a very physical presence; when he slithered catlike through a hotel lobby, eyes alert, powerful shoulders swaying slightly, people instinctively moved back to give him room. Underneath his bland gaze, one sensed a dangerous streak of violence. His voice—hoarse and reedy—did nothing to dispel the impression of menace.

In spring of 1967, Handleman had been a sergeant in Golani for several months. He was the legendary resourceful sergeant-entrepreneur of films and fiction come to life. Nimble-minded, supremely self-sufficient, he was always two jumps ahead of his comrades. In the first days of training, when recruits had to double up to share a tiny pup tent in the Negev, Handleman somehow had a tent all to himself. Desert nights were cold; Handleman somehow had not one blanket, or two, but six. When he read himself to sleep, it was by a gasoline lamp intended for a company commander.

Israeli soldiers eat simply but well: a "sabra breakfast" of hard-boiled eggs, olives, tomatoes, cheese, bread and butter, tea; a big midday meal of meat and vegetables; and a light supper perhaps comprising soup, salad, scrambled eggs and yoghurt. On border patrol, such menus became a happy memory; no one could count on eating at all. Yet Handleman was never taken completely off guard; somewhere in the bottom of his knapsack was a can of sardines or beef, and a package of mysteriously imported British cookies.

Inevitably, he moved up rapidly through the ranks. Any man who could wind up with fifty training bullets when the regular issue was ten, and then proceed to match the company commander with bull's-eye after bull's-eye on the practice range, would have to be noticed. He ran into a brief snag when a fellow soldier disagreed over whose turn it was to mop up the barracks floor, and sharp words led to flailing fists. Both boys were disciplined. But during maneuvers soon afterward, when Handleman was assigned as a message-running orderly, he so distinguished himself that there was no keeping him out of the Corporals' Course.

Here again, under grueling near-battle conditions, he thrust his way to the top. Usually, promotion from corporal to sergeant is a six-month affair. Handleman did it in one.

He proved as adept in looking after his men as he had been in caring for himself. In the Israeli Army, as in most others, the non-com is closer to his men than are the company and platoon commanders. Responsible for a group of ten to twenty soldiers, the sergeant is the man who sees that guns are kept clean, shoes are in good condition, and morale is high. If that means wangling a compassionate leave or straightening out a quarrel, he is expected to do what is necessary. His is the intimate leadership of a playing captain on a baseball team, as against the supervision of a manager on the bench.

This role was pivotal in units like Golani that had a high proportion of Orientals. Many of the newcomers were burdened with problems of finances, complex family relationships, and adaptation to unfamiliar ways. Money was a serious issue. At best, military duty in Israel entails economic sacrifice; for Moroccan and Iraqi boys with no financial reserves, the seven-dollar monthly pay for privates could be a disaster reparable only by welfare aid.

The conscripts quickly discovered that Handleman was in their corner. He would listen sympathetically to their troubles, make suggestions, pull a few pound notes from his own pocket, and, where necessary, go to bat for them with higher authority.

On only one score was he tough with the men in his section: there could be no relaxing of discipline, no scaling-down of military standards. As one of them said, the sergeant "looked not to the right or the left, but straight ahead." A man who neglected to clean his rifle would be awakened three or four times during the night; bleary-eyed, protesting, he would be told "Do it again . . . and again" in harsh, rasping tones that brooked no argument. Handleman had strong feelings about a soldier's obligations to his weapon; his own Uzzi, which never left his side, was "my wife."

A soldier dozing momentarily on guard duty could expect no mercy. Handleman gave him all the punishment that regulations would allow—plus a few reminders of his own. Thereafter, the man stayed awake.

Apart from this, Handleman was a warm and responsive officer. His own equipment was freely available to anybody who needed it: extra shoes, a canteen, even the pirated paratrooper helmet that was his special pride.

He was solid gold on the small personal issues important to the family-conscious Orientals. Was Menachem's favorite uncle ill? Handleman would badger the company commander tirelessly until a two-day pass came through.

Did Avram, brooding in a corner, need help with a letter? Not exactly. It was something a bit more serious. Maybe Yaacov remembered this girl, the one from Tiberias with the teasing eyes? Well, the eyes had been a bit too teasing to resist, somebody had miscalculated, and now there was trouble. "Would you come with me to the captain, Yaacov?"

Handleman ran a tight group, but with a light hand. He had affectionate nicknames for everybody. A boy with pale curly hair was "Sheephead"; a horn-rimmed, scholarly corporal was "the Professor." The young sergeant had put in time at sea, and nautical terms crept into his conversation: "Who's in the galley tonight?" "See if the captain is up aft," "Your turn to swab the deck." Once in a great while he could be persuaded to talk of his adventures in a foreign port, and the others would be enthralled.

But his true credentials were as a leader. The sergeant produced for his men in a pinch, and he knew they would produce for him. Handleman was offered nomination to the Officers' Course, but he turned it down. It would only mean intensive study of tactics, which did not interest him that much. He had more independence of action, and closer contact with the men, right where he was.

Openly admiring of the muscular sergeant was his friend and corporal, "the Professor." William Horn occupied the adjoining cot in the noncom barracks. A gangling, bespectacled six-footer with a gloomy-Hamlet façade, William came from a home that prized scholarship above all. His parents were Polish intellectuals who had met in a Siberian work camp, survived terrible privations, and were married after the war in Germany. William was born in a DP compound at Heidenheim outside Munich.

His mother, daughter of a pious Jew, had been educated, after her own mother's death, in a Catholic convent. Torn by conflicting dogmas, weary of turmoil over race and religion, she now wanted to pursue studies in literature as an emancipated world citizen, a dropout from Judaism. Her husband's surname had already been Westernized; she gave her boy the additional protective coloration of the Norman-Teutonic "William."

They were preparing to emigrate to the United States to begin a new life "not as Jews" when the Korean war broke out. John Horn canceled their passage west. "If I'm going to fight," he told his wife, "let it be for some permanent end to the Jewish wandering."

William was raised as a sabra, but more sheltered than most and with shakier religious underpinnings. As his mother warmed up to Israeli life, and his university-trained father settled into a bookkeeping job, their son acquired the more native-sounding middle name of "Moshe."

William-sometimes-Moshe arrived in the army as a pensive, lyre-playing eighteen-year-old torn by the self-doubts of the scholar. He was dazzled at once by Handleman who, though only a year older, moved on a free and easy basis among the officers. William was amazed at Handleman's sang-froid, whether it was in filching minor equipment from other brigades (considered not only permissible, but a matter for pride) or in volunteering for risky assignments: "Here was a man not afraid of anything." When Handleman was injured in a training mishap, William noted, he never lost his poise, but simply made a calm signal for help.

The sergeant was quietly fond of his dark, brooding friend. He respected William's depth and sensitivity, and borrowed William's paperbacks. Not as oddly matched as they appeared, shy philosopher and blunt man-of-action spent several leaves together in Tel Aviv, where Handleman's casual forays into all kinds of company began to break down his companion's reserve.

Over coffee in a Dizengoff Street café, while watching the weekend parade of Tel Aviv's pretty girls, Handleman could be prodded into a reminiscence or two of his seafaring days: a wild melee in a

South American port touched off by the epithet "dirty Jew"; the solace afforded to the weary traveler by lady attendants in the massage parlors of Tokyo and Singapore.

But for the most part, this side of Handleman's life was held back, locked away from strangers and even from close friends. It was as if the sea held meaning for Handleman too deep and personal to be entrusted to words.

Yaacov was six or seven years old when he first discovered the water. He had grown up in Tel Aviv, a sabra in all but the technicality of birthplace; his mother had brought him from Russia as a babe in arms. The Handlemans were "not rich"; his father, injured when the Germans overran the Ukraine early in World War II, considered himself lucky to land a job as a machine-tool worker. He was a kindly man, placid and retiring, with a tendency to let things ride.

The family lived in North Tel Aviv, in rather cramped quarters where two older brothers tumbled over each other, their parents and Yaacov. The boy felt stifled, restless, vaguely miserable; he was in revolt against something he could not define.

One afternoon some older boys from the neighborhood set out for the Mediterranean seashore a mile or so away; curly-haired little Yaacov trailed along.

The moment the cool water enveloped his body, he felt a surge of elation. This was release, freedom, everything he was searching for. He was a sea animal, delivered to his natural habitat. Swimming came easily, like something remembered.

Soon afterward, virtually in his back yard, he discovered the Hayarkon River. Columbus could not have been more pleased at his first sight of land.

The presence of a river in a crowded residential district was an outcome of Tel Aviv's phenomenal growth. When the city was founded among the sand dunes in 1906, the Hayarkon ran far to its north. With the steady flood of immigration, new housing spread in every direction and finally enveloped the river.

The Hayarkon is a sluggish stream with no pretensions to Mississippi status. Its waters are muddy green and too microbe-ridden for swimming; its banks are not more than one hundred feet apart.

But along those banks are great stands of eucalyptus, providing welcome shade on a suffocating August afternoon. And the glassy surface of the watercourse was ideal for the kind of boating that small boys could manage: rafts and flatbottoms. It was a modest beginning for a sea-roamer, but enough to dream by.

Yaacov had his outlet, doubly necessary because of a disturbing development at home. He had always been close to his mother. Now, at eight, he found that a sister four years younger was making greater claims on her attention; he was no longer the baby. This disappointment he drowned in the refreshing breakers of the Mediterranean and along the leaf-strewn Hayarkon. River and ocean became his real home; the flat was for interludes of food, sleep and study. Yet, he was a scrupulously "good boy," attentive to his lessons at a religious public school, respectful of his obligations at home. "From ten on, I would do my homework after school and then make deliveries for my cousin's laundry. It wasn't a question of starving if I didn't, but it paid for special treats—a cake, a movie, something beyond the necessities."

At about the same period, he joined Gadna Yam, the seagoing branch of the national youth movement. His chest already deepening from hours of competitive swimming, he had no trouble qualifying as an oarsman allowed to take out rowboats. Next step was the somewhat older Sea Scouts, who handled sailing craft if their seamanship was good enough. At thirteen he had his own boat, a fourteen-footer requiring a two-man crew. He ran it smartly before the wind down the coast to Ashdod; made a seven-day voyage to Rash Haniqra at the Lebanese border in the north; and topped off his adolescent adventures with a thrilling dash across the eastern Mediterranean to the island of Cyprus—two hundred miles of flaming sun, spanking breezes and shimmering golden isles, along a route that was old in the days of Alexander the Great.

By now the sea held a new dimension for him, a possible career of limitless horizons. Factory benches and salaried jobs had never appealed to Yaacov. From grade school, he entered the Naval High School in Acre, which offered the usual academic regimen plus courses in navigation.

Two years with books and charts were all he could stand. He insisted that it wasn't because he undervalued education; he just didn't feel it had to be confined to a classroom. A man picked things up himself every day—at home, in the street. The world was "full of things to learn."

And the sea led to every part of the world. At sixteen, Handleman signed on with an Israeli tramp steamer as an ordinary seaman. For nearly three years he bounced around the globe in ships of various registry, age and condition: to Turkey and Greece, Italy, Malta and Majorca; to Belgium, France, Holland and Finland; to Canada and the United States, then south to Ecuador, Brazil and Argentina. He got an eye-opening glimpse of the Dark Continent in Nigeria and South Africa, and a long, soul-satisfying taste of the Orient: Honolulu, North Korea, Japan, Hong Kong, Singapore, Australia.

In human relations, his unofficial seminar started from scratch; anyone who had ever been close to him was left behind in Tel Aviv. He found out from bruising experience how to handle himself with strangers—when to speak and when to keep silent, who could be trusted, how far horseplay could be carried without invading personal dignity.

He learned without benefit of Dale Carnegie how to make friends —and that it was sometimes necessary, for self-preservation, to make enemies. He could not listen meekly to anti-Semitic mouthings. At a waterfront bar in Buenos Aires, a burly stoker from the Balkans made the mistake of referring disparagingly to a passing Jewish waiter. Yaacov knocked the man across the room and forced him to apologize.

In contact with a multitude of religions and nationalities, he became more, not less, Jewish. Although drifting away from formal observance once past confirmation, he had always, following his father, taken his basic moral instruction from the Bible. A man's first duty was to behave justly, to be "correct." This was important for its own sake, not for fear of being struck down by God if one wavered from the righteous path. God was no super-policeman, nor a schoolteacher grading his flock according to their performance of petty ritual, but a complex Power, in the long run supporting the efforts of the good and thwarting those of the bad. These views became more decisive under attacks from forecastle cynics. Handleman declined to get into extensive theological debates: "A man must believe in something. I believe there's a Force up there. I can't prove it, and I don't have to."

Handleman's body was hard before he ever started painting a deck. Within a year, he had sloughed off most of the baby fat, intellectually as well. Since boyhood, he had heard glamorous accounts of life in the United States. Going ashore at Los Angeles, and wandering inland for several weeks, he quickly concluded there was a bleak side to the shiny silver dollar. "In the United States, a man works all day, then goes home and talks business half the night. If he has two million, he wants six. He's always looking down at people who have less money, and looking up hopefully toward those who have more.

"In Israel, when the day's work is done a man relaxes. He takes his wife to a movie, goes to visit friends. And he has more friends to visit; they're not split up into nasty little cliques. Everybody mixes freely—bosses, laborers, secretaries. If you don't have a car, somebody will always drop you off. Life is warmer, especially for young people."

Handleman was surprised and intrigued to find that strangers in the United States invariably asked, "Are you a Jew, or an Israeli?" Soon he decided that there was indeed a considerable difference between himself and some Jewish undergraduates at U.C.L.A. with whom he struck up acquaintance. "The American boys were full of facts, they could quote from books—but they knew nothing about how to get along in life. They had very little understanding of people, or even of simple mechanical things, like repairing a refrigerator. Israelis are at their best in unexpected situations; they never get lost."

Racial discrimination in America troubled him, the more so because he could not deny certain parallels with the snobbism of European-born Israelis toward dark-skinned Orientals. However, there were also important differences. Israel would never know race riots, he was convinced, because all citizens enjoyed the same basic rights and legal protection.

Handleman found American girls attractive, but he was appalled by the insouciant demeanor of young matrons: "For a woman who has children, and is supposed to be running a home, to go around in little pants, swishing through the streets, blinking her eyes at everybody . . . this you don't see in Israel!"

On shore leave in Europe, he found French sexual mores only slightly less objectionable. Man-woman intimacies, he felt, were not for public display.

More to his liking were the women of the Far East, or at least those among them who had resisted Westernization. Here he found subtlety and grace. It was a taste he had first acquired at home, where he decided quite early that Jewesses of African or Middle Eastern origin were generally "softer, simpler and more honest" than Europeans. They were less concerned with new shoes and dresses, and more with the responsibilities of motherhood. Handleman didn't want a submissive Circassian slave girl for a wife, but he was wary of winding up with a Tel Aviv imitation of the Westchester golf-and-bridge-club set.

He knew of his parents' prejudice against marriage to Orientals —"for them, it would be the equivalent of an American boy marrying a Negro girl"—but for the moment, it was no great problem. So long as he wandered the seas, women were a matter of only passing interest—from time to time diverting, but essentially replaceable. Still, he reflected, if one day he really wanted to settle down with a black-eyed, silky-haired Yemenite or Egyptian, "I wouldn't ask anybody. I'd do it."

Stealing an illicit midnight smoke on deck, Handleman liked the feel of the planks under his feet, the wash of the waves, the mystery of the blue-black night.

People—and by now he had seen a great many of them—were at bottom much the same. Treated kindly, the worst of them could be surprisingly docile. Under sufficient stress, the best could fall apart. There were few devils, and fewer demigods. The most you could really ask was that a person should be sincere, that "his heart and his mouth should speak the same."

One man he had been close to idolizing: John F. Kennedy. "When he was killed, I was in port at Malta. I started to cry, I don't know why. Partly it was the way he made decisions, as at Cuba. But it was something more, too."

At the other extreme, he detested the Beatles. "You couldn't get away from them anywhere, all over the world!"

Such railing was rare. Handleman accepted the visible fact that not all events were controllable, not all material rewards distributed with strict respect to merit.

However, these reflections did not blind him to the convenient business possibilities at hand. He had no intention of winding up like some of the seagoing flotsam he had encountered: a Norwegian cook in perpetual flight from three wives accumulated over the years; a Greek boatswain's mate who was always a few drinks ahead of his next paycheck.

Acting on tips from knowledgeable shipmates, he began quietly investing in a small import business of his own. Handcrafted dolls could be picked up in Ecuador and sold at a profit in San Pedro or Los Angeles. African art work was popular in Europe. There were buyers everywhere for exotic women's dresses and men's shirts. The operation skirted the edge of legality at various points, but with reasonable discretion and a strategically placed friend or two on the docks, it could be managed.

Handleman was particularly impressed by economic opportunities in Australia, where he felt a shrewd investment could yield large returns. And by the time he returned from his travels, he had something to invest: twenty thousand Israeli pounds (nearly seven thousand dollars) saved from his salary and business ventures.

But first, there was conscription ahead, thirty months devoted to national defense. In spite of his years at sea, Handleman made no special effort to join the perky little Israel Navy, consisting mostly of torpedo boats, whose largest vessel was a dumpy destroyer left over from Britain's pre–World War II fleet: "The big people at headquarters knew my background. I figured they'd put me where I could do the most good." Besides, the sea was in a way his personal preserve, to be kept totally separate from national duty, much as Dudu Sela's cello and his paratroop service existed in two unrelated worlds.

Handleman entered the army still very much a loner. His distaste for formal learning had left its mark; his spelling was deplorable, his social graces minimal. His image of himself was very different from the one he conveyed to his comrades in the Golani Brigade. "I could take care of myself all right, but I had no conception of discipline for the common good. When it came to submitting to orders, I was a rebel. If somebody said 'Don't go out,' that's when I went."

The first breach in his insularity came from army education courses in history. "I came to see Israel in a different light, as the product of a long historical development whose continuation was my responsibility . . . and privilege." From there it was a natural step to begin viewing his own actions within a wider framework. "I learned to consider the consequences for others of everything I did. Once I became a good citizen, I had to become a good soldier."

The Corporals' Course completed the maturing process. Thereafter, Handleman's considerable insights into people could be turned to the task of welding a battleproof unit.

Meanwhile, his self-education continued. He read steadily: newspapers of every political persuasion, current biography and nonfiction. He dipped occasionally into the paperback novels that litter every military camp, but only when nothing else was at hand. "I prefer something with truth, reality. It's the same with movies: James Bond is okay while I'm watching, but when I come out I feel let down, empty. *Doctor Zhivago*, on the other hand, was an experience; I learned something."

By early 1967, his army service was drawing to an end. Handleman looked forward to "a quiet life": good health, an apartment of his own, ultimately a family. But he still had an eye cocked toward Australia: "A man could do a lot there in five years." Much as he loved Israel, the thought of being cooped up permanently within its narrow borders, subjected without any break to its intense, all-Jewish environment, gave him claustrophobia. After the excitements of New York and Rio, a future spent shuttling among Tel Aviv, Jerusalem and Haifa was a pale prospect. Fortunately, there was always the sea.

Less fortunately, with discharge only months away, there was Nasser. "Sharm el Sheikh meant war. I was not pleased." He felt a flare-up of rage at the Arabs: why couldn't they live and let live? They were a primitive, treacherous lot. Then he reminded himself that he knew better. No nation was all villains; there were Arab Druses (a non-Moslem sect) in the Israeli Army.

He was sorry for his parents: his father, who winced every time a gun was brought into the house; his mother, who would have to face a war with all of her three sons at the front. But for himself he had a job to do. "The Jewish people have one home: Israel. Everywhere else they are dirt. In the ghetto, they had no chance to defend themselves. Today, we can. Our generation has the mission of protecting our achievements and perpetuating the State. Ours is the generation of the shield."

Ulysses was home. And he was ready.

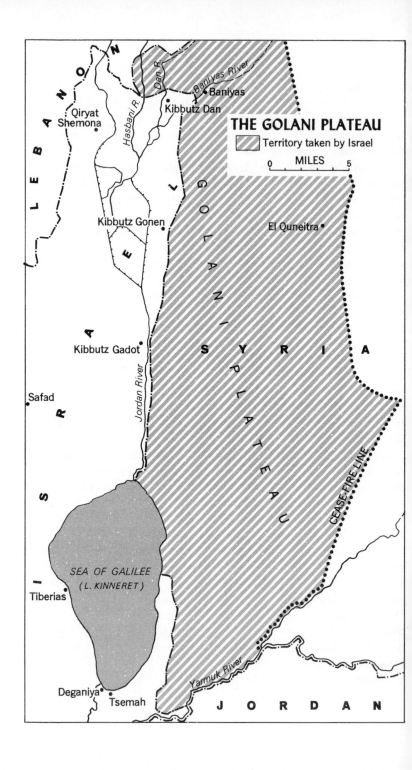

THE GOLANI PLATEAU

Territory taken by Israel

MILES
0   5

L E B A N O N

Qiryat
Shemona

Dan R.

Hasbani R.

Baniyas River

Baniyas

Kibbutz Dan

Kibbutz Gonen

Kibbutz Gadot

G O L A N I - S Y R I A N - P L A T E A U

El Quneitra

Jordan River

Safad

CEASE-FIRE LINE

S   R   A   E   L

S Y R I A

SEA OF GALILEE
(L. KINNERET)

Tiberias

Deganiya

Tsemah

Yarmuk River

J O R D A N

General Elazar's plan for the Syrian front was elegantly simple: a tank-led, head-on knockout smash straight up the cliffs near the northern edge of the ridge, accompanied by secondary thrusts elsewhere to keep the enemy off balance. Once a hole was punched in the main sector, an armored reserve would pour through and swing to the right, sweeping southeastward down the spine of the plateau along the Syrian rear. This force would join with others invading from the south and center, including paratroopers dropped by helicopter, to bite off a considerable chunk of the menacing heights.

The entire scheme, however, hinged on a hand-to-hand operation assigned to mechanized infantry from Golani. On the heels of the onrushing armor in the north, they would tear through the same gap and turn sharply to the left, fanning out to assault the three key bastions anchoring Syria's northern flank. Tel Azaziat, a steep and ugly jutting known to the Galilee farmers below as "the Monster," would be the objective for Yaacov Handleman and his comrades.

At 6:00 A.M. on Friday, while the B.B.C. was announcing Syrian acceptance of a cease-fire, shells came crashing down into several border kibbutzim. Four hours later, Elazar answered back, not with random pot shots but with a sustained artillery barrage backed by the full fury of Mordechai Hod's air force. The real war in the north, for which the generals in Damascus had long been clamoring, was on.

Israeli jets roared in continuous sorties across the border, rattling the walls of the kibbutz bomb shelters. Their role was as much to unnerve the entrenched defenders as to silence gun positions.

Back with his Mystère squadron was Major Avihu, for his second foray into the north. On Tuesday, after the abortive ground assault on Kibbutz Dan, the Syrians had dumped massive salvos of Katyushka rockets into settlements farther south, setting dozens of fires. Avihu had swooped down through a curtain of flak that afternoon to pinpoint the low rectangular silhouettes of the electrically-controlled firing platforms, then blasted a row of them to rubble: "When I saw all those beautiful fields and homes burning, I was ready to do anything." This time, he was grimly pleased to see that the thick smoke in the north hung over Syrian territory, not Israeli. He plunged deep inland to attack anti-aircraft batteries around El Quneitra southwest of Damascus.

From their encampment at Qiryat Shemona several miles to the west, the Golani troops watched the air strikes and wondered when their turn would come. They had been assembled in half-tracks since 7:00 A.M., alternately depressed and elated by a flurry of conflicting reports. The evening before, when a cease-fire had seemed certain, many had wept in frustration: the Syrians would go unpunished, and Golani troopers would stand abashed before their rivals in the Paratroop Brigade.

Now things looked more promising. Handleman, ever-equipped, turned the dials of his transistor radio in search of news. The half-track under his command, carrying eleven men, held the No. 3 position in the column, behind those of the company commander and a platoon commander. Its weaponry included light mortars and machine guns, two Uzzi submachine guns, and four Belgian-made FN rifles. Several vehicles back rode Handleman's friend, William "Moshe" Horn.

Far across the field, near the battalion headquarters tent, a roar went up, spreading rapidly along the line. Men started to sing, loudly, exultantly. The word to move had come.

At the peak of the excitement, a soldier named Shmuel Lichtenstein pulled up with a friend in a jeep. Shmuel, a farmer in a moshav, was a crack performer with the heavy grenade-throwing rifle. He had lost an eye in training, but he didn't want to be left behind. Comrades enthusiastically hauled him aboard a half-track.

The trek eastward took the troops across flat, open country in plain view of the Syrian mountain artillery. This part of the battle, at least, would have gone more easily by night. But the Israelis had to strike for a decision at once, if the Syrians were not to be rescued by international pressure for a cease-fire.

Smoke plumes rose in the hills, and shells started streaming toward the advancing column. At first the Syrian gunners, evidently unsettled by the aerial pounding, were badly off target. Then the mortar and howitzer bursts began closing in.

William Horn looked up anxiously as a finned five-foot rocket sailed overhead. He had gone into battle in excellent spirits, fresh from word that his father, long ill, was being discharged from the hospital. As he wrote home, "The news takes down the stone weighing on my heart, makes my feet feel light and my head clear."

Now he scanned the sky in dismay. Moments before, at the order to open ranks, his half-track had dropped back slightly—and all but wound up in the path of a huge projectile that shattered the road behind it. "Fighting up close, you don't have time to think or worry; you're too busy. But when you're standing in the open and hear the whoosh of shells, it's paralyzing. You know they're coming at you, you see one land forty yards away, then come closer and closer— and there isn't a thing you can do about it."

Handleman, like a good infielder in a tight situation, concentrated on reviewing what he would do in event of various battle circum- stances. He knew he might be hit, and had reflected on previous days about how it would affect his family, especially his mother. But now that was behind him—except for the fleeting thought that when it came to the Syrians, he would prefer death to capture.

He had no doubt of an Israeli victory. Tanks and half-tracks would undoubtedly be blown up, men would fall—but others would rush to fill their places. The momentum of the whole would never be stopped. "We might die, but for the next generation, Israel would be here."

He was glad Golani training had been so tough and comprehen- sive, including even realistic charges through Syrian-style trenches: the rougher the training, the easier the battle.

At 11:31 A.M. the half-track battalion joined up with the tanks from Nablus waiting at the foot of the plateau, and the push was on. Two single-file columns a half-mile apart, spearheaded and inter- laced by Shermans and Centurions, ground their way up the steep, twisting slopes under a hurricane of deadly fire.

Tanks reeled back, toppled sideways, clanked to a halt; but the slender twin lines slowly lengthened up the incline. Losses from close-range antitank and bazooka fire were matched by those from mines; sappers groped forward on their knees to probe with knives for the hidden explosives. Where great boulders blocked the way, bulldozers crunched a path, each bearing two stand-by drivers for instant replacement of men who fell.

The Golani infantrymen in their half-tracks crept upward, feeling like toy soldiers among the thundering guns but bolstered by the presence of the tanks scattered through their ranks. A great shout of excitement went up when, rounding a hairpin curve, they saw loom- ing far overhead the jagged outlines of their objective, Tel Azaziat.

Less heartening was the sight that greeted them on the Syrian- occupied hilltop of Givat Hayim, in the supposedly demilitarized zone some three city blocks south of Tel Azaziat. Two half-tracks had been blown apart by direct mortar hits, their occupants dismembered and flung among the rocks. Across the lopped-off engine section of one lay the flaming lower body of a soldier.

William Horn recoiled, trembling, nauseated by the smell of burning flesh. "We wanted so to believe that it was a Syrian half-track, not ours. But the military identification number left no room for doubt. The friends who a few minutes before had been singing and laughing with us were gone, mutilated remnants. Tears filled my eyes; hatred swept over me; and I swore to myself they would be avenged. I wanted to shout, burst, shoot; my rage and bitterness were like coiled springs waiting for the command 'After me!' "

The command would come, but only after further perils. By now the armor had slashed a breach in the Syrian line, and the Golani half-tracks were careening through to enter the decisive sector, a strip about a mile wide embracing the fortresses of Tel Azaziat on the far west, Tel Faher a mile farther east, and Bourj Bravil to the southeast.

Suddenly the lead tank rumbled over a mine, shattering its treads and halting the entire column. Demolition engineers, including one from Handleman's squad, raced forward to clear the area. While maintenance men worked furiously to replace the treads, savage fire from the covered bunkers of both Tel Azaziat and Tel Faher poured down on the vanguard elements.

In Handleman's half-track, amid the hail of shells and bullets, a rifleman pulled out the pocket prayer book issued to all members of the brigade and started reading aloud. The others listened attentively. "He wasn't," as Handleman later pointed out, "a particularly religious guy. But in trouble, everybody turns to God. He kept it short—just a plea for protection. When he finished, like everybody else, I said 'Amen.' "

Handleman was summoned to company command to receive new instructions. By the time he had been fully briefed, the damaged tank was mended and was blasting away at Syrian armor in the fortresses. Engineers reported that the path immediately ahead was clear.

Under protective fire from five Israeli tanks on Givat Hayim, Shermans and half-tracks began the last stage of the climb. Tel Azaziat was directly ahead: black, desolate, and spurting flame like some fork-tongued, super-size Gila monster of antiquity.

The ragged Israeli column aimed straight for the maw of the fortress. The going was painfully slow. Blocked by boulders, shales and sharp outcroppings, the crawling vehicles were wide-open targets for Syrian gunners enjoying perfect 300-degree fields of fire.

Handleman gripped his Uzzi and looked upward for a target. Everything in sight was as battened down as the deck of an ancient freighter wheezing around the Cape.

A loud explosion a few yards ahead knocked him backward in the half-track. As Handleman peered into the murk, trying to see what had happened, a second blast lifted him off his feet. For a moment the air was filled with smoke, flying stones and confused shouting.

Handleman ran his hands quickly over his body. No pain, nothing broken. He checked his men one by one: there were only bruises and scratches. Apparently they had run into a nest of antipersonnel mines. They were still in business, but the half-track was not. Worse, it had been blown sideways so as to block the narrow approaches to Tel Azaziat.

So much for the original attack plan, Handleman decided. They would have to scale the remaining seventy-five yards on foot, advancing from rock to rock, hoping for luck against the mines scattered on the ground and the volleys of fire from above.

A moment later the order came from the company commander: "Dismount and attack." Handleman jumped down, waved his men to follow and started sprinting toward Tel Azaziat.

William Horn, farther back in the column, had been chafing at the repeated delays. Over and over he had been rehearsing in his mind the long-memorized layout of the enemy position, and his own vanguard assignment: to lead two other men forward against the "edges" of the objective.

Approaching the last narrow incline, William heard a series of mine explosions and then a volley of machine-gun and small-arms fire. He stuck his head over the side, and a bullet whizzed past his ears. The half-track he was riding shuddered to a halt, smoke curling up from its front wheels.

Some hundred yards away, William saw a Syrian rifleman crouching behind a rock, steel helmet camouflaged with prickles and burrs. "His weapon was trained on us. It seemed to me that he even smiled; in any case, I saw his white teeth." The Israeli corporal fired his Uzzi instinctively from the waist.

The Syrian doubled up. William shifted his automatic to single action for greater accuracy, and fired several more times. The enemy soldier fell back among the rocks.

All around William, Golani men were jumping to the ground for the final charge uphill. "The Professor" followed suit.

Higher up the slope, Handleman had outdistanced his men and reached the barbed-wire perimeter of the fortress. Under a battle-field shift of directives, he now bore responsibility for leading an entire platoon of thirty soldiers, normally handled by a lieutenant.

He found that a single half-track—the battalion commander's—had penetrated the outer Syrian fence and reached the lip of the compound. Handleman plunged through the breach after it.

At first, billows of smoke obscured the scene. Then, to his left, he was able to make out the lowest row of trenches, just where they should be. He jumped into the corner of the seven-foot pit.

A rifle bullet cracked off the basalt-lined wall behind him. Twenty yards away, where the trench angled upward and bulged out into a bunker, he caught a glimpse of an enemy helmet.

Uzzi pumping, Handleman advanced rapidly toward the bunker. One man pitched forward lifeless, then another. "It was a question of reflexes—and luck. I managed to finish off all four men in that first position."

Now more Israeli troops were joining him. Handleman's harsh voice carried down the trench: "Follow me!"

The Israeli tactic, here as with tanks in the desert, was to slam full-speed ahead, unnerving the enemy by creating the impression of a huge surrounding force. Bypassed pockets would be left for mopping up later.

Erratic but intensive fire sliced across the Israelis' path. Against the massive concrete bulwarks of bunkers and round pillboxes, the attackers could only hurl hand grenades, sometimes at eyeball range.

Rifles poked out of a square bunker directly ahead. Handleman reached for the grenades at his waist: one, two, three went sailing over the wall. With the last grenade he broke into a run and burst into the position, Uzzi blazing. A single Syrian, surrounded by fallen comrades, fired back.

Handleman felt an empty click; his ammunition magazine was

exhausted. A Russian Klatchnikov rifle stood against the wall. "I grabbed it as the Syrian bolted for the exit, and brought him down in his tracks."

Returning to the trench labyrinth, he ran into William Horn at the next crossroads. "Take the right trench," he shouted, and continued up toward the center of the compound. William rallied a few men together and disappeared southward.

Handleman surged forward, his men trailing after like trains pulled by an onrushing locomotive. He had no sense of the Syrians as human beings: "It was war, and they were targets." He was conscious only of a "technical" thought: it had been a very good idea to load up with extra grenades for this mission.

He was down to his last of them when, coming around another of the endless turnings in the maze, he found his force under fire from a large pillbox. "I pitched the grenade with all my strength and followed it up by storming the position with the Klatchnikov. I counted seven Syrian dead."

Now Handleman had nearly reached the junction point where he was to link up with the company commander. However, harassing fire continued from another trench on his flank. He picked up a Syrian submachine gun (the Klatchnikov in its turn had run out of ammunition) and gathered two comrades. Advancing across open ground, they silenced the position.

Orders came to send part of his force to another sector, and organize the rest for a holding action. As Handleman was regrouping the platoon, he came upon the quiet "Professor" assembling a long stream of prisoners. The Syrians were filing forward meekly from an apparently bottomless tunnel.

William Horn was winding up the most exciting adventure of his young life, begun nearly two hours before when he had gone loping at a half-crouch through the iron gate to the compound. After a few moments of bewilderment—"it was nothing like a training exercise, here nobody was smiling"—he had teamed up with a fellow soldier to clear a bunker, "running and shooting like an automatic machine," then set out as ordered by Handleman to explore the trench system leading southward.

The first two tiers of trenches in the new sector seemed to have been abandoned. The next was anything but. Heavy fire spurted from an overhanging bunker fifteen yards away.

William clambered up from the trench. "I pulled out a No. 26 grenade and, signaling my intentions to the man behind me, pitched it through the window of the bunker. There was a terrible explosion. I dashed forward, but just as I reached the entrance I discovered my Uzzi was out of ammunition. Fortunately the other man was right on my heels, and he finished mopping up the position.

"Suddenly I heard loud shouting in Arabic. I peered out of the bunker, and advancing toward me from the far side of the trench were five or six Syrians. Their hands were high over their heads, and they were crying 'Salaam, salaam" (the Arabic equivalent of 'Shalom' or 'Peace')."

The Syrians had knives dangling from their waists, but they had already discarded their firearms. More men poured out behind them; William had evidently stumbled on a deep underground command post. "They were mature, husky men—the first one could have been my father—but they were weeping like children. They complained that their officers had abandoned them, they were hungry, they longed only to see their wives and families at home."

In spite of himself, William felt a wave of compassion. As he wrote to his parents, "They began to cry, and we pitied them and did not shoot." On Handleman's orders, he herded the prisoners toward a swimming pool near the edge of the compound where, stripped to their underwear, they shrank back from entering the water: "The pool is for officers only."

William was struck by the terror in their eyes. He considered reassuring them that they would not be harmed; then he remembered the murderous reputation earned by Tel Azaziat, "the Monster." "I asked one of our Arabic-speaking boys to question them: why had they fired on our kibbutzim all these years, and on us when we had done nothing to them? The answer was, 'Our officers forced us to.' I thought of Adolf Eichmann. He too claimed he was 'just a small cog' obeying orders."

One last position was not yet taken: the central command post at the heart of the fortress. Handleman led a group out into the open for a flanking attack.

Immediately, they came under fire from one of the lower trenches, bypassed earlier. Handleman resumed his one-two technique. A couple of borrowed grenades, followed by a head-on charge, silenced the position.

Resistance at Tel Azaziat ended at about 2:00 P.M., when the Syrian officer in charge emerged with hands up from the command dugout. The Israelis embraced each other happily—"no Tarzan roars of victory, just a sense of satisfaction." A corporal of Iraqi parentage shinnied up a gnarled olive tree to plant the blue-and-white flag on top of the fortress.

Samson had toppled pillars with his bare arms. The soldiers of Golani brought down mountain strongholds with rifles, hand grenades—and the sabra spirit. It was an achievement that, in the eyes of the American military expert General S. L. M. Marshall, "transcended technical explanation and mortal understanding."

Yaacov Handleman, neo-Maccabean sea rover, trader and earnest seeker after "the quiet life," alone accounted for more than half a Syrian platoon. He was at the time about ten weeks short of his twenty-first birthday.

Although the forts were in Israeli hands, the General Staff was taking nothing for granted. Still to be executed was the rest of Dado Elazar's plan: the wide flanking movement southeastward, and the synchronizing stabs east across the border. As the Golani armored columns swept down the Syrian heights, Mota Gur's paratroopers were ordered up from Jerusalem to form a strategic reserve.

The paratroopers took the short path northward, through the heart of the Jordanian West Bank, completely under Israeli control since late Wednesday. They rolled up through an area rich in historical associations. Part of the original territory of Solomon's Palestine, it included such emotion-loaded place names as Jericho; Nablus, where royal Shechem "defiled" Dinah, the daughter of Leah and Jacob; Ramallah, birthplace of the prophet Samuel; and Shiloh, where the ark of the covenant was placed after the conquest of Judah. South of Jerusalem were Bethlehem and Hebron.

Under the U.N. partition plan rejected by the Arabs in 1947, the West Bank had been designated as an independent Arab state. The following year, during the multiple Arab invasion of Israel, the area was seized by Transjordan's King Abdullah, father of Hussein.

In 1967 it was a thick Jordanian belly protruding westward into Israel, squashing the Jews at one point into a corridor only ten miles wide between the Arab lines and the sea. Instead of the natural barrier against infiltration afforded in biblical times by the Jordan River, the Israelis were obliged for nearly twenty years constantly to defend a straggling land frontier of 350 miles—more than double the length of the border with Egypt.

In less than three days the entire territory had been retaken. Driving simultaneously against the heights above Jerusalem, vital to the capture of the Old City, and down from the north against Jenin, Israeli armor slashed through rugged mountain passes to chop up the Jordanian defenses. Early Tuesday, the southern column barreled through to the mountaintop crossroads above the capital, intercepting and wiping out a force of twenty Pattons coming up from Jericho; within hours, the Israeli Shermans and Centurions were linking up with Mota Gur's paratroopers west of Mount Scopus.

By midday Tuesday, after heavy losses on both sides, Jenin was overrun; by dusk, Ramallah at the other end of the north-south highway was also in Israeli hands. On Wednesday the two main arms of the Israeli pincer closed against Nablus. The Jordanians threw in what was left of their two hundred tanks, but to no avail. Later in the day other Israeli columns occupied Jericho, Bethlehem and Hebron with little resistance.

The Paratroop Brigade started north toward the Syrian front around noon on Friday. Among those in the convoy was First Lieutenant Karni Bilu. Karni was now on liaison duty, riding in a liberated Arab Legion fire brigade car with an Operations officer and an Intelligence sergeant.

By midafternoon, they had cleared the bulge and reached Afula, twenty-odd miles southwest of the Sea of Galilee. The sergeant had an inspiration: they could take a left fork toward Nazareth, pick up useful Syrian maps and information at army headquarters there, then rejoin the main body of the brigade at Tiberias. The necessary permission was obtained.

However, the detour westward took longer than anticipated. By the time the sergeant had rounded up his intelligence data, the day was over. Under blackout instructions, they had to make their way up to Tiberias without lights. The night was murky and movement slow.

Finally they reached the balmy Galilee capital to find that the rest of the convoy had already moved on—according to a local M.P., to the police station at Tsemah. They swung southeast along the shore.

Tsemah was on the extreme southern tip of the Sea of Galilee, half a mile from the Syrian border. It was a small outpost with a large history. At the time of the Second Temple, Tsemah was a Jewish settlement. In the post-Roman era, its population became more diverse. During the First World War, it was the scene of a major battle for control of the Damascus-Jerusalem railroad line, with Australian cavalry finally overrunning the Turkish defenders. In 1948, as the gateway to the Deganiya settlements directly westward, it was again bitterly contested as Haganah forces threw back the Syrian invaders. In recent years the ancient town had been deserted, although the Israelis manned a police station built by the British during the mandate period.

As Karni and her comrades approached Tsemah, lights out, ominous rumblings to the east reminded them that they were heading straight into the artillery positions at the southern anchor of the Syrian line. Flashes lighted up the mountainside, and a shell crashed, uncomfortably close, in the woods alongside the road. The sergeant speeded up, but the shelling only grew heavier.

As they pulled into the courtyard of the police station, a mortar blast made the car rock like a toy. It was obvious that they were under full-scale bombardment. The three Israelis scrambled from the car, the Operations officer pulling Karni after him toward the stone façade of the station. "Stick close to the wall," he shouted.

They ran through the darkness, Karni clinging to his hand. Outside the station, soldiers from the local garrison were already clustered. Karni dived into the group and made a space for herself on the ground, sitting against the cool stones, wishing she could melt into them.

The booming from the east continued. Somebody asked if she had a cigarette. Karni nodded, reaching into the leather bag slung over her shoulder. By the half-hidden light of a match, the man sitting alongside saw that the newly arrived officer was a girl. He was astonished; more so when he learned that Karni was from the famed brigade that had taken Jerusalem.

No, he told her, there were no paratroopers in Tsemah. But, as she could see, there was plenty of action. Evidently those Syrian gunners who had not yet been overrun in the south were, in a last burst of frustration, pouring in everything they had. Doubtless to the dismay of their Russian "advisers," they were concentrating their fire not on the advancing Israeli legions but against their old targets along the border.

Karni could find small comfort in this. The eastern sky was aflame. Another mortar shell landed in the courtyard, and the station building trembled violently. A few feet away, the Intelligence sergeant berated himself for the "clever" expedition to Nazareth.

Karni huddled miserably against wall and pavement. She had never been so terrified in her life, never felt so utterly exposed. If only she had a helmet, or a rifle—not that a gun would have done any good. Instead, she clutched a soccer football given to her by one of the paratroopers in Jerusalem for her young brother . . . and prayed.

Around her, some of the local troops speculated calmly on the location of the Syrian firing positions, and tried to guess where the next shells would land. A thunderous crash shook the courtyard, leaving her ears half-deafened and her body quivering. "That was a close one," somebody murmured.

When would there be a shell so close that they would hear nothing at all?

She shivered, and thought of her parents. They would take the news badly. Her brother Dudu would be brave—dear, sweet Dudu who complained bitterly that although "nearly seventeen" he was not allowed to fight. Her grandmother she didn't want to think about.

Never again to see them all, or to browse through the comfortable rambling apartment on Shprintzak Street. Suddenly she saw her home in intimate loving detail; in her mind's eye, she walked through room after room, saying a farewell to the green-cushioned sofa where she had spent hours reading, the immaculate little kitchen, the white toy dog at the foot of her bed.

She thought back to her departure when the army recalled her three weeks before. She had been proud and happy, until she saw the tears in her mother's eyes, and the possibility crossed her mind that she might not come back.

She dismissed the idea, but it recurred as she was going down the stairs, until she pushed it firmly aside as childish.

Now she could only pray that her death would not be too devastating a sorrow for them. She had seen the families of this war's casualties, and she sobbed aloud at the prospect of her parents undergoing such suffering.

The Operations officer was bending over her. He wanted to return to the car and drive north—he didn't know where, but they had to find the brigade. Karni persuaded him to look for a telephone first, and call paratroop general headquarters for information.

It was a good hunch. In a few minutes the officer was back, with definite word on the brigade's whereabouts. Karni welcomed the idea of heading north—any movement would be better than waiting here. At the first lull in the shooting, they piled back into the fire brigade car, which was happily still untouched. Karni, eyeing the possibilities for protection against shrapnel, squeezed into a far corner in the back.

Once on the road, even driving in darkness, she felt relieved. The explosions were not as numerous now, and the mere fact of being in motion was a help. The night sank into near-silence, punctuated only occasionally by a far-off explosion. Stiff-limbed, Karni clung with both hands to the football, her private life raft.

A sliver of moonlight poked through the clouds, and she recognized the terrain. The kibbutz where the brigade was encamped would be only minutes away.

When they rolled through the gates, Karni jumped down before the car had come to a complete halt. She threw her arms around the first paratrooper she saw—who happened to be Major Arik, the brigade's chief of Intelligence. Arik was surprised if not displeased. He found sleeping quarters for the late arrivals. But it was a long time before Karni could sleep.

The paratroopers did not have to fight in Syria. As Karni was speeding away from Tsemah at 8:30 Friday evening, the important village of Baniyas east of Dan, with its Crusader castle that had been too impenetrable for Saladin, fell to the Golani attackers. Elsewhere along the front, enemy artillerymen were being blasted from their deeply-sunk positions to begin a long, wild retreat. Although fighting was to continue for another day, sometimes desperately, the tide of battle in Syria was irreversible.

At long last, the Jordan Valley could breathe freely. Children came dancing out of the bomb shelters. Parents wheeled their pram-borne infants into the sunlight. Adolescents gawked in pride and wonder at crater-pocked roads and shell-flattened dining halls. And old settlers could say, "The War of Independence is finally over."

But the conquest of the Syrian battlements had been costly, by small-country standards. Total Israeli casualties came to more than 400. At Tel Faher alone, 20 of the attackers died and 45 were wounded. Officers and noncoms accounted for 70 percent of the losses in the Golani Brigade.

Death in battle is a personally-felt sorrow in Israel, never an anonymous statistic. The limited size of the country, the intimacy of the shared struggle, and the heavy contribution demanded from each individual, reinforce the biblical emphasis on the high value of human life. When Premier Eshkol mourned publicly before Parliament that "every living soul is an entire universe," and Moshe Dayan told his soldiers, "Victory is ours—and so is bereavement," they were speaking for the whole nation, the reunited tribe that feels with the intensity of a single family. Just as the State belongs to all, so does every soldier in the field. And Israel lost nearly 800 men, the proportional equivalent in American terms of 70,000 dead and more than 200,000 wounded.

Enemy casualties are hardly received more joyously. A story in the Midrash, the traditional Jewish interpretation of the Scriptures, tells of God's reaction when the Egyptian chariots pursuing Moses were swallowed up in the Red Sea. Heaven's angels began singing loud praises of the Almighty. He silenced them sternly: "How can you sing, when My children are drowning?"

Today as historically, no nation is less consoled than Israel by "favorable" casualty statistics, less cheered by a high "kill ratio" of enemy losses, less exultant in triumph. The parades and celebrations that followed the Six-Day War took place in Washington and Paris, not Tel Aviv. No brass bands greeted the returning sabra heroes; as quietly as they had gone off to war, they slipped back behind their grocery counters and the wheels of their taxis. As one brigade commander summed it up, "A non-militarist army suits an antimilitarist nation."

The Sixth Day

THE PATRIARCH

THE Israeli pilot was in trouble. Twenty-five miles inside the Syrian lines east of the Sea of Galilee, his squadron had been dive-bombing long columns of retreating enemy armor since early Saturday morning. On the road below him sprawled a grotesque pile-up of mangled metal: tanks, gun carriers, trucks and jeeps mashed into the eerie shapes and blurred colors of avant-garde sculpture, a grim "happening" that the Syrians must have wished hadn't. Huge vehicles, overturned in the fields, lay on their backs like giant beetles, helplessly clawing the hot midday air.

But the endless Syrian columns with their modern Soviet equipment still boasted prodigious fire power, and in a dangerously low swoop the pilot had caught a burst from a heavy machine gun in the engine of his swift, delicately-balanced Mirage. The Israeli flyer, although a colonel and base commander, was helpless in a plane that could not stay aloft and in fact might explode at any moment. He would have to ditch, in full sight of the Syrians below, and within easy range of their guns.

The pilot swerved away from the road, radioing his situation to the other three members of his flight. Some five hundred yards south of the enemy column, he released his overhead canopy and pressed the button of his ejection seat. He shot forward into space. Seconds

199

later, his parachute billowed out gracefully behind him. The abandoned Mirage spun dizzily for a moment, plummeted, and burst into flames.

A roar went up from the Syrians on the ground. Rifle and machine-gun fire crackled around the descending flyer.

The pilot looked down. He was over a low mound of jagged black volcanic rock, intermittently broken by relatively flat shelves but in most places thrusting skyward like giant spikes. It would be a difficult landing at best.

He was not to have the best. As he neared the ground, a rifle bullet smashed into his left leg, knocking his balance awry. In the desperate attempt to protect his injured leg and at the same time swing over toward a sheltered area, he crashed into a jutting ledge with an impact that broke his right arm and leg.

Two jeeploads of Syrian troops promptly raced southward toward the crippled pilot. Other vehicles, and groups of foot soldiers, began splitting off from the retreating lines to join them.

The Syrians had not reckoned, however, with a cardinal principle of Zahal: never, under any circumstances, to abandon dead or wounded to the enemy. In one action several years ago, fourteen Israeli soldiers in succession were cut down before the body of a comrade was finally retrieved. Sizable offensives have been launched simply to recover a handful of missing men. While to other armies this might seem foolhardy or irrational, in Israel it is considered "an absolutely indispensable attitude, a necessary price we must pay for maintaining high morale." The feudally oriented Arab, trained to self-concern, cracks under pressure into fragments of rank, sect or geography. But the Israeli soldier, in the words of Chief Education Officer Bar-On, "knows he will never be left behind on the battlefield, alive or dead. He is part of an indissoluble body, and by that fact has a thousand times his own strength. To abandon this principle would undermine the whole character of our fighting force."

At the colonel's first radioed word of his plight, his No. 2 man had peeled off to organize a protecting screen. Now all three Mirage fighter-bombers came screaming down at the Syrians, recklessly low, cannons blazing. As the pilot began a long, painful crawl toward a larger hill some two hundred yards away, whose huge boulders might offer some protection, Israeli planes engaged Syrian ground gunners in a furious duel.

The fending-off action could not last long; the Mirages had limited fuel. When they were forced to quit the field, the injured pilot would be at the Syrians' mercy—unless he could be pulled out first by helicopter.

At air force headquarters in Tel Aviv, Mordechai Hod had been alerted. The commanding general took over direction of rescue operations. He ordered a relief flight of Mirages into the air. The rescue itself would be entrusted to a four-man helicopter crew posted near the border under Captain Yair. A backup helicopter would be placed on emergency stand-by.

Yair, thirty-two, was a former fighter pilot removed from jet service in 1961 because of a minor heart defect. He had stayed on in the air force, accepting duty with the helicopters while hoping to requalify for the jets. By now he was reconciled to the slower craft: "Even though you love only your wife, you can appreciate the qualities of another woman."

Yair was asleep when Hod's order came. He had been on duty much of the preceding twenty-four hours; earlier Saturday morning, he had scooped up in a single operation two pilots who had been forced down separately.

A quiet sabra who refused to discuss his exploits except under direct command, Yair quickly gathered his crew: a reserve pilot-navigator; a mechanic to make repairs and control the rescue wire; and a medical corpsman.

The briefing received by Yair was marred by faulty radio connections. He took to the air knowing little except that a pilot had been shot down and that his chopper would have to fly east, directly over the Syrian gun emplacements. Beyond that, he hoped he would be able to make contact with the Mirages on the scene. He estimated he would need about twenty-five minutes to get there—a long time for the jets to hold the enemy ground troops at bay.

As he crossed the border into Syria, Yair found himself in the center of a crisscrossing swirl of Mirages. Evidently the two Israeli flights had combined to hem in the Syrians on the road. Whenever a Syrian straggler dodged free of their cordon or burst through it, a Mirage would swoop down from the clouds to give chase and eliminate the threat.

The helicopter flew into the scene at five thousand feet, unarmed and easily inflammable, an inviting and highly vulnerable target for enemy anti-aircraft guns. At this point Hod, following the action by radio and knowing the unpleasant percentages, told his stand-by helicopter to be ready for take-off.

Yair radioed the jets overhead: would somebody please come downstairs and point out where he was to make his pickup? He saw one Mirage peel off from the group, then turn sharply and zoom off westward, evidently running out of fuel. But another plane dropped down and signaled for Yair to follow.

The jet pilot led the helicopter to a bony, rock-strewn hillside south of the highway. Yair circled slowly overhead, looking for the downed flyer and also for a suitable place to land.

His mechanic shouted and pointed. Peering down, Yair saw a crumpled parachute among the rocks . . . but no airman.

He made another exquisitely slow, deliberate turn around the area, hovering almost motionless over the ugly outcroppings. In a pitted gully between two hills, he and the mechanic simultaneously spotted a prone figure, dark air force overalls all but invisible against the black rocks.

Yair braced himself for a bumpy pinpoint landing. But as he started coming down, the pilot struggled erect and moved forward. Yair then guided the helicopter to a flatter stretch of terrain nearby. His crewmen sprinted over to the wounded man.

The pilot stumbled forward, arms around his rescuers, so bloodied and battered that Yair did not recognize his own base commander.

A radio message from the Mirage overhead sputtered into Yair's headphone. "Hurry up! You've been spotted!"

The wounded colonel was lifted gently to safety; the others tumbled after. In ten seconds Yair was airborne. As his wheels left the ground, an artillery shell crashed into the rocks, followed by a rain of mortar fire that swept the hillside.

Within an hour the pilot–base commander was undergoing treatment at Tiberias Military Hospital. He was the sixteenth Israeli flyer to bail out of a damaged plane successfully during the war.

The parachute that had braked his passage earthward lay in the hills of southern Syria, its hardy nylon blasted by an exploding mortar shell. On a patch of lining, caught face-up in a crevice among the rocks, a thin strip of tape fluttered in the late-afternoon breeze stirring from Lake Kinneret. The tape bore the printed words: "Inspected by J. Ochayon, Corporal."

The "J." was for Jacqueline.

Corporal Jacqueline Ochayon is a twenty-year-old parachute inspector born in Casablanca. She is part of a special unit attached to the paratroop brigades (*too* attached, for a time, when the tradition developed that after a successful training jump a trooper should kiss the girl inspector whose name appeared on the inside of his chute. Headquarters ruled this a "distraction").

Viewing Jacqueline, one sees their point. She is a tall, slender girl with a brooding dignity that seems of another time and place, almost medieval. Her profile is long and fine under a mass of high-piled jet-black hair, and the graceful line of her legs sweeps upward into firm, womanly thighs.

Tense in strange company, she speaks quickly in a high nervous voice, gesturing with her left hand. As she relaxes a little, a creamy smile breaks through, followed by another agreeable surprise: a dimple in her cheek. As is the case with many Israeli girls of Oriental origin, a subtle aloofness clings to her, quite beyond the range of the camera to capture.

Jacqueline could not be more proud of her job if she sat behind the desk of the Chief of Staff. As it happens, she rarely sits at all. Parachute folding and inspection is a stand-up, bend-over job. Rough on the feet, the hands, and the eyes, it is assigned only to volunteers, usually robust outdoor types from the kibbutzim. City-bred Jacqueline is an exception.

She is very conscious of her responsibility as a corporal-inspector. "For six months I was allowed to do only simple folding. Now, every time a nylon is brought to camp after a jump, I supervise its examination for holes, rips, even dirt. We keep a file on every chute."

Jacqueline is the eldest of eight children. Her father, a carpenter, came from a family that had lived long in Morocco, "perhaps since the days of the original tribes"; her mother escaped to North Africa from a Vichy concentration camp during World War II, aided by a gentile family that smuggled her aboard a warship.

Jacqueline came to Israel from Casablanca at the age of eight, settling with her parents in Beersheba, ancient biblical site of shrines dating back to Abraham and Jacob. The uprooting was difficult. It meant learning a new language and very different ways. Casablanca had been like Cairo, a flavorful city, European in sophistication, with an overlay of the languorous Orient in its native bazaars and flowing galabeahs. Its crowded shops, abundant beaches, and heavy humid air were a far cry from the Spartan desert life of Beersheba. Casablanca was also strongly French in culture, with a strict middle-class sense of propriety. Accustomed to the formality of its schools, Jacqueline was dismayed at the casualness of Israeli teacher-pupil relations: "To this day I can't bring myself to address a teacher as 'Moshe' instead of 'Professor.'"

There were deeper sources of turmoil. The Ochayons had known prejudice in Morocco: religious restrictions, biased courts. The shift to Israel did not end these humiliations. In high school, Jacqueline ran into chatter about the "crude family life" of Orientals. Sensitive, close to her French-speaking, music-loving mother, she suffered. It didn't help when one of her Western classmates was barred by parental edict from marrying a Tunisian-born boy.

In her late teens, she had her own disillusioning adventure in cross-cultural romance. A young army officer of Polish extraction, stationed in Beersheba, began courting her. Evidently sharing her interest in the arts—Jacqueline plays the accordion and guitar—he took her to concerts, brought over books for discussion. In line with the close family life of Moroccan Jews, where tribal tradition is reinforced by Gallic clannishness, he was "welcomed as a son" in her home.

On closer acquaintance, however, the officer's "intellectual interests" seemed to develop in a distinctly physical direction. Jacqueline broke off.

Soon after, army service intervened, as with Naftali Cohen, drastically. Suddenly Jacqueline was plunged into another new environment, not only reassuringly disciplined, but focused on a common aim. Visiting paratroop bases, attending seminars on Jewish history, Jacqueline began gradually to feel an enveloping sense of solidarity. "I belonged to the country, and the country belonged to me."

With a new core of purpose came a crystallization of personal plans. She would make a post-army career of teaching retarded children—not because so many Oriental youngsters fell into this category, but because "with the handicapped there is a bigger challenge; you have to give more of yourself." She would marry only a man who had a comparable dedication to national service. And, unlike her mother, she would raise a small family: "There ought to be a better balance between what a mother does for her children, and what she does for herself."

More sabra in spirit than the sabras, Jacqueline has gone beyond confidence to a positive condescension about mores other than those of her Israeli generation. She dismisses the modern Western woman complex of miniskirts, psychedelic art and casual sex as "a childlike manifestation of emptiness . . . people groping to fill the vacuum of meaningless lives."

She is even more impatient with the disciples of an uncompromising past. Her voice becomes low and passionate as she describes an encounter with a group of bearded orthodox men at the reconquered Wailing Wall. "There they were, bending over their prayer books, and a few yards away was a pile of stones commemorating the fallen paratroopers. They had walked right past the memorial without even a glance.

"I had to speak up. I said, 'Those boys made it possible for you to pray at your Wailing Wall. Don't you think you should honor them?'

"They looked at me as if I was crazy. 'The war was a miracle,' one of them replied, 'an act of God. If certain boys fell in battle, that was God's will. Their sacrifice was nothing in itself.' The others nodded, and they all went back to their books."

Jacqueline takes a harsh view of her orthodox countrymen. But then, she has never crossed the path of Eliezer Eckstein.

Shaari Zedek Hospital stands at the top of Jaffa Road in New Jerusalem, its massive two-story façade assembled from great handhewn slabs of tawny Jerusalem granite. Overshadowed by the sleek modern Hadassah complex, venerable Shaari Zedek ("Gates of Mercy") nonetheless performed quiet marvels during the war. More than four hundred paratroopers were treated there. An eleven-year-old Arab girl, "physiologically dead" on the operating table from shrapnel wounds in the neck, was saved by Jewish surgeons. Some two dozen newly-born babies were successfully shifted from ward to ward as Jordanian shells thumped into the building, twice tearing huge holes in the masonry.

Since Monday, the soberly orthodox doctors had risen to crises with ingenious improvisation. But on Saturday afternoon they had to admit pleasant bafflement—not by any diagnostic riddle or elusive microorganism, but by the extraordinary person of Eliezer Eckstein.

Eliezer had been brought to the hospital, his lower left leg ripped off and second-degree burns on his right arm, after a misadventure the previous afternoon. He had been in a command car carrying a four-man recovery team from the Military Rabbinate, all reservists assigned to bring back dead and wounded from the battlefield. On this mission—to reclaim the body of a pilot shot down south of Jerusalem three days before—they were accompanied by a demolition expert, a captain of engineers. The area they would be searching, the hills along the Bethlehem Road, was thickly studded with mines.

Eliezer, as Second Lieutenant in charge of the recovery unit, rode up front, a grizzled, heavily-bearded figure squeezed between the driver and the captain, who was a construction foreman in civilian life.

The captain, round-faced and youngish, was nervous. Earlier in the week he had slogged through a series of murderous mine fields in the Sinai, probing forward in the darkness on hands and knees while men were blown up on either side of him. How long could his luck hold out? Besides, he knew something that the others did not: a regular-army team, attempting this same operation yesterday, had been forced back by mine-caused casualties.

The downed plane was reported to have crashed on the outskirts of Bethlehem, between the Mar-Elias Monastery and the Tomb of Rachel. Winding through the stony, sparsely-planted mountain landscape, the captain fingered a detail map. "It should be about a mile this side of Bethlehem," he said.

"No," said Eckstein. "It's closer. I know this terrain very well. I fought all through here in 1948. And I remember it from British days, before I was married." His manner was positive without being overbearing. The captain stole a curious glance at the older man. Eckstein was surely well over fifty, although clear-eyed, ruddy-cheeked and sturdily built.

"You probably have children," the captain ventured. "You could have left this war to them."

"I have children," Eliezer nodded. "I also have grandchildren. But a man is still responsible to God for his own actions."

The car was approaching the top of a small rise. "Stop here," Eliezer told the driver.

"This is a good lookout point," Eckstein explained to the captain.

"Below here, the ground starts sloping down." The two got out, and Eliezer led the captain toward an abandoned blockhouse. "From this roof we will have a good view."

Eckstein walked with a slight limp, the captain noticed. But when they reached the blockhouse, the bearded lieutenant planted a foot in the ruins and swung his 180 pounds lightly onto the roof. To the astonished sapper clambering up beside him, he remarked, "I am a plumber. I climb a lot."

They had a sweeping view of the terrain: undulating bleak brown hills fading toward the Dead Sea in the east, and broken by patches of olive groves below them to the south. Eliezer's bright blue eyes searched piercingly. "There!" he pointed.

In a grove just off the road, some 150 yards away, the tip of an airplane wing glistened among the olive leaves.

They got back in the car and drove down to the edge of the grove.

This was the bad moment: traversing the uncharted twenty-five or thirty yards between the road and the wrecked plane. Squinting toward the closely packed trees, silvery-sheened in the sunlight, the captain frowned. "Perfect terrain for antipersonnel mines," he murmured.

Eliezer regarded him calmly for a moment. "Whatever God wishes, so it will be done."

The captain went first, carrying a mine detector. Eliezer followed in his footsteps. The rest of the rescue team, including a stretcher-bearer, came after in single file.

The young engineer threaded his way gingerly through the trees, eyes fixed on the pebble-strewn ground. The faintest bump might conceal a deadly charge. The grove thickened perceptibly, then opened to a clearing. Directly ahead loomed the undercarriage of the plane, bullet-scarred and twisted. A few feet away, alongside the demolished cockpit, lay the body of the pilot.

The dead man was moved carefully to the stretcher, and the group started back. Again the captain led the way, retracing his original path. But now the others, one man at each corner of the stretcher, were obliged to step slightly outside the captain's trail.

Halfway through the trees, Eliezer felt something crunch under his left foot. Simultaneously he heard a loud explosion and found himself flung to the ground. For a few seconds he was stunned. He looked down to see blood streaming from his leg, cut off about six inches below the knee.

He had stepped on a small plastic antipersonnel mine, designed with cruel ingenuity not to kill a man outright, but to tear off part of his leg, putting out of action not only the victim but others who would have to aid him.

Eliezer pushed himself up and got his weight onto the right leg. Following the captain's shouted instructions, he hopped in a zigzag course back onto the road. One other man had been wounded by the blast, but less seriously.

A tourniquet was wound around Eliezer's thigh, and a blanket thrown over him. Lifted into the command car, he sank back against the rear seat. He asked to be taken to orthodox Shaari Zedek.

After intravenous injections and a blood transfusion, Eliezer had been rushed to surgery, where the leg had been amputated below the knee to enable the fitting of a prosthetic appliance.

Now, twenty-four hours later, he was sitting up cheerily in bed with a half-dozen young paratrooper patients gathered around him, looking like a man who had just been elected chancellor of the world. His vast, tangled gray beard flowed down like a wayward stream over his chin and cheeks; a reddish mustache added a note of color.

Smiling constantly, he flung out homily-sprinkled anecdotes of the 1948 war: "We didn't know how to march in formation, but we could fight!" In his eyes twinkled a genial acceptance of the absurdity as well as the dignity of the human condition.

A paratrooper born in Cairo hung silently on the edge of the group, his right arm reduced to a stump. Eliezer caught his eye: "With your legs and my arms," he boomed, "we'll defend Jerusalem another one hundred years!" Under the patriarch's gaze, the young soldier found his lips curving in an answering smile.

Eliezer was quick to dispose of his own injury. Like everything else on earth, it was God-ordained, beyond the challenge or comprehension of man, but undoubtedly balanced in the heavenly accounts: "God is His own bookkeeper."

He even found an angle to be grateful for. "I can still work. A one-legged plumber scampering up a scaffold, I'll grant you, that's unusual. But it's not impossible. Suppose I had lost both legs. From that point of view, what happened to me was a miracle!"

Eliezer's vitality radiated to every corner of the ward. Teen-age orderlies hovered over him in eager attendance; nurses paused in their rounds. Courage was hardly new to the hospital, nor humor nor philosophy. But never had they been seen in such abundant combination. A surgeon of Brazilian origin peered in from the corridor disbelievingly: "One man like this is worth a ton of medicine."

Over lemonade and cookies in the hospital's spotless kosher restaurant, the doctors ruminated. What was the source of Eliezer's ebullience? No books held the answer; none, at least, in the Shaari Zedek medical library. They might have found a clue, however, in the private office of their white-haired director, Dr. Falk Schlesinger, where an obscure shelf held several ancient volumes of rabbinical philosophy. . . .

It had not been a good winter for Eliezer Eckstein. Unusually heavy rains had drenched Jerusalem in January and February of 1967, and damp weather was bad news for his injuries from the War of Independence. The rains also interfered with his business as a free-lance plumber. People didn't get around so freely, so there were fewer of the word-of-mouth recommendations on which, lacking a telephone, he was completely dependent. Furthermore, the tiny basement apartment under a synagogue in one of Jerusalem's orthodox sections was getting a bit crowded; it had never been intended for a family of eight.

But Eliezer was not complaining. After all, what was there to complain about? His children had suffered no serious illness. There was—thank God—enough food to cover the table, carefully repaired clothing to cover their backs, a drawerful of candles for the Sabbath. If he was not flourishing like the Rothschilds, that was something to take with an amiable shrug and a smile. "We are men, human beings; we must expect good times and bad. Myself, I am always happy."

Eliezer was a Hasid, member of a mystic pious sect that rejoices in a continual celebration of God's beneficence: "Life is a good thing; one must make the most of it." Face aglow, he strode briskly through the twisted streets of the old Mea Shearim district, a picturesque and arresting figure in broad-brimmed black hat, with long black caftan flapping about his ankles. Like the Zeus of Greek mythology, he managed to be majestic without surrendering a certain earthy humor: "Am I going to have more children? What will happen will happen. It's up to God. Do I decide these things?"

Eliezer had no office. On the other hand, he paid no rent; his building was owned by the community, established some forty years before by immigrants from Hungary. To friends who inquired how things were going, he would reply in Yiddish, in his hearty, resonant voice, "We're not dead yet!" He might throw in a genial reminder from the Mishnah, or early oral law: "That man is rich who is content with his lot."

And he meant it. Eliezer owned no silk shirts or turtle-neck sweaters—but he didn't want them. His white cotton shirt, black knickers and round felt hat looked fine in the synagogue. He would have been pleased to sit down to an occasional steak, but candles and sweet wine for the Sabbath were far more important.

After all, he had riches he would not trade to any man. There was his plump, spectacled little wife, no glamour queen to the casual viewer but in Eliezer's eyes incomparable, a marvel at cooking chicken or potato *kugel*, a clever improviser with the needle, a flawlessly clean housekeeper and a thrifty shopper. And withal, unlike some shriller helpmeets he could mention, a mild and agreeable companion, daughter of a Bible scholar who had devoted himself entirely to religious studies in Europe.

Could a man be more blessed? Only with a large and lively family. And here, too, Eliezer had been dealt with kindly. Three sons and a daughter were happily married, providing him with six grandchildren, while five boys and a girl were still at home. In the weekly Sabbath observances, when the rewards of being surrounded with family were joined with those of serving the Lord, Eliezer overflowed with contentment. And on special holidays like Passover or Sukkoth, he soared as close to paradise as is permitted to mortal man.

The Eckstein home was in Beit Hungareen, literally "Hungarian Courtyards," a residential enclave of small houses, synagogues and religious schools in the orthodox sector of Mea Shearim northwest of the Old City walls. Within the four square blocks of Beit Hungareen are some four hundred families and five houses of worship.

Long before reaching the orthodox area, the visitor senses its pungent flavor. Buses traveling northward from the business district of New Jerusalem are crammed with bearded men in the quaint, formal, medieval garb copied from fourteenth-century Polish aristocrats. Pale young students, likewise dressed in solid black, display the long twisted curls of piety below their ears.

Approaching Mea Shearim, females from outside the quarter are reminded that they are expected to display more-than-maidenly modesty here. Street signs spell out ground rules suggesting Puritan New England or austerely Moslem Saudi Arabia: tight sweaters are strictly forbidden, as are miniskirts, cigarettes, and painted lips. Arms and legs are to be thoroughly concealed, any hint of nakedness being regarded as a temptation serving the interests of the devil. This is the district where even fellow Israelis, driving through on a Saturday afternoon family outing, are liable to be stoned for desecrating the Sabbath.

The main thoroughfare of the quarter is lined with shops offering religious articles and curios. Behind are courtyards and alleyways that pay little obeisance to Western European mores—or to the twentieth century. Oriental-style open markets feature exotic herbs and spices. Narrow, dimly-lighted jewelry stalls offer a remarkable array of craftsmanship from Persia and Morocco, the Sudan and India. And through it all scurry the citizens of the sector on their obscure errands, long cloaks trailing on the ground, vivid relics of another age, seemingly fresh from the Amsterdam ghetto etchings of Rembrandt or the pages of Sholem Aleichem.

Tucked into a far corner of the orthodox quarter is Beit Hungareen. It lies at the end of a labyrinthine trail too narrow for auto passage and best not ventured without a compass or, preferably, a local guide. Its unmarked "streets" merge, overlap and intertwine with casual disregard for the conventions of man.

Small boys frolic underfoot, looking much like the preschool set in Peoria or Baton Rouge except for the ever-present skullcaps. Girls, as befits their modesty, are less visible in public; small curly heads poke out curiously from behind laundry lines and ample maternal derrieres.

A dim humming of voices rises to a lusty shout, then recedes again. Students at a nearby Talmud Torah are reciting the day's lesson in the Pentateuch. From the time they begin their education at three or four until they finish a religious secondary school at eighteen, their only instruction is in the Bible and the copious commentaries, oral and written, derived from it. Secular studies are forbidden.

Several times a day, just inside the entrance to the community, the chanting voices are not childish but deep and spirited. Follow them and you will arrive before the "apartment" of Eliezer Eckstein. Eliezer and his brood live in a synagogue building that reverberates night and day to the prayers and songs of the Hasidic faithful. The basement area occupied by the Ecksteins formerly housed a Talmud Torah; echoes of its earlier role linger in the many-arched ceiling and the frequent wall niches.

The uncertain visitor approaches via a shallow courtyard, a few steps down from the street. A door stands at its far end. Cross its threshold and you are in the Eckstein living room. You are also simultaneously in the dining room and kitchen, and unless you stop walking very soon you will be in one of the two bedrooms on either side.

To the right is the master bedroom, set off by a wooden partition of Eliezer's creation to give him a flat of three rooms instead of two. Here there is a three-quarter-size bed, with neat blankets that have seen better days; a large cupboard; and a series of wall niches converted into closets by ingeniously arranged cloth coverings.

The center room, some twenty feet wide but not more than ten feet deep, is largely filled by a long and versatile mahogany table. It serves for prayer, cooking, dining, sewing and homework. On the rear wall are several parental photos in the starched poses of nineteenth-century Europe, and an oil reproduction of a vaguely devotional character. The floor is stone and mirror-polished.

To the left is the dormitory of the younger Ecksteins. At first glance it seems barely big enough for one moderately active boy. But an adroit juggling of space and folding cots provides sleeping room for four of them, ranging from ten years down to six. Eliezer's eldest son, nearly twelve, has a bed in the Talmud Torah, and the one daughter at home manages to pass the night comfortably on a cot in the kitchen area. Eliezer concedes affably that the establishment is something less than a Mediterranean villa, but he makes no apologies for it.

In such close quarters, sharing the uncertainty about the next day's bread, children grow up thinking not so much of themselves as of each other. Besides, did not the immortal Baal Shem-Tov, miracle-working father of Hasidism, live in a rude mountain cabin and work as a common lime-burner? Was not poverty extolled in the parables of his great-grandson, Rabbi Nachman, as the path to purification, a very root (along with Belief and Fear of God) of the great tree whose trunk was Truth?

The Baal Shem-Tov, or "Master of the Wondrous Name," is one of the giants of Jewish folklore. The title refers to the magic powers exercised by a certain Rabbi Israel, who by his secret knowledge of the Wondrous Name could invoke the aid of the Almighty to confound the wicked with dazzling miracles. Rabbi Israel started Hasidism ("Ecstatic Piety") as a reaction against the stuffy scholasticism of medieval rabbis who, he felt, in their day-long wrangling over the significance of a single phrase were losing sight of the Almighty.

Instead of their relentless pedantry, Rabbi Israel offered the direct, uninhibited worship of God through nature and man, leavened with the intriguing mysteries of the ancient cabala, or coded interpretation of the Scriptures.

According to legend, the Baal Shem-Tov was born some 250 years ago in the foothills of the Carpathian Mountains. His father, for whom Eliezer Eckstein was named, was chosen for the honor of bearing such an illustrious son because he was one of Heaven's few Innocent Souls, pure spirits who escaped the taint of Adam's sin by hiding in a corner of Chaos while the first man was being created. Rabbi Eliezer further demonstrated his worthiness on earth when, enslaved by Tartar conquerors, he refused to escape because it would have involved killing a man. Still later, awarded a beautiful young bride by a king grateful for his counsel, Eliezer insisted on remaining faithful to the Jewish wife who had been waiting home for him for seventeen years.

His son, Israel, early fled the schoolhouse to wander in the woods and fields, communing with plants and animals. He found the Living Glory of God in all things: rocks and streams, beech trees and bumblebees and men. Growing to young manhood, he became learned in the Scriptures but still placed feeling above mechanical ritual. Around him sprang up the Hasidic cult, taking joy in every living thing, available to the humblest peasant or artisan, typified by the shepherd who worshiped his deity by leaping back and forth across a brook.

The Hasid preached delight in being alive: "Tears may open the gates, but joy will tear down the very walls." He was less concerned with the absolute accuracy of his rendered prayer than with the richness of its emotional content. A man unable to write his name could still "know the song of the sparrow." And he should deliver it thunderously, with full voice, as befitted an offering to the Lord. The grape was a welcome ally: "Drinking together, men are friendly and their joy is purest worship."

In prayer, a man could join his soul to the universal soul. But his actions were no less vital: "Every act serves God directly; therefore be joyous, whatever you are doing."

The murkier side of the cult was in its mysticism: fabulous tales of the Baal Shem-Tov bringing back brides from the grave, flashing across oceans, defying polymorphous satans through occult powers derived from his study of cabala.

The standard work on cabala is the Zohar or "Book of Splendor on the Torah," compiled by a thirteenth-century rabbi in Spain from the writings more than a thousand years earlier of Rabbi Simeon bar Yohai in the Holy Land. Cabala asserts that all the wisdom of the world is secretly embedded in the Torah or first five books of the Old Testament; the seeker for knowledge needs only the key.

Since each letter in the Hebrew alphabet has a numerical equivalent, the key is conceived in mathematical terms, with a wide-ranging variety of formulas from simple addition tables to elaborate code-schemes that would tax a modern cryptographer. Generally, cabalistic equations were used to "prove" core propositions, such as the triumph of the human soul over evil, or the infallibility of the Torah.

After the death of the Baal Shem-Tov, Hasidism descended for a time into magic and demonology, with dynastic rabbis frequently abusing the credulity of their flocks, until the movement burst into full spiritual flame again with the appearance of Israel's great-grandson, Rabbi Nachman of Breslau.

Nachman, founder of the sect to which Eliezer Eckstein belongs, was another riverbank dreamer who delved deep into cabala, traveling to the graves in the Holy Land of such philosopher-mystics as Isaac Luria, who lived in the Galilee hill town of Safad in the middle of the sixteenth century. Returning to Breslau, Poland, in 1802, Nachman declared that "a teacher must clothe his thoughts in wondrous raiments," and proceeded to turn out a remarkable series of poetic parables.

Through them drift lost princesses and personified planets; pirates and robbers and holy men, all woven into dramatic adventures that speak to the reader or listener at many levels. Nachman, eyes lifted to eternity, sought to illuminate "the meaning of the thing within the thing."

On his deathbed, Nachman decreed that he was to have no dynastic successor: "I will still be with you in the grave." His parables were gathered together by a disciple, and form the fundamental literature of the Hasidim of Breslau, or the "Hasidim of the Dead One."

Eliezer Eckstein's forebears stayed strictly within the fold. One of the sect's practices, to safeguard against contamination by outsiders, was child marriages. Continuity could be assured by arranging betrothals between the children of followers well in advance. Eliezer's father was eight years old when, soon after arrival of his family in the Holy Land, he was pledged to a girl of the same age, the daughter of a neighbor.

The boy became a married man at fourteen, entering at once into his father's profession of shohet, or kosher-slaughterer. Unfortunately this was hardly a unique specialty in the orthodox quarter of Jerusalem, and Eliezer's father could not keep pace with the needs of a rapidly growing family that included four girls; daughters require dowries.

When Eliezer was two and a half years old, his father moved the entire household to the United States, where there were relatives. His slaughtering skills were more in demand there, but his wife missed Jerusalem. In less than a year she went back, taking half the family including Eliezer with her. For the next three and a half decades, separated by economic necessity, the Ecksteins lived in two hemispheres, with the father making pilgrimages to Jerusalem whenever he acquired enough capital.

Promptly on his return from America, Eliezer was enrolled in the Talmud Torah. To wait much longer would be a disgrace; he was already past his third birthday. Day after day, hour upon hour, he grappled with the Word of God, sheltered from such time-wasting frivolities as geography and basketball, wrapped up in the intricate oral tradition of Jewish law.

At eighteen, his elder brothers had gone on into higher religious studies in the Yeshiva. But Eliezer, contemplating the family's empty larder, got a job as a plumber's assistant. There was no contradiction between Hasidic piety and humble employment. Judaism was a commitment, equally binding on king and cobbler; and the highest flights of cabala were not banned to the serious-minded layman.

At twenty, Eliezer became eager for a family of his own. Child marriages were less common in Israel; as God willed it, he was free to make his own choice—within, of course, strict limits. He picked himself a suitably pious partner and set up house. Although he still had a long stretch of poorly-paid apprenticeship ahead, he never regretted the move.

With children came the delights of the Sabbath, "celebrated with us as it never could be in a nonreligious home." The whole week revolved around the twenty-four-hour period ushered in at sundown Friday by Eliezer's sonorous song of welcome to the Sabbath-bride. His wife, her head covered, would light the candles, murmuring the appropriate prayer. The head of the house drained a glass of wine, cut the ceremonial hallah bread, and launched a meal featuring "all sorts of things" not on the Eckstein table during the week: kugel, chopped eggs and onion salad, gefillte fish, a big sponge cake. "Each Sunday, we are already looking forward to the next Sabbath."

The traditional climax to the Friday evening feast was the testing of the children. Each boy in turn was required to identify the section of the commentaries he had studied during the past week, and then to field sly questions tossed out by his father. "Who was the first carpenter?"

Noah, of course—likewise identified as the first man to send a telegram, via his pigeon.

Later, Eliezer would dip into the lore of Rabbi Nachman. Had one of the boys neglected to finish sweeping the yard of the widow across the street? He was reminded of the mitzvoth, the good deeds, to which every Jew is exhorted; and of Nachman's observation that every good deed gave birth to a good angel in heaven, and every bad deed to a bad one—"but unfinished deeds create incomplete angels, missing a head, or eyes, or arms."

Or the talk might turn to worldly possessions, and Eliezer would recount Nachman's "The Sage and the Simpleton." The magnificent

Simpleton lived in happy fantasy, praising his wife for the "splendid roast goose" as he nibbled a dry crust, admiring a tattered rag as his "fine velvet coat." Strong in faith, he rose to govern a country, while his intellectual but cynical friend, the Sage, had to be saved from the devil's pit of horrors by the Baal Shem-Tov. A favorite of the children was "The Wind That Overturned the World," telling of the ineffable Kingdom of Money-Worshipers where, depending on their income, men were ranked as Insects, Dogs, Horses or Lions. After various magically-induced tribulations, the people were brought to wisdom by the revelation that "the stench you smell is your money."

The annual peak of excitement came on Passover, "each year the same and each year marvelous." The traditional feast, liberally laced with wine, generated the hand-clapping fervor of a revival meeting in America's Bible belt.

Eliezer's peaceful regime was jarred by World War II and the swiftly-emerging crisis over emigration from Europe to Palestine. He joined the tough Irgun Zva'i Leumi underground, because it was "standing up aggressively to the British." When independence came, he was commissioned a lieutenant in the Haganah and assigned to escort convoys between the coast and beleaguered Jerusalem.

Returning from operations at Ramat Rahel, he learned that a slain Israeli soldier had been lying near the Mandelbaum Gate for four-teen days. The area was still being raked by Arab sniper fire; nobody—"not the Red Cross, not the U.N."—was willing to pull the man out for proper burial.

Eliezer reflected on the comment made by Rabbi Hillel, head of the rabbinical academy in Jerusalem in Roman times, when a man came to him offering to embrace Judaism if he could be taught "the whole Torah while standing on one foot." Hillel replied, "Do not unto others what you would not like them to do unto you. That is the whole Torah. The rest is commentary."

Eliezer translated this into terms of the present problem. "How would I like to be lying out there under the blazing sun day after day, neglected by friend and enemy alike, denied a proper burial? I wouldn't like it at all."

He devised a plan. After nightfall, with Israeli soldiers covering him from villa walls nearby, he would slip out into no man's land carrying a stretcher, a blanket and a length of rope. A second, longer rope would be wound around his chest, its other end remaining in the hands of a comrade. "That way, if I got hit, I could signal like a deep-sea diver and at least they'd be able to drag me back."

Darkness came. Before the rise of the moon, Eliezer crept forward from the Jewish-held barricades at the end of Mea Shearim. He passed a discarded helmet, an overturned truck, an empty fuel can —and came to the fallen Israeli. Quickly he bound the body to his stretcher and lifted the load to his back.

A shot rang out. From his friends on the Jewish side, came answering fire. Eliezer started back in the darkness, a few eet at a time, sliding, wriggling on the ground, changing course from ·ide to side. Bullets ripped around him, one chipping the road a few inches from his head.

It was the longest, slowest journey of his life; seventy-five minutes to cover as many yards. But the next morning, the fallen Israeli had a decent burial.

In the summer of 1948, Eliezer battled along the slopes of every hill surrounding Jerusalem. The worst part of combat for him was to see men fall and know they would never get up again, that there was nothing he could do to help.

During the bitter struggle for the Musrara district north of the Old City walls, Eliezer was hit twice himself. Machine-gun fire smashed the toes of his left foot, and a ricocheting rifle bullet glanced off his chin. Doctors smilingly suggested that the tangled matting around his face might have blunted the impact and helped save his life, giving Eliezer a miracle of his own to match those of the early Hasidic wonder-workers; he was the man with the bulletproof beard.

His wounds were severe enough to plague him for subsequent winters, and to keep him out of the Sinai campaign in 1956.

But 1967 was a more serious threat to Israel. Eliezer felt a righteous fury at Nasser. The Arab masses, he thought, were a pitiable lot, ignorant pawns of their ambitious leaders; the Egyptian dictator, however, could not be viewed as anything but a crafty cynic, a modern embodiment of Satan.

On the eve of war, after the children had gone to bed, Eliezer sat sipping tea with his wife at the long, smoothly polished table. Dayan and Rabin, he conceded, were not begging him to take over a company command as in 1948. But there ought to be some way he could serve.

He was in his fifties, his wife pointed out gently; a father and a grandfather many times over. Israel had younger men to fight its wars.

What was this talk of time and age? demanded Eliezer. She knew as well as he the story of the Seven Beggars, which demonstrated that time could not be measured in mere hours, but was meaningful only in terms of mitzvoth.

In this classic tale by Rabbi Nachman, the heart of the universe is portrayed as looking ever-yearningly toward a spring bubbling on a far-off mountaintop, the sight of which keeps the heart alive. Toward nightfall each day the spring falters, and the heart is on the verge of perishing; but both are restored by the good deeds collected from the ends of the earth since early morning by the Godly Man: "Each deed becomes a melody; from this melody the Godly Man makes a day; and the heart makes the gift of another day's time to the spring on the peak."

Eliezer and his wife sat in silence for a moment. She knew his decision was taking shape. "The *met mitzvah*," he ventured, "is one of the highest *mitzvoth* in the eyes of the Lord."

Under Jewish tradition, the Commentaries provide guidance to all aspects of human behavior. As codified by the twelfth-century sage Maimonides, there are 248 affirmative exhortations ("support the needy . . . aid your neighbor with his burdens . . . honor scholars and the aged") and 365 prohibitions, corresponding to the number of days in the year ("A married man must on no account leave his bride during their first year together").

The *met mitzvah* concerns the obligation to uphold the dignity of a fellow man even after his death. The devout Jew, coming upon a body in a field, is enjoined to provide a decent and proper burial, honoring the departed but immortal soul. The obligation applies even to Cohens, persons of high priest lineage who are normally forbidden to touch the dead.

On Monday morning, Eliezer volunteered for the Chevra Kadisha, an orthodox burial society mobilized under the Military Rabbinate to recover casualties from the battlefield. Operating on the heels of advancing troops, Chevra squads brought back wounded to the field hospitals, and delivered those who were beyond help to the burial grounds on Mt. Herzl. Eliezer commanded a small unit engaged most of Tuesday in the Mandelbaum Gate area, where they worked with doctors and nurses under constant sniper fire. The next day he followed Mota Gur's forces into the Old City. He was at Latrun on Friday, seeking to extricate and identify men who had been trapped in burning tanks, when word came of the need for someone familiar with the heavily-mined Bethlehem area.

Late Saturday afternoon Eliezer's family started trooping to his bedside, the children big-eyed and trembling in the whitewashed halls. With his left hand—the right was still swathed in bandages—Eliezer patted their heads. "It's all right, I haven't gone to heaven, I'm still with you here on earth." Soon he would be home to tell them stories and lead them in prayers again. Meanwhile, he assured them, he was in excellent hands in this wonderfully observant hospital where no doctor touched a pencil on the Sabbath, but communicated his instructions by pointing to pages previously marked by paper clips. If a prescription absolutely had to be written, the job was turned over to an Arab orderly.

Mrs. Eckstein had already been there the day before, murmuring her relief at learning that it was her husband's bad leg, not the good one, that had been hurt. But now, seeing his brawny frame encased in bandages, she winced. Eliezer squeezed her hand comfortingly. "God has been good to us. I will be able to walk, and to work. The arm is nothing; in two weeks it will be like new. We will go to the Old City together, and kiss the stones our fathers could only dream about."

Meanwhile, Eliezer had work to do at the hospital. He beckoned a doctor over to his bed. "There's a boy across the hall—Aaron, from Haifa—he has a chest wound." The doctor nodded. "He is very lonely," Eliezer continued. "If you could perhaps telephone his fiancée, and arrange transportation for her?"

The doctor smiled. "I'll see what I can do."

Eliezer raised a finger. "One other thing. Perhaps tomorrow, when the Sabbath is over, you could find a fiddler? Music is good. It will remind the boys that they still have ears to listen with, voices that can sing."

Some of the doctors found Eliezer's constant counsel a little wearing. But he was undeniably a strong factor in building morale.

After Eliezer's family left, the paratroopers drifted back. So did a passing medical resident from Canada, and an ultra-orthodox orderly, a confirmed pacifist. Eliezer expounded freely on man, war and piety.

He saw no sin in fighting. "The Gemara says, 'If someone comes to kill you, you should kill him first.' The land of Israel is historically ours as a grant from God. The Arabs seized it, the British occupied it, but it has never stopped being ours. To hold Israel is worth any personal price."

In Eliezer's eyes, the Israeli has evolved into a "Jew of stronger beliefs" because of his sufferings in building a state. "We had no option but to fight Nasser and Hussein; we had to show that we have a home, that Israel lives."

Peacetime military training, however, is something else: "Why should young boys run around with women soldiers and be corrupted?" His eldest son served in the army, but it was in a Nahal agricultural unit, where "at least they were kept away from the girls." (In Eliezer's Hasidic sect, mixed folk dancing is permitted on festive occasions—but only with a handkerchief separating each man and woman in the circle, so that they never touch hands.)

Eliezer acknowledges the admirable contributions of generals and political leaders. He concedes that even the "corrupted" boys of the discotheques, whose worldliness he had condemned before the war, "stopped dancing and settled down" when the country needed them. "They knew what they had to do. They gave everything they had, and they should get full credit." However, he still clings to his own code, which gives primacy to the rabbis and the sages as "the inspiration, the source."

Eliezer's way of life has its critics. There are the objectors on political grounds, who complain of the strangle hold maintained by the religious parties on matters of marriage, divorce, Sabbath travel and official diet in Israel. (Defenders counter that Israelis of all persuasions are secretly pleased to have the orthodox as a kind of "national conscience," answering an inner hunger for ancient roots that, if left to the casual traditionalists, might go unsatisfied.)

Then there are the humanists who maintain that children raised in Mea Shearim are frozen in medievalism and superstition, isolated from the world's advances in science and understanding as well as from their contemporaries. Men like Eliezer Eckstein are accused of lacking ambition for their families, dooming the women in particular to a chattel status bereft of the blessings of female emancipation. (For centuries, Hasidic women have been drilled to regard acquisition of a pious husband as their highest dream.)

Eliezer admits that his own secular education has been limited, and that his children might benefit from a broader knowledge of man's transitory world. But he is not yet ready to pay the price for letting them attend ordinary public schools, even those that combine secular and religious programs; he feels that in such compromises the spiritual side tends to get watered down. "They would learn some good things, yes; but they would be exposed to too many negative influences that would distract them from God and the exploration of His word. Better that they should stay in the Talmud Torah, even if it means missing some types of learning."

For Eliezer, his approach indisputably works. He can claim a serenity of spirit untasted by those who rail at him. He has little enough else to bequeath his descendants; but in an age of turbulence the sons and probably the grandsons of Eliezer Eckstein will grow up to rejoice in the Lord, share the burdens of their fellow man, and regard the defense of Israel as a holy obligation.

AFTERMATH

THROUGHOUT the week of the June war, Azgad Yellin's mother had moved like a woman in a trance. She had two sons in combat; she refused to feel, see, think anything.

Her main fear was for her younger son, thrown without preparation into a new command. She was sure he wouldn't do anything irresponsible—"after all, he was a man of twenty-two"—but the hazards of war were great enough, without last-minute complications.

She was dimly aware of a visit from a young friend of David's, kept out of the army on medical grounds, and of the boy's anguish at being left behind. She envied his mother. She did not expect to see both of her sons alive again.

Even at the capture of Jerusalem, she kept her feelings reined in. Once loosed, she knew, they would be beyond control.

After the Saturday cease-fire, she lived only for the mail. The letter came at noon Tuesday, delivered by a bicycle-riding ten-year-old from the neighborhood (the mailman was still at war). Trembling, Mrs. Yellin took it from the box.

The first thing she saw was the heading "Saturday, with the war over"; then, at the bottom, David's signature. She read the hastily scrawled message: "Both of us are well and in good spirits. Regards from the Red Sea."

She brought it in to her husband "like someone frozen." Then she collapsed and let the tears flow.

Along the newly won border on the Syrian heights, Israeli forces were engaging in house-to-house defensive maneuvers. The exercises were being repeatedly interrupted by a huge, nondescript dog who prowled in and out of buildings, snapping menacingly at the troops. The animal refused to be coaxed or driven away.

When the dog knocked over and damaged a field radio unit, the captain in command stopped the maneuvers. He turned to Yaacov Handleman, standing beside him in a shattered doorway: "Get rid of it."

Yaacov stared back at him. He shook his head.

The captain started to repeat the order, then glanced more closely at the blond, sinewy sergeant. After a pause, he drew his own revolver, took a few paces forward, and fired. The dog yelped once, and pitched forward.

The captain returned to the doorway. "What's the matter, Yaacov?"

Again Yaacov had no words. He knew only that for him this particular bullet, after all the others he had fired at Tel Azaziat, would have been one too many.

The wounded resumed living. Within days, Eliezer Eckstein was leading an impromptu entertainment on the lawn of the Tel Hashomer rehabilitation clinic outside Tel Aviv. Surrounded by young amputees in wheelchairs, the bearded Hasid hopped up and down on his good leg, brandishing a crutch overhead like a baton, as he sang lustily of man's happy destiny under God: "Drain your cup, lift your heart, be thankful to Him for the gift of Life!"

For Dudu Sela, the trip back was more tortuous: skin grafts and operations, and the slow painful process of restoring nimbleness to fingers stiffened and shortened by flames and inactivity. On his left hand, several of the five microscopic layers of skin had been burned away; the new tissue was thin and excruciatingly sensitive, especially to the knifelike pressure of the high A string.

Day after day, alone with his instrument and his determination,

Dudu went through exercises in muscle-stretching, bowing, scales. The curled-up fifth finger of his right hand impeded his bowing; stubbornly he struggled to work it loose, and to perfect his rapid left-hand arpeggios. Before winter, he was performing in public again.

Who was the "architect" of Israeli victory? Western media, attuned to the notion of supermen, seized upon the picturesque Dayan. Certainly the Defense Minister provided the thrust that took the nation to war. But he was far from alone. It was Yitzchak Rabin who shaped the army that Dayan inherited, and who coordinated a campaign in which every unit carried its objective. It was Mordechai Hod who designed the crushing air strike. And beyond stood a long row of unpublicized prodigies who for a decade had guided the nation's broad operational planning. Typical of them was Brigadier General Amos Chorev, Israel's Deputy Chief Scientist. As Chief of Ordinance through four successive military administrations, M.I.T.-trained Chorev virtually rebuilt the American Sherman tank for Israeli use. It may be something of a wrench for westerners, raised on the cult of the individual hero, to accept the notion of interchangeability at the top. But that is the Israeli way.

Moreover, all of the brilliancies in leadership would have been wasted in 1967 if not for the performance of the untried Orientals. Sabra and refugee alike, the newcomers delivered unforgettably on every front, nowhere more so than in Jerusalem.

At 8:30 A.M. on Monday, June 12, almost exactly a week from the time he had bombed Fayid airfield, Major Avihu was completing a routine patrol in the north. Flying back by way of Jerusalem, he looked forward to the still-unfamiliar thrill of hearing a Jewish voice from the control tower of the capital's airport. Now it was coming over his radio, in response to his initial identification call: a request in Hebrew for his position, from the captured field at suburban Kalandia. Avihu reported his location, altitude, and heading, savoring the final phrase: "One minute flying time from Jerusalem. Repeat: one minute to Jerusalem."

Below him, incredibly lovely in the clear blue-tinted morning air, lay the sparkling domes and the tranquil, tree-shaded villas of the Holy City. Flags fluttered in profusion, the contrasting emblems of surrender and of victory, creating to his left on the Arab side of the old border a field of unbroken white, and to his right, where Israeli banners flew, a blue-and-white medley.

From twelve-thousand feet, the walled Old City looked like a woman's bracelet, its mighty battlements reduced to the size of gleaming, jangling links . . . so small a gem for so much striving. Avihu cut his speed and dipped lower.

In the area of the Temple Mount, vehicles were circling in businesslike patterns. He saw a huge civilian bus pull up and disgorge a long stream of troops. The soldiers were Mota Gur's paratroopers, assembling for a ceremonial parade.

Under the multicolored pillars of the Dome of the Rock, Karni Bilu waited for the colonel to finish arrangements with his battalion commanders. Karni had never ceased to be astonished by Gur: his abrupt halting of a convoy on the trip back south to empty his water canteen for a refugee Arab family; his dreamy absorption when looking down on the lights of Old Jerusalem from the roof of the Mount of Olives Hotel; his unabashed tears after a tour of the wards at Hadassah Hospital.

Now the colonel came forward to lead Karni, his official escort, across the great paved square of the Temple Mount to the broad stone stairway on the east. Here, under the Scales of Judgment arch, the first soldiers were starting to arrive. Freshly-polished helmets and rifles gleamed in the bright morning sun, but there had been neither time nor supplies to permit a change of uniform: most of the men still wore the baggy, dirt-soaked field outfits in which they had fought.

Mota planted himself at the top of the steps, offering a quiet "Shalom, boys" to all who passed. There were no salutes; the commander's hands were held out to anyone who wanted to grip them. As the men poured through, they formed up into companies on the vast natural parade ground of the Mount.

A siren screamed. Through the wooden-framed gate where Moshe Ben-Tsur had first crashed into the Temple area five mornings before, down along the time-smoothed Turkish flagging, sped two ambulances from Hadassah Hospital. A moment later a jeep appeared with a medical orderly at the wheel; then came a private car driven by a woman, with a pale soldier alongside, and more ambulances, from Shaari Zedek and Tel Hashomer.

The vehicles pulled up and the men tumbled out—bandaged, limping—a cavalcade of the wounded, everyone who could be helped or carried from his hospital bed. Many were accompanied by nurses. Some rode in wheelchairs, military shirts tucked into their pajamas, with the brigade patch on their shoulders and paratroop wings glittering on their chests. Karni knew every one of them by sight, by name—and by injury.

As the new arrivals started hobbling up the stairs, marching ranks on the mount dissolved, orders were forgotten. The hale swarmed joyously around the wounded. It was the first time most of the reservists had seen each other since the fury of the battlefield; more than one of the returnees had last been glimpsed lying motionless in a trench or on a stretcher.

In the excitement of the occasion, the hospital contingent forgot their injuries. Wan, with cheeks unnaturally bright, they waved bandaged arms or hopped about thumping shoulders in a one-legged happy delirium.

Karni noticed that Mota did not have hands enough to greet and caress his youngsters. Obviously moved, concern showing in his mobile face, he smiled only in extending a specific welcome.

Reunions finally accomplished, the wounded reluctantly retired. The paratroopers lined up again in rows facing the mosque. Regimental colors—green, black and white on a deep red background—were unfurled, and faces grew more serious. Mota's deputy patrolled the area with a bullhorn, calling the troops to order.

Karni, moving toward her place with the headquarters staff in the front row, took a long look to fix the scene in her memory. The square was a sea of dazzling light, sparkling upward from hundreds of steel helmets and rifles, capped by the blazing golden dome of the mosque. A faint breeze rippled through the eucalyptus grove below. The men were still, suspended in anticipation.

Karni's eye traveled along the first few rows. She caught her breath. Wide gaps split the ranks—two spaces here, three there, nearly an entire line in one of Noah's platoons—representing the fallen and disabled. Nowhere had the place of a missing man been filled. *The whole brigade is here,* she thought to herself. *The living and the dead.*

The ravaged ranks bore testimony to the brigade's losses at Jerusalem: seventy-five killed, three-hundred wounded.

Karni stepped into line, conscious of the haunted expressions on every side.

The dignitaries had arrived. A crisp command snapped the soldiers to attention. Another sharp order, and twelve hundred rifle breeches clicked in unison (Zahal *could* drill, Karni reminded herself; they just didn't very often feel like it).

The ceremonies opened with a trumpet call, ushering in two minutes of silence in memory of the dead. The flags were lowered, the breeze died down.

The Central Front commander, Brigadier General Uzzi Narkiss, thanked the brigade on behalf of the nation. He was followed to the rostrum by Mota. The brigade chief had spent his eloquence the night before, in the Hebrew University amphitheater on Mt. Tzofim, where he told the paratroopers: "The western wall, toward which the Jewish heart beats, is in our hands. You fought as a single body that smashed anything standing before you, without regard for your own wounds. You never complained, you never protested. One thing you did always: advance and conquer. Jerusalem is yours forever."

Now he simply let his gaze wander over the throng and said softly, "Thank you all."

A young paratrooper named Ariel stepped forward to recite—with apologies to composer Naomi Shemer—his own somber battlefield version of "Jerusalem of Gold." Miss Shemer's lyric had dwelt on the aching in Israeli hearts because no Jew stood on the sacred Temple Mount, walked in the deserted market place, or made the winding trip down to the Dead Sea by way of Jericho. Ariel told a fiercer tale, commemorating a capital not of tawny gold and light but of "steel and lead and blood," where "mother followed mother into the congregation of the bereaved."

The men started singing after him. The words burst forth in a torrential release of feeling, climaxed by a return to the original refrain: "Let me be the violin to all thy songs." The melody soared exultantly across the spiraling rooftops and the minarets.

Centuries before, the Psalmist had made his passionate commitment: "If I forget thee, O Jerusalem, may my right hand forget its cunning"; and in countless Passover services, from Shanghai to Warsaw and New York, the vow had echoed incessantly with undiminished fervor: "Next year in Jerusalem." Now the young paratroopers had redeemed the ancient pledge.

Rarely in history had men been so closely bound together—not in mindless hysteria but by conscious choice. United around the sabra core, they had accomplished the impossible in battle. With peace, they might do as much in building a truly humane society: not out of any innate superiority, but because as a people they had suffered more.

Whatever was to come, on this bright morning the circle stood completed. Among these stones, under the sun that had shone down on Abraham and Isaac, the blood of the paratroopers mingled with that of the Maccabees; the voice of the sabra merged with that of Moses; the Jewish future linked up with the Jewish past.

ACKNOWLEDGMENTS

MY first debt, of course, is to the people who lived this book, and who supplied me with notes, recollections, letters and guided tours . . . of their personal histories as well as the battlefronts.

In particular I want to thank reservist First Lieutenant Karni Bilu and Brigade Commander Mota Gur of the paratroopers; the colonel for opening many doors, the lieutenant for indefatigable assistance in finding and talking with widely scattered soldiers, as well as for her graphic account of the final paratrooper assembly on the Temple Mount.

The bulk of responsibility for interpreting was generously assumed and articulately fulfilled by banker and Lieutenant Arie Shein. Others who helped bridge the language gap were the Misses Yona Nelson, Varda Gill, Dalia Carmel and Mrs. Basia Horn.

Valuable cooperation in arranging interviews came from Lieutenant Colonel E. Bar-Lev of the Israeli Government Press Office and members of his staff, including Lieutenant Bennie Barak. At the fighting sites, Major Amos and Lieutenant Zvi kept me out of mine fields while recapping the action.

Among Israeli writers and journalists who provided useful insights were the poet Chaim Guri, Lieutenant Colonel Gershon Rivlin of

Ma'arahot (through whose permission the verses of Amos Eplinger are quoted), Gabriel Zifroni, and Dan Raviv of Kol Israel Radio. I am indebted also to Mrs. Yitzchak Rabin, Brigadier Generals Amos Chorev and Vivian Herzog, Colonel Moraleh Bar-On, Mayor Teddy Kollek of Jerusalem, Joel Blau, and my old Middle East colleague Winston Burdett of the Columbia Broadcasting System, as well as his associate Peter Kalischer. A word of gratitude is in order likewise to Elchanan Pels of Shaari Zedek Hospital, Dr. Michael Bar-Zohar, and Arnold Sherman of El Al Israel Airlines.

Of the many military accounts of the war, I found most authoritative the French *Bazak*, by Julien Besançon; Brigadier General S. L. A. Marshall's *Swift Sword;* Paratroop Captain Ely Landau's *Jerusalem the Eternal*, and Moshe Natan's *The Battle of Jerusalem*, from which the detail map of Ammunition Hill on page 47 was derived. To readers intrigued by the folklore of Hasidism, I commend Meyer Levin's *Classic Chassidic Tales.*

Able editors are too often slighted in these postscripts. Mine was Mrs. Judy Sklar Rasminsky.

INDEX

ABOUT THE AUTHOR

Edward O. (Ted) Berkman was born in Brooklyn, New York, in 1914. He was educated at Cornell University, and has had a long career as a newspaperman, screenwriter, composer, and United Nations official. From 1943 to 1946 he was in the Middle East as an American intelligence executive and later as foreign correspondent for the ABC radio network and the Overseas News Agency. His first book, *Cast a Giant Shadow*, published in 1962, was the biography of Mickey Marcus, the American colonel who fought in Israel's war of independence in 1948. Mr. Berkman is currently at work on a novel.

Format by Katharine Sitterly
Set in Linotype Caledonia
Composed, printed and bound by The Haddon Craftsmen, Inc.
HARPER & ROW, PUBLISHERS, INCORPORATED

ISRAEL AFTER THE SIX-DAY WAR

▮ Territory taken by Israel during the Six-Day War

O ⊢━━━━━━━ MILES ━━━━━━━ 1OO

M E D I T E R R A N E A

32°

Alexandria

30°

Cairo

Nile

U N I T E D   A R A B

(E G Y P

28°

30°

J. P. TREMBLAY